Hezekiah Butterworth

South America

A Popular Illustrated History of the Struggle for Liberty in the Andean Republics and

Cuba

Hezekiah Butterworth

South America
A Popular Illustrated History of the Struggle for Liberty in the Andean Republics and Cuba

ISBN/EAN: 9783744693202

Printed in Europe, USA, Canada, Australia, Japan

Cover: Foto ©ninafisch / pixelio.de

More available books at **www.hansebooks.com**

BOLIVAR'S ENTRANCE INTO CARACAS.

SOUTH AMERICA

A POPULAR ILLUSTRATED HISTORY
OF THE STRUGGLE FOR LIBERTY IN
THE ANDEAN REPUBLICS AND CUBA

BY

HEZEKIAH BUTTERWORTH

AUTHOR OF "OVER THE ANDES," "ZIGZAG JOURNEYS," ETC.

"Where Liberty is, there is my country."
—LA FAYETTE.

NEW YORK
DOUBLEDAY & McCLURE CO.
1898

PREFACE

THIS volume relates the story of liberty and progress in Latin America. It is also an introduction to a study of the Andean republics and those on the Spanish Main.

The struggle for liberty in Cuba but follows the events of the Latin republics of the Andes, and throws a new light on those heroic endeavors.

South America is one of the lands of the future. The immigration to that country is now rivaling that to North America, and to the overcrowded populations of Europe the south temperate zone is the waiting world.

An English poet of prophetic gifts is recorded as saying that in the progressive development of America, South America, or the table-land of the Andes, was not unlikely to become the theater of great achievements, an opinion also shared by the author of "Social Evolution." It is objected to this that much of South America is tropical, and that the lands of the Sun are unfavorable to the development of the virtues and arts of peace. But out of nearly such conditions of mingled temperate and tropical climates came the poems of Job and Homer, the arts of Egypt, and the sacred literature whose principles govern the conscience of the world. Sarmiento, the educational President and prophet of Argentina, once said that Buenos Ayres would become the greatest city of the three Americas. This may be too large a vision. But whatever may be the future of South America, her growth is such as to make her recent history a very interesting study to the popular mind.

To write an adequate history of South America and Central America would require a lifelong preparation of study and travel, and more than ordinary ability, insight and vision, to which gifts the present writer can make no claim. He has wished to interest others in the story of liberty in these lands, to picture Bolivar's march to the south and San Martin's to the north, the meeting of these heroes, the central campaign in the Peruvian highlands, and the progress of the new republics after the Congress of Panama. If such be but history in outline and picture, it is a story most pleasing to write, and, we may hope, not uninteresting to read.

In 1895 the writer visited Buenos Ayres, went over the Andes to Valparaiso, and up the west coast to the ports of Tarapacá, to Callao, Lima, and Guayaquil, and afterward to Cartagena and Costa Rica. These excursions led him to spend much time, on his return, in reading works on these countries in the Boston Public Library, which is rich not only in the collections made by Ticknor and Prescott, but in books of travel in South America, and local narratives of South American cities, and in biographies of heroes like Don Ambrosio O'Higgins, Lord Cochrane, General William Miller, and many South American leaders of English descent or of English education. The reading of these books, and that of the travels of Humboldt, has been followed by the reading of the popular works of Sarmiento, Mitre, Pilling, and of local poets, some of whose poems are events in picture. Strongly partizan pamphlets, and books forged out of some special experience, like Larrazabal's vivid " Life of Bolivar," of which only the first volume was published, and like James Briggs's "Life of Miranda," give episodes in strong colorings, which are interesting to collect and reproduce in an historical order.

In this course of reading, following his excursions, the writer was led to wish to tell the story of South American liberty for popular reading, as an introduction to a study of South American history. He has sought to explain events so clearly to the reader that his narrative may prepare the way for more philosophical studies of a most interesting phase of the recent progress of mankind.

South America, after the manner of the lesser countries Japan and Mexico, seems about to surprise the world by her industrial achievements. The liberators of the viceroyalties and the pioneers of science are the heroes of a great preparation, and in harmony with this spirit of patriotic educational and industrial progress this interpretation is written. As much as South America owes to Bolivar, San Martin, and Sucre, the emancipators, she feels her obligation to men like William Wheelwright of Newburyport, Massachusetts, who made for her shores, ports, lighthouses and harbors, founded the South American Steam Navigation Company, caused the railway across the pampas to be built, created the canal of Ensenada, and planned the railway over the Andes from Buenos Ayres to Santiago de Chili and Valparaiso. This captain of industry has two grand monuments in South America, and a more humble memorial in his native town of Newburyport.

The immigration of the eastern world to South America is becoming so great that already this eastern movement across the placid seas of the equator is laying the foundation of a new Latin race under the peaks of Tupungato, Aconcagua, Illimani and Chimborazo. The "purple empire that England lost," resourceful Argentina, extends her ports and multiplies her cities, in which float the flags of Italy, Germany, England and the East. Buenos Ayres has now a population of nearly seven hundred thousand souls, and may number nearly a million at the close of the century.

A land of wonder awaits these new immigrants. South America embraces an eighth of the globe. The whole area of the United States could find room in the marvelous valley of the Amazon, whose fertile fields would sustain an incalculable population. The Mississippi would be lost in the river that drains the Andes. The glittering domes of the Cordilleras surpass by a mile the highest peaks of the northern part of the hemisphere. Cotopaxi lifts her snowy chimney five times as high as Vesuvius.

The stupendous table-lands where the Incas ruled in their glory, and that begin at silver Potosí, the highest large city on earth, and end at Quito, in the shadow of Chimborazo, have an area of more than four times the State of New York. Lake Titicaca, the supposed crater of a volcano, is twelve thousand feet high. The Bolivian highlands, the region of the alpaca, the vicugna, and of the crags of the condor, are capable of maintaining a population surpassing that of France or Spain. And in these temperate altitudes are to be found all varieties of climates, and the productions of all zones.

Here spread the coast solitudes of Atacama, with its resources of silver, and the white desert of Tarapacá, the natural laboratory of vegetable food, that causes the outworn gardens of Europe to bloom again.

The early history of these vast regions that await the future is one of moral and spiritual suggestion, of heroism and romance. The period of the Spanish and Italian discoveries has been a tempting theme to the writers on human achievement, and the ideal civilization of the period of the Incas has interested the historian. The Spanish conquerors have been pictured in romance and song, and by the regretful pen of the philosopher. But the story of the heroes of the *republics* of South America, though it has found a considerable place in narrative and critical history, has not often been told in popular form. It is the purpose of this volume to tell this story, as the like story of our own land has often been told, for home reading, for the social club, the school-room, and for the pioneer of opportunity.

In regard to the style of the book, the writer has aimed to make vivid and picturesque what seemed to him the heroic and prophetic. His purpose has been to interest the reader in what is most noble and promising, to be true to the spirit of events, and accurate in noting progress from the liberal and optimistic point of view. He has undertaken this introductory work less in the spirit of authorship than in the hope that *he who reads this will read more* from the authors cited, and be led to study the more adequate sources of information about a country of heroic achievement and wonderful resources, that promises to take a foremost place in the new history of the New World.

28 WORCESTER STREET, BOSTON, MASSACHUSETTS,
July, 1898.

INTRODUCTION

THE whole of South America for the two centuries after the Columbian discovery was a viceroyalty of Spain. At first it had but one viceroy, the seat of whose government was in Peru. From a very early period Lima, which came to be called, in the poetic language of the conquerors, the "Pearl of the Pacific," was the "City of the Kings." In the golden days of the Spanish Main colonial settlements multiplied in the viceroyalty, and some of the most important of these were on the eastern coast. There New Granada arose, with the city of Cartagena, whose gigantic fortifications and walls are still a wonder.

As the population grew the viceroyalty was found to be too large for the administration of the government. For this reason Spain created another viceroyalty in New Granada in 1718, and a captaincy at Caracas in 1734. During this period of subdivision a viceroyalty was founded at Buenos Ayres, and a captaincy in Chili.

South America was wholly governed by the kings of Spain, who maintained for the judgment of its common affairs the Council of the Indies, or of West India. This council instituted a local court of inspection, called the *Audiencia*. This was also a court of appeal. The authority of these bodies was only advisory. The King of Spain governed all; his will was supreme.

The viceroy, or vice-king, represented the Spanish

throne. He was president of the Council of the Indies. His salary was sixty thousand dollars, or *pesos*, in Peru, and forty thousand dollars in New Granada and Buenos Ayres. The viceroy, as a rule, held his office for five years.

The *cabildo* was a popular assembly somewhat corresponding in purpose and form to a council of a mayor and aldermen. An *alcalde* was a judge, or a justice of the peace. A Spanish creole was a Spaniard born in the colony. He was little more than a Spanish slave.

These simple explanations are a necessary introduction to Spanish-American history for popular reading.

The purple flag of the liberation of the north of South America went from Venezuela to New Granada, and thence to Ecuador and over the Peruvian Andes. It was first thrown to the breeze by Miranda, and was borne on its march of flame and blood to Peru by Bolivar. This was the southward march of liberty.

The purple flag of the liberation of the south of South America went from Buenos Ayres (Argentina) over the Andes, and emancipated Chili and Peru. The flag was borne by San Martin, and the banner of the southern army of the Andes was emblazoned with the emblem of the Sun. This represents the northern march of liberty.

The two flags of liberation, that of the north and that of the south, met in Peru, in Lima, the " City of the Kings." General Sucre completed the liberation in the Peruvian Andes.

It is our purpose to describe the march of the two flags of liberation, the victory of the united banners in Peru, and to trace in outline the industrial and educational progress of the republics of the Sun.

Ducoudray-Holstein, an officer under Bolivar in the war of the liberation, thus clearly presents the march of events in the Atlantic provinces of South America from the beginning of the revolution to the battle of Carabobo, near Valencia, Venezuela, which was the Yorktown of the war of the patriots of the north:

"The following are the principal revolutions and changes of government on the Main, from April 19, 1810, until December, 1819, when Venezuela and New Granada united under one government, which took the name of the Republic of Colombia.

"In Venezuela the Spanish government was changed by a revolution which took place at Caracas, April 19, 1810, when the Captain-General Emparan and the Real Audiencia were arrested, and a provisional junta was formed, under the name of 'Junta Established for the Preservation of the Rights of His Majesty, the King Ferdinand VII.'

"On March 2, 1811, the Congress of Venezuela opened its sessions at Caracas. It was composed of the deputies of the following provinces: Margarita, Caracas, Mérida, Cumaná, Barcelona, Barinas and Truxillo. By an act of July 5, 1811, Congress declared the republic of Venezuela free and independent of Spain. On the 21st of December of the same year it sanctioned a constitution which bound the provinces together by a federal act, like that of the United States of America. But these several provinces, being exposed both to internal faction and to invasion from without, were scarcely able separately to bear the expense incurred for their own preservation, so that the expenses of the general government, and the support of the army and navy, fell chiefly upon Caracas. Congress was in a prosperous state, when the dreadful earthquake, together with the loss of Puerto Cabello, and the capitulation of Vittoria, between Generals Miranda and Monteverde, ruined the government, and destroyed the Congress and republic of Venezuela (July, 1812). The country was left to anarchy, and subjected to the power of the sword.

"On August 14, 1814, General Simon Bolivar entered the city of Caracas as conqueror, and assumed the title of 'Dictator Liberator of the West of Venezuela,' and established an arbitrary military government. General San Iago Marino had done the same before in the provinces of Cumaná, Barcelona, etc., under the title of 'Dictator Liberator of the Provinces East of Caracas.'

"July 17, 1814, the Spaniards again entered the city of Caracas. In consequence of the battle of La Puerta, where the two dictators were beaten by Boves, the Spaniards shortly after took possession of the provinces, which the two dictators and their troops had evacuated. In the night of the 24th and 25th of August the dictators embarked at Cumaná.

"Venezuela again became subject to the bayonet, and each military chieftain governed despotically the territory occupied by his troops.

"May 5, 1816, Simon Bolivar, with some armed men, entered again the territory of Venezuela (the island of Margarita), and assumed the title of 'Supreme Chief, Captain-General of the Forces of Venezuela and New Granada,' etc.

"On the 6th of July of the same year he lost that title and Venezuela, when he suddenly embarked at Ocumare for the Dutch island of Buen Ayre.

"On December 31, 1816, General Bolivar landed again at Barcelona, and reassumed the title of 'Supreme Chief, Liberator of the Republic of Venezuela, Captain-General,' etc. He had been called through the powerful influence of Admiral Louis Brion, but under the express condition that he should, upon his arrival, assemble a congress at Barcelona. He not only neglected to do so, but he persecuted the members of the Congress at Cariaco, May, 1817.

"In consequence of General Bolivar's unfortunate campaign in 1818 against Morillo, the general dissatisfaction of the inhabitants of Angostura with that campaign, and the strong representations of Brion, Zea, Manuel Torres, Dr. Roscio, Dr. Carli, and other patriots, the supreme chief was compelled at last to assemble a congress at the city of Angostura, under the name of the Congress of the Republic of Venezuela. Bolivar was chosen President of the republic."

After the battle of Boyacá, Bolivar united Venezuela and New Granada, under the name of Colombia.

The revolution against the Spanish rule in America began in Buenos Ayres, and in the north at Caracas at about the same time. The two movements met in Alto, Peru.

Under the rule of the viceroys the people of South America had practically no rights. Spain only allowed them certain privileges in return for obedience and service. They were made slaves and were robbed in the name of the government. Out of their servitude and enforced labor Spain became one of the richest of nations. It was death for a creole to protest in any open way against injustice. One of the greatest forms of injustice was the mita, or the enforced labor of the native population. On the Spanish Main the tyranny was as great as it was on the land.

There were enlightened and patriotic priests; some of the leading heroes were priests; but in general the ecclesiastical tyranny was as rigorous as that of the state. (See Appendix.) The church as well as the state enforced the view that America was the gift of the Holy See to Spain, and that it was the divine right of the king to rule, and that the king could do no wrong. Any plea for justice outside of royal authority was both treason and heresy.

Such was the civil condition in South America when the first revolution arose under Tupac Amaru.

CONTENTS

	PAGE
PREFACE	v
INTRODUCTION	xi

CHAPTER
- I. TUPAC AMARU, THE INCA REVOLUTIONIST . . . 1
- II. THE KNIGHT ERRANT OF LIBERTY—THE DREAM OF MIRANDA . . . 19
- III. JOSEPH BONAPARTE, KING OF SPAIN AND OF THE INDIES . . . 28
- IV. SIMON BOLIVAR, THE WASHINGTON OF THE SOUTH . . . 34
- V. THE INDEPENDENCE, 1811—THE EVENT OF JULY 4—THE DECLARATION . . . 43
- VI. THE EARTHQUAKE AT CARACAS—AN HEROIC EPISODE—MONTEVERDE—THE UNLOCKED DOOR—THE FAILURE OF MIRANDA . . . 53
- VII. THE COLONIAL SYSTEM—WHAT LATIN AMERICA SUFFERED—THE SPANISH VICEROYALTIES—THE MANIFESTO OF ARGENTINA—THE EXPULSION OF THE JEWS FROM SPAIN—THE PERSECUTIONS OF THE NATIVE AMERICAN RACES—CUBA—THE CREOLES . . . 69
- VIII. THE LIBERATING ARMY OF THE NORTH—THE TRIUMPH OF BOLIVAR—THE BATTLE OF ARAURE—PÉTION—PIAR—BOLIVAR ELECTED PRESIDENT—THE MARCH OVER THE CORDILLERAS—THE BATTLE OF BOYACÁ—ANGOSTURA—COLOMBIA . . . 93

CONTENTS

CHAPTER		PAGE
IX.	The Battle of Carabobo — Paez — The Liberty of the North — The Magnanimity of Bolivar.	114
X.	Argentina — The Liberating Army of the South	119
XI.	Cuzco — The Banner of the Sun	126
XII.	The Battle of Maypo — Chili — Peru — The Meeting of the Two Liberators — Abnegation and Moral Heroism of San Martin	131
XIII.	Ayacucho, the Decisive Battle of South America — Its Dramatic and Thrilling Events — Bolivia — The Triumphal Entrance of Bolivar into Potosí	139
XIV.	The Panama Congress of 1826 — The Union and Peace of the American Republics — The Last Days of Simon Bolivar	149
XV.	William Wheelwright and the Industrial Heroes	154
XVI.	The Monroe Doctrine — The Venezuelan Boundary	160
XVII.	Brazil	170
XVIII.	The Progress of Argentina — The Tyrants Quiroga and Rosas — Mitre — The Period of Progress	174
XIX.	The Tyrants of Paraguay	184
XX.	Education in Argentina and the Other Republics — Sarmiento	192
XXI.	Dom Pedro II. and the Progress of Brazil — The History of the Amazon	200
XXII.	The Congress of the Republics at Lima, 1847 — The Progress of the West Coast — Balmaceda — Guiana — The Pan-American Congress, 1889-90.	210
XXIII.	The Chili-Peruvian War — The Affair of the "Esmeralda," and the Heroism of	

CHAPTER		PAGE
	Arturo Pratt — The Battles of Tarapacá and Miraflores	224
XXIV.	History of Liberty in Cuba — The Cuban Heroes — The Destruction of the "Maine"	230
XXV.	Porto Rico	246
XXVI.	The South American Orators — The Orations of Bolivar — The Farewell of San Martin	248
	Appendix	259

LIST OF ILLUSTRATIONS

BOLIVAR'S ENTRANCE INTO CARACAS . . . . *Frontispiece*

Facing page

BOLIVAR ON MONTE SACRO 36
VIEW OF CARACAS, VENEZUELA 40
STREET SCENE IN CARACAS, VENEZUELA, SHOWING CAPITOL ON THE LEFT 46
INNER COURT OF THE CAPITOL, CARACAS, VENEZUELA . 50
BOLIVAR AT THE EARTHQUAKE OF CARACAS 56
STREET SCENE IN LA GUAYRA, VENEZUELA 60
MAP OF SOUTH AMERICA 80
PIAR BEFORE HIS EXECUTION 104
WASHINGTON PLAZA, CARACAS, VENEZUELA 118
THE BANNER OF THE SUN 126
MAUSOLEUM OF SAN MARTIN, IN BUENOS AYRES 138
CHART SHOWING STEAMSHIP ROUTES TO AND FROM AMERICAN AND WEST INDIAN PORTS 158
QUIROGA AND THE TIGER 176
A SCENE IN THE CATTLE-RAISING DISTRICT ON THE PAMPAS OF THE ARGENTINE REPUBLIC 182
SCENE ON THE GREAT GERMAN RAILROAD OF VENEZUELA, CONNECTING VALENCIA AND CARACAS 198
CHILIAN VOLCANO, IN THE ANDES IN CHILI. HEIGHT 9446 FEET 214
A PARTY OF INDIANS CONDUCTING A BAGGAGE-TRAIN OF LLAMAS, CHILI 224

CHAPTER I

TUPAC AMARU, THE INCA REVOLUTIONIST

THE first struggle for liberty against the Spanish dominion in Latin America was made by a descendant of the Incas—Tupac Amaru. The effort was a spasm; it ended in one of the most cruel and pitiable scenes of history; but its influence lived. The sympathetic reader may well inquire, after reviewing the tragedy of Amaru, will the spirit of the events that made Tupac Amaru the first apostle of liberty in the Peruvian highlands ever return again to the Quichua race in the ancient Incarial empire?

Visions become history, and patriots build, like the Hebrew legislator, after the pattern shown them on the mount. Washington, following the example of Cincinnatus, laid down the sword and took up the implements of husbandry, and dreamed, in Mount Vernon's gardens, of the time when all the nations of the world should make a compact of peace. This larger faith in humanity found expression in the International Conference of 1890, called the Pan-American Congress, whose inspiring spirit was the Hon. James G. Blaine, then the Secretary of State. Near the close of that memorable congress of the representatives of seventeen American republics, Mr. Blaine said:

"If in this closing hour the conference had but one

deed to celebrate, we should dare call the world's attention to the deliberate, confident, solemn dedication of two great continents to peace, and to the prosperity which has peace for its foundation. We hold up this new Magna Charta, which abolishes war and substitutes arbitration between the American republics, as the first great fruit of the International American Conference. The noblest of Americans, the aged poet and philosopher Whittier, is the first to send his salutation and benediction, declaring:

"'If in the spirit of peace the American Conference agrees upon a rule of arbitration which shall make war in this hemisphere well-nigh impossible, its sessions will prove one of the most important events in the history of the world.'"

Such are the hopes of Latin and English America, for whose liberties from foreign dominion Tupac Amaru struck the first blow, and made himself the earliest martyr. The memory of the past haunted this native hero of liberty. In his veins flowed the blood of benefactors of his race who had reigned a thousand years. One of his ancestors, bearing his name, had dared to lead a rebellion against the tyranny of Spain in the dark days of the viceroyalty.

Tupac Amaru I. (too-pak ah-mah-roo), the Inca after whom this later hero was called, was born in Cuzco about 1540, and died there in 1573. He was the grandson of Atahualpa, and the second son of Manco Iñca Yupanqui, who succeeded the unfortunate Atahualpa on the throne. The eldest son of Yupanqui, Sayri Tupac, submitted to the Spanish crown, and was baptized and given a place as sub-chief under the rule of the conquerors. On his death the Incarial succession fell to Tupac Amaru. This Indian had the spirit and pride of his ancestors. He refused to renounce his family claims in favor of the Spaniards, and aspired to restore his race to their pristine glory. He sought refuge in the mountains of Vilcabamba. The Peruvian Indians recognized him as the true Inca, the royal representative of the children of the Sun. For this reason the Spanish viceroy, Francisco de Toledo, determined to bring him within reach of his power. In 1572 the viceroy pretended to be sending troops to Chili, but he ordered two hundred and fifty of these auxiliaries to explore the mountain fortresses of Vilcabamba, and to capture the young prince and bring him to the viceroyalty.

Tupac Amaru met the invaders like a hero, but was again and again defeated by their superior arms and skill.

He then fled, with his family and followers, to the mountain fortresses of his principality, which he deemed impregnable. Before the rugged mountain walls rolled a stream which he believed no foreigner could cross without destruction.

Captain Martin de Loyola, in the service of the viceroy, resolved to cross this stream with twenty intrepid followers, under the cover of night. He suddenly appeared in the camp of the Inca, captured the prince, and carried him to Cuzco. He was there accused of leading a revolt, and was beheaded.

His descendant, José Gabriel Condorcanqui, Amaru II., seems to have inherited his purpose and spirit. He dreamed of the independence of his people, and of the return of the first Inca in the glory of the rising sun.

Before we narrate the incidents of this hero's history, let us glance at the race from which he sprang.

There are great legends, worthy of noblest representation in poetry and art, that belong to the dusk of American tradition, to the twilight of the gods. They are fanciful, but they are parables, and are full of the noblest suggestions. One of these relates to Quetzalcohuatl, the mythic apostle

from the eastern world to Guatemala, and to the golden age that arose under his preaching, when the birds sang never so sweetly, when the flowers bloomed never so brightly, when a single ear of corn taxed the strength of a man, and no violence was allowed to bird, beast or man. Quetzalcohuatl, of whom the beautiful bird of Guatemala, the quetzal, is still a reminder,—a bird that, according to John Lloyd Stephens, the explorer, is " the most beautiful thing that flies,"—is associated in an agreeable fable with the person of St. Thomas, the doubter, the apostle who said to the disciples, when Christ was about to take the ways of peril, " Let us go, that we may die with him." According to the old legends, which have received color from the beautiful sculptured cross found at Palenque, St. Thomas went to the Indian peninsula of Malabar, founded there the church that has lived in the Nestorians of Persia, and, according to an extension of the same fable, came to Mexico by the supposed way of Chinese Tartary, Bering Strait, and the West Pacific coast, and there appeared as Quetzalcohuatl. The legend, which has many forms, has, notwithstanding its absurdities, left us a picture of the golden age in America as poetic as Vergil's " Pollio," and as interesting as the prophecy of the Cumæan sibyl.

The second great legend that awaits poetry and art is that which attributes the origin of the Peruvians to Jewish wanderers from Armenia, or from other parts of the Orient. This legend also has many forms.

A most interesting work published in 1854, entitled " Peruvian Antiquities," by Mariano Eduardo de Rivero and Johann Jakob von Tschudi, translated by Francis L. Hawks, D.D., thus pictures some of the incidents of this great but improvable tradition:

" Passing by the proofs, more or less ingenious, advanced by Heckewelder, Beltrame, De Laet, Emanuel de Moraes,

Beatty, Samuel Stanhope Smith, William Penn, Count Crawford, and many others, we will make particular mention of Adair, who lived forty years among the Indians, and who, after the most thorough examination and minute comparison, assures us that the origin of the Indians is Israelitish, founding his assertion principally on the religious rites, which plainly present many points of agreement with those of the Hebrew people.

"Like the Jews, the Indians offer their first-fruits; they keep their new moons, and the feast of expiation at the end of September or in the beginning of October; they divide the year into four seasons, corresponding with the Jewish festivals. According to Charlevoix and Long, the brother of a deceased husband receives his widow into his house as a guest, and after a suitable time considers her as a legitimate consort. There is also much analogy between the Hebrews and Indians in that which concerns various rites and customs, such as the ceremonies of purification, the use of the bath, the ointment of bear's grease, fasting, and the manner of prayer. The Indians likewise abstain from the blood of animals, as also from fish without scales; they consider divers quadrupeds unclean, as also certain birds and reptiles; and they are accustomed to offer as a holocaust the firstlings of the flock. Acosta and Emanuel de Moraes relate that various nations allow matrimony with those only of their own tribe or lineage, this being, in their view, a striking characteristic, very remarkable and of much weight. But that which most tends to fortify the opinion as to the Hebrew origin of the American tribes is a species of ark, seemingly like that of the Old Testament. This the Indians take with them to war. It is never permitted to touch the ground, but rests upon stones or pieces of wood, it being deemed sacrilegious and unlawful to open it or look into it. The priests scrupulously guard their sanctuary, and the high priest carries on his breast a white shell adorned with precious stones, which recalls the urim of the Jewish high priest, of whom we are also reminded by a band of white plumes on his forehead.

"According to the credible testimony of Adair, the Indians of North America celebrate the feast of first-fruits with religious dances, singing in chorus these mystic words: 'Yo Meschica, He Meschica, Va Meschica,' forming thus, with the three first syllables, the name of Je-hovah, and the name of Messiah, thrice pronounced, following each initial. On other occasions may be heard in their hymns the words *Aylo, Aylo*, which correspond with the Hebrew word *El*, 'God.' In other hymns occur the words *hiwah, hiwah, hydchyra*, 'the immortal soul,' and *Schiluhyo, Schiluhe, Schiluhva*, of which Adair thinks that *Schiluh* is the same with the Hebrew word *Schaleach*, or *Schiloth*, which signifies 'messenger' or 'pacificator.' The use of Hebrew words was not uncommon in the religious performances of the North American Indians, and Adair assures us that they called an accused or guilty person *haksit canaha*, 'a sinner of Canaan'; and to him who was inattentive to religious worship they said: 'Tschi haksit canaha' ('You resemble a sinner of Canaan'). Lescarbot also tells us that he had heard the Indians of South America sing 'Alleluia.'

"Those authors who attribute a Hebrew origin to the American tribes do not agree among themselves touching the coming of the Israelites into the New World: some think that they came directly from the eastern hemisphere to the West, and established themselves in the central and southern parts of this hemisphere; but the majority are of the opinion that they crossed Persia and the frontiers of China, and came by the way of Bering Strait."

A writer named Montesinos would have us believe that the Peruvians came from Armenia, that here were King Solomon's mines; and he dates the events of poetic history from the deluge, of which the Peruvians seem to have traditions.

Several curious writers have attempted to prove that the first Inca, Manco Capac, and the poetic divinity of Mexico, Quetzalcohuatl, were Buddhist missionary priests.

In a work like ours, which seeks to tell the story of liberty and progress in Latin America, to picture an advance in civilization by incidents, a study of the Incarial period would not be expected; but a glance at that wonder of romance is permissible, as it associates itself with an heroic revolution in which one of Inca blood was a leader.

Gonzalo Pizarro and Prescott have pictured the Incas in their glory. The authority of the Peruvian monarchs exceeded that of the most powerful kings of the eastern world. Under the dominion of Huaina Capac the Inca empire extended from the regions north of Quito to the river Maule in Chili, or eight hundred leagues, thus exceeding the greatest empire in Europe, and was bounded on the west by the Pacific, and on the east by the pampas. It contained some ten millions of inhabitants,* a number that greatly diminished after the conquest.

Over this glittering empire the Inca was the absolute lord. "The very birds will suspend their flight if I command it," said Atahualpa to the Spanish invaders, in the fabulous language of the Peruvian kings.

According to Garcilasso de la Vega, himself of Inca blood, the government of the Incas was paternal. One only needs to read Garcilasso's wonderful book to be convinced that Mr. Bellamy's prophetic retrospect entitled

* According to some authorities, thirty millions.

"Looking Backward" has already largely been enacted in the theater of the Andean world. Some of the accounts of the glory of the Incas seem to belong, indeed, to the dazzling epoch of fables. Plutarch tells us that the birds in the air were affected when the Roman herald proclaimed the liberty of the Greeks; and Sarmiento, in his "Revolution," says the shouts that hailed the Inca on his pilgrimages among his people caused "the birds to fall to the ground."

The ancient Peruvian realm was one of equality and fraternity. The people were like one family, of which the Inca was the father. None were rich, none poor. All labored for the good of the whole, and the labor was not exacting. Age and infancy were alike protected. The temples were opened to all; the delights of the festivals were shared by all; the bards sang for all; and the people rejoiced together in the golden gardens of Yucay.

The memory of the Incarial festivals was the light of the past. In those days the highways were strewn with flowers. The worshipers on the hills acclaimed with delight the rising of the sun, wondering if that would be the day when the first Inca would return to the world again. The sun's rays filled with a golden light the crystal crowns of the Andes; hymns were sung in the white processions bearing the Inca lilies; drums were beaten, trumpets were blown, and bells, silver and golden, added their music to the choruses of joy. The sun's rays met the rays reflected by the gold in the great temple, from the golden roof of which were taken seven hundred plates, each as heavy as four men could bear, for the redemption of Atahualpa. The priests bowed down to the reflected splendor.

The scene is Cuzco. A mighty and shadowy fortress lifts itself over the city. The wall facing the city is precipitous, is twelve hundred feet long, and sustains three colossal towers. This Cyclopean wall has been so built that it seems to be but a single stone; the blade of a knife could not be inserted into its seams. The sun appears above the mountains. The city bursts into song. A long procession, led by the royal family and priests, takes up its march for the golden gardens of Yucay, which surpassed those of Cashmere. The young Inca, just proclaimed, walks beside his father. He wears on his head the insignia of the *llanta*, with two feathers from the sacred bird of the kingdom, the *coraquenque*. In his ears are hung golden *orejones*, or heavy pendants. He supports a girdle of jewels, the colors of which typify the virtues. The sun in the sky becomes a fiery splendor as the procession approaches Yucay, the gardens of delight, some twelve miles from the Temple of the Sun. The maize that adorned the temple was made of gold, with husks of silver and tassels of silk. The flowers were of gold, emeralds and precious stones. In front of the procession is borne the jeweled banner of the iris. The procession enters the gardens amid the songs of bards, the music of viols, and banks of flowers. Dances follow. At a festival given in the gardens of Yucay in honor of the birth of Huascar, son of Huaina Capac, the nobles danced to a chain of gold seven hundred feet long, with links nearly as large as a man's wrist. A festival was held at Quito during which the rising moon shone upon a temple of silver situated on a high hill. It filled the temple with living splendor.

The people were happy. They believed in an ineffable God that ruled all the world. The sun was his message to them, and the Incas were the human interpreters of his will.

The meridional world, or what is now Alta Peru, or

Ecuador and Bolivia, may not, indeed, have been the Ophir of old, but it was a golden empire. Francisco Lopez de Gomara thus describes the house of the Inca: "All the service was of gold and silver, except copper, which was used for strength. They say that the Incas had a flower-garden by the sea, where the trees and flowers were of gold and silver." * To this the opulent Garcilasso de la Vega, of Inca blood, adds: "In all of them were gardens and orchards, where the Inca refreshed himself. In them were planted all the fine and beautiful trees and odoriferous plants which abounded in the kingdom, after which models they imitated in gold and silver many trees and other smaller bushes most perfectly, with their leaves, flowers and fruits; some seemed about to bud, others were half ripened or matured, and others entire and perfect in their size. Besides these and others, they made counterfeit resemblances of various species of corn, with their leaves, ear and stem, with their roots and flowers; the fibers which are found in the ear and stem were of gold, and all the rest of silver, soldered together. The same difference was made in the other plants, so that the flower, or whatever other part inclined to yellow, was imitated in gold, and the rest in silver. There were also to be seen animals, large and small, cast in gold and silver, such as rabbits, lizards, snakes, butterflies, foxes and mountain-cats; also birds of all descriptions, some placed in the trees as if singing, others flying about and sucking the honey from the flowers. There were also deer and fawns, lions and tigers, and all the other animals and birds which the country produced, each in its place, as true to nature as the reality. In many houses there were baths with large jars of silver and gold, from which water was poured into the baths. Where there were natural fountains of warm

* "Peruvian Antiquities."

water there were also baths of great splendor and richness. Among other displays of wealth, there were collections of billets of wood, imitated in gold and silver, as though they were deposited to be expended in the service of the houses."*

The Inca roads, a part of which were constructed in the period of Yupanqui, were as marvelous as the temples and golden gardens. Humboldt describes these roads, which filled him with wonder. Lopez de Gomara says:†
"There were two royal roads from the city of Quito to that of Cuzco,—very costly and noble works,—the one over the mountains, the other across the plains, each extending more than a thousand miles. The one which crossed the plains was walled on both sides, was twenty-five feet broad, with ditches of water outside, and was planted with trees called *molle*. The other, which was on the mountain, was also twenty-five feet wide, cut in some places from the solid rock, and in others made of stone and lime; for, indeed, it was necessary to cut away the rocks or fill up the valleys to bring the road to a level. It was a work which, as all agree, exceeded the pyramids of Egypt, the paved ways of the Romans, and, indeed, all other ancient works. Huayna Capac restored, enlarged, and completed these roads; but he did not build them entirely, as some assert, nor could they have been wholly constructed in his lifetime. These roads went in a direct line, without turning aside for hills, mountains, or even lakes. For resting-places they had certain grand palaces, which were called *tambos*, where the court and royal army lodged. These tambos were provided with arms, food, shoes and clothing for the troops. In their civil wars the Spaniards destroyed these roads to impede the march of their enemies. The Indians themselves de-

* " Peruvian Antiquities." † *Ibid.*

molished a part of them when they waged war and laid siege to the cities of Cuzco and Lima, where the Spaniards were."

The betrayal of Atahualpa, the last Inca before the conquest, and his tragic death, have often been pictured.

There was one Spaniard, by name Lejesema, or Lequizano, a conquistador of quick conscience, who, although a soldier, came eventually to see the robbery of the Inca empire in its true light. He was the last of the conquerors. In his old age he was truly penitent for the part he had taken in the great crime against humanity, and he trembled before God. He had received as his share of the robbery of the Incas the golden image in the Temple of the Sun—the golden sun of the empire. The latter was a huge plate of burnished gold, round like a shield, with rays that spread over the sacred face of the temple, that reflected the sun at its rising.

In his early life Lejesema was a noted gambler. Gambling seems to have been a passion with him. After receiving the golden sun of the gods as his share of the robbery, which would have brought him wealth and fame, it would seem that he could desire nothing more. But the passion for gambling haunted his soul. He staked the golden sun of Peru one night, and lost. Hence arose the proverb in Spain in regard to an all-controlling passion: *"Juega el sol antes que amanezca"* (" He gambles away the sun before sunrise ").

When this man had repented he desired that Spain should know the truth in regard to the nobility of the Peruvians, and the wrong that had been done them in the name of religion. So out of his tortured soul was wrung a remarkable confession, for which we are indebted to Prescott.

The line of the Incas was as follows:*

" 1. Manco Capac began to reign in the year 1021, and died in 1062, after reigning forty years.

" 2. Sinchi Rocca reigned thirty years, from 1062 to 1091.

" 3. Lloqque Yupanqui reigned thirty-five years, from 1091 to 1126.

" 4. Mayta Capac began to reign in 1126, reigned thirty years, and died in 1156.

" 5. Capac Yupanqui inherited the power in the year 1156, reigned forty-one years, and died in 1197.

" 6. Inca Rocca began to reign in 1197, and died in 1249, after having reigned fifty-one years.

" 7. Yahuar Huaccac had a reign of forty years, from 1249 to 1296; seven of these he passed in private life, after having renounced in 1289, in favor of his son Viracocha.

" 8. Viracocha occupied the throne from the year 1289, and died in 1340. This Inca predicted the ruin of the empire, and the arrival of white and bearded men. His son, Inca Urco, reigned only eleven days, being deposed by the nobles of the empire as a fool and incapable of governing.

" 9. Titu Manco Capac Pachacutec came to the crown in the year 1340, reigned sixty years, and died in 1400, after having lived, according to tradition, a hundred and three years.

" 10. Yupanqui inherited the regal power in the year 1400, reigned thirty-nine years, and died in 1439.

" 11. Tupac Yupanqui reigned from the year 1439, and died in 1475, after thirty-six years' reign.

" 12. Huayna Capac succeeded Tupac Yupanqui in the year 1475, reigned fifty years, and died in 1525. This chief was considered the most glorious of all the Peruvian monarchs.

* " Peruvian Antiquities."

"13. Huascar received the crown in 1526, reigned seven years, and died in 1532.

"14. Atahuallpa, or Atahualpa, began to reign in the year 1532, governed the whole empire for one year and four months, after having reigned six years in Quito only, and died on the scaffold, by order of Pizarro, in the public square of Cajamarca, the 29th of August, 1533.

"After the conquest of the Spaniards, the brother of both the preceding monarchs was crowned as Manco Capac II. He reigned with a light shadow of royal dignity until the year 1553. He was succeeded by his three sons, Sayri Tupac, Cusititu Yupanqui, and Tupac Amaru. This last was beheaded in Cuzco, in the year 1571, by order of Don Francisco de Toledo, fifth viceroy of Peru."

Tupac Amaru the younger was the fifth in descent from Inca Tupac Amaru, who had been put to death in 1571. His name as a subject of the viceroy was José Gabriel Condorcanqui. He was educated at the college at Cuzco, amid scenes that daily recalled the glory of his ancestors· and the injustice that had been done to his race. The college had been founded for the education of Indian chiefs. The youth learned the Spanish language. He seems to have been an apt scholar. To a high spirit and natural gifts he added many polite accomplishments. But his heart throbbed for his people. The Spanish rule over them had reduced them to slavery. The mita, or forced labor, not only made them slaves, but victims of merciless cruelty. They toiled without recompense, and suffered without justice. They were helpless.

Tupac Amaru began his career as a petitioner for justice to his race. He was brought into association with Spanish priests and officers, and to them he presented the misery of the Indians, and begged them to reform the laws in regard to servitude. His appeals met with no response.

Labor under the lash went on, and the young Inca's heart could do little but bleed. He had an income from an estate. Out of this he assisted those in need, paid the taxes of the poor, and sheltered those who in their poverty and despair turned to him for assistance. He seems to have been a man of great dignity of deportment, and of a philosophic temperament. He was one who loved others better than himself, and whose deeds were an honor to humanity.

His father was a cacique, or tributary chief. Tupac Amaru succeeded him at the age of twenty. His province was Tungasuca, a high plateau of the Andes, one of the winter lands of the sea. The cry of the wrongs of his race found him there, and gave him no peace. He sought in every way to obtain redress for the slaves of the hateful mita. His mission was met only by excuses or scorn. The thought of the liberation of the Indians became sweet to him in his Andean fortress. The Spaniards were merely robbers of the country, who put might for right. The whole land groaned under their tyranny. Why could not their power be overthrown by the union of all the people whom they oppressed, and why might not the lands of the Sun be made independent and free? His dream of liberty grew, and was stimulated by new cases of cruelty and injustice. It was but the dream of an Adams, a Lafayette, a Miranda, a Bolivar.

The governor of Tinta, near Lima, was one of the most merciless of the oppressors of the Indians. Tupac Amaru formed a plan for rescuing his people from the power of this tyrant. He led a force against him, arrested him, brought him to Tungasuca, and put him to death. The Indians now flocked around Tupac Amaru. An army was formed. The oppressed people were eager to be led against their taskmasters. Tupac Amaru descended from the hills with an army that constantly grew stronger. He faced Cuzco, and found the city of his ancestors in his power. He liberated the workmen in the Spanish factories, and set at naught the mita. He was advancing like a conqueror when the Spanish officials met and asked for negotiations. With a sense of his own honor, and trusting to the justice of his cause, he consented to open negotiations with his crafty enemies. He formed a protected camp, and issued a proclamation setting forth the grievances of his race, and calling upon all the people to rise and make a common cause for liberty. The proclamation was circulated throughout the country. The people flocked to Tinta, and hailed the Inca as their deliverer. The Peruvians, with arms in their hands, for a brief time breathed the air of liberty.

Tupac Amaru now addressed letters to the bishop and to the officers of the municipality, asking for those measures of justice which are the birthright of all men. The whole population of Peru was now rising. The viceroy was alarmed. In February, 1781, a Spanish force was gathered to march against the Inca, who was still proposing a negotiation by which reforms might be secured peaceably. It was justice that the Inca desired, not blood. The answer came, as brutal as if from the regions beyond mercy: "We refuse all negotiation. If you will surrender now, the torture of your execution may be lessened." Tupac Amaru could do but one of two things: conquer a peace for the liberty of the people, or surrender and die. He was at the head of two hundred thousand men who were looking to him for salvation from a living death. The people thought that they saw in him the return of the Incas and of the golden age. He must strike for the independence of the slaves of the mita. A battle was fought. The rude army of patriots under the Inca was defeated, and driven back in disorder at the point of the Spanish bayonet. Tupac Amaru and his family were made captives.

On May 18, 1781, the conqueror issued a proclamation which caused humanity to shudder. The Inca with his family was to be publicly executed. His tongue was to be cut out; he was to be tied to four horses by his arms and legs, and to be drawn asunder as the horses should be led four different ways. It was a refinement of old Spanish cruelty. The infernal imaginations of the tyrants of those dark days have found but few equals in the records of mankind. The Inca was first made to suffer mentally and emotionally by witnessing the torture of his family. His uncle, an old man, had his tongue cut out, and was then strangled by an iron screw. His son, a youth of twenty, was then subjected to the same horrible tortures, in sight of the Inca. Then his wife was led into view, and her tongue torn out, and the screw applied to her neck. His youngest boy of ten years was compelled to witness these scenes. The Inca was then tortured by the knife, and lassos tied to the girths of four horses were fastened to his arms and ankles. The horses were headed in four different ways. They moved, and the bleeding form of the Inca rose in air. As the young son of the Inca saw the spectacle, he uttered a piercing shriek. The hearts of the Spaniards who heard that cry shrank with horror. It is said that the boy's voice haunted for a lifetime the people who heard it. Says a writer: "It was the death-knell of the Spanish colonial dominion." For there were Spanish hearts that could feel, even in the days of the viceroys. An evil priest had said to Pizarro, "I absolve thee," as he urged Pizarro to seize Atahualpa. But there were good priests as well as the agents of cruelty. There were patriot priests whose country was the world, and whose countrymen were all who live.

Liberty in South America began in the patriot clubs of London and Caracas. There was formed a club in Lima in silent memory of this and similar events. It was a club of silence, but it had a powerful purpose. Sympathetic priests, literary men, and Spanish women with the hearts of mothers joined that club. It grew. Its purpose was to secure justice to all, and the protection of the rights of all men. The club prepared the way for liberty. Tupac Amaru's death was to abolish the mita and to liberate his people. Of all martyrs of liberty, none ever died under more heartrending circumstances than he who was torn asunder in the great square of Cuzco, amid the fallen temples of his despoiled people.

So sadly but nobly perished the last son of the Incas, the first apostle of liberty in Latin America.

CHAPTER II

THE KNIGHT ERRANT OF LIBERTY—THE DREAM OF MIRANDA

HUMAN events are often preceded by visions. It is possible that Columbus, as he watched the stars on the quays of Genoa, saw America in a vision. Certain it is that he had more faith in his intuitions than in his scientific studies. "God," he said, "made me the messenger of the new heavens and the new earth, and told me where to find them. Maps, charts, and mathematical knowledge had nothing to do with the case."

The emancipation of South America began in the youthful visions of Francisco Miranda (1756–1816), a young cadet of noble family, born at Caracas,* in the Maritime Andes. He was a splendid dreamer, but he had not the sublime creative faith of a Columbus. He could see in his mind what he was incapable of carrying into execution; he had the prevision of liberty in South America, but was able only to show by failure what might be wrought by a mind that was practical. The patriot's character has been severely handled by the soldier and the critic; but the victories of the vanquished count for much in the ultimate values of human history. Miranda failed, and seldom has a high heart had a disappointment more pathetic. Mi-

* Some authorities state Santa Fé, in New Granada, in 1754.

randa, however, did not dream his young dream of the liberty of the South in vain. Though a visionary, he led the way to the independence of his country.

He rose to the rank of captain in the army, when his mind became thrilled with the cause of the patriots in North America struggling for independence. He was also inspired by the conduct of the French republicans. He came to North America, and served in the French contingent of the Continental Army from 1779 to 1781. At this time he was twenty-three years of age. As he witnessed the splendid achievements of Lafayette, and as the English power in America went down at Yorktown, he thought of his native land. He aspired to be the Washington of Venezuela, the emancipator of the slaves of the Spanish viceroys, the hero whose sword should lead armies under the fiery arch of the equator, and make free the populations of the meridional world. He went to Cuba and to Europe. He traveled through England, Germany, Turkey and Russia, dreaming always the dream of South American emancipation. The French Revolution fired his heart. He went to Paris, entered the army of the patriots, and rose to the rank of major-general. His name adorns the Arc de Triomphe in Paris, in the list of the heroes of the Revolution. In 1797 he incurred the displeasure of the French Directory, and fled to England, where he mingled in official society. He told his dream of South American liberty to William Pitt, and asked his aid in a scheme to proclaim liberty in the Andes. In Russia he won the favor of the Empress Catherine.

What was the true character of this lonely man who was passing from country to country, and who was filled with these dazzling visions?

In "The History of Don Francisco de Miranda's Attempt to Effect a Revolution in South America," by James

Briggs, who was an officer under Miranda, we find a description of the hero: "He [Miranda] is a great moralist or moralizer. Vice and meanness in every degree or shape are, according to his own declarations, entirely against his taste and judgment. If you take his word for it, he is a lover of virtue even to enthusiasm. To use his own language, he 'abominates tyranny, hates fools, abhors flatterers, detests pride and laments the corruption of modern days.' He loves freedom, admires candor, esteems wise men, respects humility and delights in that noble and beautiful integrity and good faith which distinguished the golden times of antiquity." Briggs further says of him: "He would renovate the perverted minds of mankind and restore the ancient beatitudes, when every excellence and virtue prevailed among men, for the happiness of the present race, and the perpetual prosperity of future generations." This is a qualified but not wholly unpleasing picture of one who might indeed have been a follower of Cincinnatus and Washington.

A letter from Miranda to President Thomas Jefferson, who had predicted South American liberty, dated "New York, January 22, 1806," confirms the view of Officer Briggs. Miranda says: "If the happy prediction which you have pronounced on the future destiny of our dear Colombia is to be accomplished in our day, may Providence grant that it may be under your auspices and by the generous efforts of her own children. We shall then in some sort behold the arrival of that age the return of which the Roman bard invoked in favor of the human race:

> "'The last great age, foretold by sacred rhymes,
> Renews its finished course: Saturnian times
> Roll round again, and mighty years, begun
> From this first orb, in radiant circles run.'"

A mind whose dreams of life thus sought the sublime interpretation of the Fourth Eclogue of Vergil was one of no common order, and must ever command admiration.

Officer Briggs brings his volume of letters to a close with these criticisms: "After all, this man of renown, I fear, must be considered as having more learning than wisdom, more theoretical knowledge than practical talent. He is too sanguine and opinionated to distinguish between the vigor of enterprise and the hardness of infatuation."

A man may have good morals and every polite accomplishment, and yet fail in a noble cause, if self-seeking be not eliminated from his purpose. The critics of Miranda have said that the hero sought to advance his own interests more than those of his country, and was more willing to imitate the achievements of Washington than to be a Washington. Men must be judged largely by their ideals, which are their true selves, and we must place ourselves among those who would give credit to the high purpose for the welfare of mankind that everywhere led the young steps of Francisco Miranda. Miranda suggested to the world the cause and method of South American independence. Wendell Phillips used to say that there were two kinds of men in the world—one who went forth and accomplished something, and the other who showed how the accomplishment should have been done in some other way. Miranda belonged to those that plan but do not successfully execute.

Miranda was rich, but his property was sacrificed to the cause. He lived in London as one in another world; for he thought of nothing, talked of nothing, sought for nothing, but South American independence. Failing to secure aid for his cause in England, he came to New York, organized an expedition of ardent and adventurous spirits, and sailed for Venezuela to proclaim a republic.

He met with disaster at sea, and the Venezuelans at the port where he landed were not prepared to respond to his call. Disappointed, but not disheartened, he returned to England. His effort seemed to have been fruitless, but it was powerful in suggestion. The very discussion of it stimulated the cause of Venezuelan independence.

In 1814 there appeared at Albany, New York, a book entitled "History of the Adventures and Sufferings of Moses Smith during Five Years of his Life, from the Beginning of the Year 1806, when He was Betrayed into the Miranda Expedition." The book is not friendly to General Miranda, for Smith was led by false representations of a recruiting-officer named Fink to join the patriotic expedition. The narrative is graphic. It furnishes a picture of the ideals and methods of Miranda, and of the first attempt for South American liberation. We quote from this narrative: "On the 15th of February we arrived at Jaquemel in St. Domingo. There our tricolored flag was displayed, and our printing-press was set to work on board the *Leander*. Proclamations were struck off, addressed to the people of South America by Don Francisco Miranda, commander-in-chief of the Colombian Army of South America. In them were set forth the griefs of the people, their wrongs and hardships, and the intention of the general to emancipate them. The officers, who were constituted before by brevet, now received their commissions from the general, by virtue of the power vested in· him. It was announced that the *Cleopatra*, Captain Wright, was to join us at this port, and there was a constant lookout for her. It was also expected that we should be joined by another American merchant ship, called the *Emperor*, commanded by Captain Lewis. To effect this junction, Captain Lewis and Major Smith went to Port au Prince, but returned without success. Two unarmed American schooners, one called the *Bee* and the other the *Bacchus*, were, however, chartered, and various modes of recruiting resorted to in order to increase the army, which, after all, did not amount to more than two hundred men, seamen included. An oath was administered to the officers to be true and faithful to the free people of South America independent of Spain, to serve them honestly against all their enemies, and to obey the orders of the supreme government of that country, and the officers by them appointed. The officers, on receiving their commissions, signed a promise to be governed by the articles of war of the United States, with such formal alterations only as might suit them to the different government under which they then were or might be. From this time the discipline, which had been strict before, became rigorous."

It was Moses Smith's lot to be put, with those enrolled by Mr. Fink, on board the *Bee*, and anchored close to the *Leander*. The alarm and discontent of these sailors were great, but their murmurs were silenced by the terrors of the articles of war. They concerted plans of escape, and once rose to effect their deliverance; but their officers hailed the *Leander*, which sent an armed force to subdue them. They were unarmed, and easily overcome. Some were wounded, others punished summarily by imprisonment or put into irons. They still, however, held to the determination to effect their escape on the first favorable occasion, or to sell their lives dearly.

"After being ten days at sea," the narrative continues, "instead of making the place of our destination, which was the small island of Bonair, on the coast of the Spanish Main, we were, by some mistake of the pilot, or by other mischance, deeply engulfed in the bay of Venezuela, seventy miles to leeward, with current and trade-wind against us. We therefore directed our course for the island of Aruba, which we reached on the 4th of April.

"We were joined at Aruba by an English schooner called the *Echo*, Captain Philips, a smuggler, to whom it was said the general gave sealed orders, but who left us after a few days, and never appeared again. We beat up toward Bonair, and on the 24th of April had the mainland and the islands of Little Caracas and Bonair in sight. An officer, Major Donahue, was ordered to go in the *Bacchus* to Bonair, to see whether any English frigates or other vessels of war were there, as we expected to be joined by such. There were no English vessels in the port, nor did Major Donahue bring intelligence of any. On the following day, the 25th, a proclamation was issued, offering to the sailors who should enlist as soldiers, to serve under the Colombian standard on shore, thirty dollars per month, a bounty of fifty at the close of the campaign to each one who should distinguish himself, a bounty to the non-commissioned officers, and to all who, having distinguished themselves, wished to return to their families, a gratuity proportioned to their courage and fidelity. With these promises, and much haranguing and persuasion, many were prevailed on to agree.

"Many of these men had been forced into this expedition against their will. They had not yet shed blood nor taken any active part in warfare. The laws of their native country were not intentionally violated by them, and they had not incurred the vengeance of any other. They determined to escape. Two undertook to sound the others. They were Benjamin Davis and Henry Sperry. Every one of the men engaged by John Fink agreed cordially to coöperate, and some of the sailors promised to join; but before the time arrived for executing their plot it was discovered. Their plan was to mutiny, take command of the schooner, and steer for the nearest port where they could escape; but the ships were discovered by two Spanish *guardacostas*, one a brig of twenty guns, the other a schooner of eighteen. They were hailed by the captain of the *Leander*, and ordered to prepare for action. After some broadsides exchanged between the armed vessels on both sides, they were ordered to board the enemy on the lee side, while the *Leander* was to attack and board the ship on the weather side. They obeyed their orders, but before they could accomplish them, to their inexpressible astonishment, they saw the *Leander*, with Miranda on board, haul down her colors and make off. The remaining ships were boarded and taken by the Spaniards. The men were plundered, stripped, and rifled; and so impatient were the conquerors for the booty that before they took the time to pull the clothes off they first cut the pockets to make sure of the contents. So expert were they in this inglorious kind of warfare that they seldom failed to clear away the pocket with a single stroke. The prisoners were next pinioned and secured, tied back to back, and in that humiliating posture conveyed to Port Cabello. There they were disembarked, and driven into the castle of St. Philip, chained two and two, and loaded with irons. They were divided into two parties of about thirty each, the whole number taken in the two schooners amounting to about sixty. They were then thrown into two separate dungeons, and suffered indescribable privations.

"Their trial took place toward the end of June. It was not till the 20th of July that their doom was announced to them. On that day their prison doors were thrown open, and they were told by an interpreter that they must come out to be hanged. The names of ten of the prisoners, all officers in Miranda's army, were first called, and the interpreter read this sentence from a paper he held: 'In the morning of to-morrow, at six o'clock, you, and each of you, are sentenced to be hanged by the neck until you are dead; after which your heads are to be severed from your bodies, placed upon poles, and distributed in the most public parts of the country.' The remainder, being nineteen in number, were sentenced to eight years' imprisonment in the castle of Boca Chica, near Cartagena, which sentences were all executed."

The conduct of Miranda in this case has been severely criticized. It would seem that it was not only the sailors who had been deceived, but that he himself had been. Had he not escaped, he must have found himself either a prisoner of the enemy or have been deserted by his own men. So ended his first vision of the emancipation of his country.

CHAPTER III

JOSEPH BONAPARTE, KING OF SPAIN AND OF THE INDIES

WE must glance back to Spain, to "the Peninsula," to understand the relations that existed between that empire and her colonies. It was Napoleon I. who opened the door of opportunity to South America by deposing the quarrelsome family of Charles IV., and placing his own amiable and faithful brother on the throne of the Bourbons.

It was the time of Ferdinand VII., son of Charles IV., who was born in 1784. In his youth Ferdinand VII. was subject to the intrigues and jealousies of his family. The father and son quarreled, and on March 19, 1808, King Charles, in the interests of peace, abdicated in favor of his son, who became king under the title of Ferdinand VII. Soon after this change the old king became unsettled in his resolution, and wrote to Napoleon I. that his abdication had not been voluntary, but had been forced. The most bitter enmity had arisen between father and son. Napoleon was ambitious to govern Spain himself through his own family, and make it a dependency of France. He refused to recognize Ferdinand as king, and sent troops over the Pyrenees, who occupied the Spanish capital. Ferdinand was induced to surrender the crown of Spain to

Napoleon, and the latter planned to govern the country by one of his own family.

The American colonies were faithful to the cause of the deposed Ferdinand VII. They regarded themselves as without a government, and set up their own governments in the name of Ferdinand VII., whom they held to be living in exile, and whom they expected to see returned to the throne.

It is necessary that the reader should know how the throne of Spain was filled during the critical period of South American history, when those revolutions which ended in the independence of that continent were occurring.

Napoleon had a favorite brother, Joseph, who was born in Corsica, January 7, 1768. Joseph was the eldest brother of Napoleon, and the stay and support of the family after the death of his father. He removed with his brothers and sisters to Marseilles in 1793. The affections of Napoleon seem to have been capricious, but he loved this brother devotedly. The affection was reciprocated. Joseph Bonaparte was true to his brother through all the vicissitudes of the latter's stormy life.

Napoleon had made his brother Joseph King of Naples. But Joseph was a lover of literature and art, and was not born for camps and courts. He had married the daughter of a wealthy citizen of Marseilles, an unambitious woman, for whom the splendors of royalty had but little charm. Her health was precarious. She did not go with him to Spain.

It has been said that Napoleon really loved none of his family but Joseph, who was a father to him in his youth. This is more easily asserted than proved, but certain it is that his affection for Joseph was most touching. It was Napoleon's delight to make Joseph King of Naples, but

he wished to give him a nobler and more historic throne. It was this affection and ambition that made Joseph Bonaparte "King of the Indies," a position that not one of the South American provinces would recognize.

The struggle of Napoleon in behalf of his amiable brother is one of the pathetic chapters of his history, and few things are more touching than Joseph's fidelity to him under all conditions and circumstances. Their correspondence tells the affecting story of this wonderful friendship; of its beginning, its decline on the part of Napoleon, and the fidelity of Joseph.

We will give the story in extracts from the letters of these brothers, some of the passages of which are the deepest revelations of Napoleon's heart:

"In whatever circumstances you may be placed by fortune, you know well, my friend, that you cannot have a better or dearer friend than myself, or one who wishes more sincerely for your happiness. Life is a thin dream, and it will soon be over. If you are going away, send me your portrait. We have lived together so many years, so closely united, that our hearts have become one, and you know how entirely mine belongs to you."—Napoleon to Joseph, June 25, 1795.

"Good-by, my dear friend; be cautious as to the future and content with the present. . . . As for me, I am happy, and only want to find myself on the battle-field; for a soldier must either conquer or perish gloriously."—Napoleon to Joseph, Paris, August 9, 1795.

"Brother Joseph, what would father say, could he see us now!"—Napoleon, in his coronation robes, Notre Dame, 1804.

"The glorious emperor will never replace to me the Napoleon whom I so much loved."—Joseph to Napoleon, 1806.

"King Charles by his treaty surrenders the crown of Spain to me. The nation asks me for a king. *I destine the crown of Spain to you.*"—Napoleon to Joseph, Bayonne, May 21, 1808.

"Only a fool remains long in a false position. In forty years of life I have learned only what I knew almost from the beginning, that all is vanity except a good conscience and self-respect.

"As soon as it becomes necessary I shall retire. During my whole life I shall be your best, perhaps your *only*, friend."—Joseph to Napoleon, February 19, 1809.

"I am here surrounded by the ruins of a great nation. . . .

"If you take from me the army of Andalusia, what shall I be? A porter of the hospitals, a jailer of prisoners.

"Sire, I am your brother. You presented me to Spain as your second self. I felt the praise. I shall not fall below it in honor, in the magnanimity of my heart, and the tenderness of my love for my brother. . . .

"I implore your Majesty to see in this letter only what I have desired to write—the simple truth which attached me to you in your cradle, and, whatever may happen, will accompany me to my tomb. . . .

"I weep over the weakness of human nature; over a family scattered, once so united; over the *change in the heart* of my brother; over the fading of immense glory, which would have been better preserved by generosity than by any acquisition of power.

"If the conclusion of my letter does not recall to you the tender and cherished friend of your infancy, if it does not tell you that I am to you what no other man can be, I have nothing to do but to retire."—Joseph to Napoleon, Madrid, August 8, 1810.

"*You are no longer King of Spain.* I do not want

Spain, either to keep or give away. What will you do? Will you come to the defense of my throne? Are you able to do this? Have you sense enough to do this? Then retire to the obscurity of some country house near Paris. *You will be useless, but you will do me no harm."* —Napoleon to Joseph, December, 1813.

In 1813 Napoleon again placed Ferdinand VII. on the throne of Spain. Joseph Bonaparte, King of Spain and the Indies, was a man who would have sought only the welfare of the South American colonies. But the colonies to the end refused to recognize him as king, and rejected all of his attempts to gain their favor. They were true to Ferdinand VII. in the early period of his banishment, but their experiments in self-government had led to the desire to become wholly independent of Spain. Ferdinand VII., after his return to power, became a tyrant, and was opposed to all liberal ideas. He reëstablished the Inquisition that Napoleon had overthrown, and sought to replace French republican ideas with those of absolutism. The reader will need to have in mind these events of Europe in order to see clearly the trend of Spanish history in the American colonies while they were disturbed by France.

The three parties in these colonies at the time of the rise and growth of independent republican ideas were the adherents of Ferdinand VII., the few partizans of Joseph Bonaparte and the French succession, and the heroes of the independence. The last steadily grew. It was composed for the most part of the creoles, or those born in America of European ancestors. Most of these were of Spanish or of Portuguese blood. The free air of America had given to these men a more liberal character. They became lovers of liberty, justice and human progress. A new race had formed under the Andes. It was a race of a fearless and noble spirit. Adequate justice has never been done to this new liberty-loving race. The splendid deeds of their heroes have never been deservedly told or sung or recognized among heroic achievements. When the creoles caught the spirit of liberty they gave to it their lives. It is the story of their struggles that we would tell.

Napoleon crowned his own family, and Europe discrowned them. His rise and fall tended to carry republican ideas into all lands, as the crusades wrought new relations in the whole human family of the East. The personal ambition of Napoleon did not destroy the ideal of the government of the people through chosen representatives. The short reign of the amiable and true-hearted Joseph, who loved all men and hated none, who helped all men and hindered no beneficent purpose, was an influence that aided the cause of South American independence, though the patriots had little sympathy with the French king when he occupied the throne.

Although the creoles did not recognize his authority, they found in the character of Joseph Bonaparte much that was favorable to their cause beyond the mere accident of the change of thrones. Joseph was a man of such democratic tendencies as to present to the revolutionary viceroyalties that liberal type of a leader of men which the world was not fully prepared to receive. The coming and going of Joseph Bonaparte in Spanish political history, as we view it to-day, brought to South America her great opportunity.

CHAPTER IV

SIMON BOLIVAR, THE WASHINGTON OF THE SOUTH

SIMON BOLIVAR, who united the inspiration of the cause of liberty in the South to the perseverance that fulfils great designs, was cradled in the Andes. This genius, who, with an army unschooled in the arts of arms, liberated his own country, and who stands next to Washington in the glories of the liberties of the West, was born in Caracas, Venezuela, July 24, 1783. While there is some uncertainty as to the exact date of his birth, the above is probably correct. His father was a wealthy landowner in Peru. The child seems to have early shown that brightness of intellect that made his life a success. He was, however, destined to be left alone in the world. His father died in 1786, and his mother lived long enough to direct only his early education.

The child was placed in the care of the most competent and inspiring instructors. Don Simon Rodriguez, who is said to have been "a kind of Diogenes," was his first instructor. He was followed in the work by accomplished ecclesiastics. At the age of fifteen, on the death of his mother, Don Carlos Palacios, the Marquis Palacios, his uncle, became his guardian. The family was wealthy and noble, and the boy was sent to Spain to complete his education. He spent several years in studying law in

Madrid, and in traveling in Europe. He was particularly attracted to those countries of the South from which the great immigration to South America is now tending. He was introduced at the court of Spain by his maternal uncle, Don Esteben, who had the favor of the king. Bolivar thus relates an experience of this period: " The Prince of Asturias, Ferdinand, invited me, on one occasion, to play rockets. In doing so I struck him on the head with a shuttlecock. Ferdinand got angry; but his mother was present, and obliged him to continue the game because, having invited a young gentleman to play with him, he had put himself on the same level. Who would have announced to Ferdinand VII. that this accident was only an omen, and that I should one day wrench from his crown his most precious jewel! "

Bolivar then went to Paris, and there witnessed the closing scenes of that great spasm of social forces, the French Revolution. Returning to Madrid, he married, at the age of nineteen, a most beautiful and accomplished daughter, then sixteen years old, of a family of rank. He embarked for America, with the intention of caring for his estates; but his beautiful young wife died of yellow fever. He again returned to Paris to soothe his grief, and there remained for five years.

The death of his wife had wrought a change in him. He now desired to wed his life to a cause. "I loved my wife much," he said, "and at her death I took an oath never to marry. I have kept my word. If I had not been bereaved, perhaps my life would have been different. I would not have been general of liberators. I would not have made my second voyage to Europe. I would not have had the ideas which I gained by my travels, nor would I have had the experience, or made the study of the world, of mankind and of things, which has been of so much service to me during the course of my political career. The death of my wife placed me early in the way of patriotic effort, and caused me to follow the chariot of Mars rather than the plow of Ceres."

In 1805 he went to Italy, accompanied by his friend and preceptor Don Simon Rodriguez. Napoleon at that time was summoning his conquered empires to rise against Great Britain. The world, as it were, stood in awe of the victorious Corsican. Bolivar crossed the Alps on foot, visited Chambéry, reputed to be once the home of Rousseau, and was present at the coronation of Napoleon as King of Italy. He saw Napoleon place the iron crown of the Lombards on his own head, with the imperious declaration: " God has given it to me!" He also saw the grand review of the Army of the Alps by Napoleon. Bolivar then visited Florence, Venice and Rome.

At Rome he was a dreamer. The time was drawing near for him to leave beautiful Italy and the purple city of the Tiber. " Let us go to Monte Aventino [the Sacred Mount]," he said, one morning, to Rodriguez. They went. Ascending the hill, the city of the living and the dead, the seven hills, the Tiber and the Campagna were before their eyes. They stood upon the Sacred Mount, and they spoke of another sacred mount that rose over Caracas, awaiting heroes such as gave the Roman republic its glory. Bolivar was agitated. He read, as it were, the book of the world. He talked of the liberty of the land of the Andes, and then he held out his hand to Rodriguez. " Let us here make an oath," said he. " Let us here, on this sacred hill, pledge our lives to the liberties of our own country." Rodriguez's heart responded to that of Bolivar. Then and there they pledged themselves to the cause of South American independence. With that resolution the republics of the Sun were born.

BOLIVAR ON MONTE SACRO.

From Rome Bolivar went to Hamburg, and sailed for home. On his return to his native country in 1809, he passed through the United States, and studied its institutions.

In that sublime resolution on Monte Aventino were the battle of Boyacá, the emancipation of New Granada, Venezuela and Ecuador, the restoration of liberty to Peru, and freedom for the whole of northern South America. That resolution was to guide his feet to the land of Washington from that of Cincinnatus. It was to cause him to enter Caracas in triumph, amid strewing of flowers and pealing of bells. It was to send him into self-exile. It was to lead him, in defiance of nature, to dare the Cordilleras, and snows, storms and perils, and live where animals perished. It would rob him of fortune, and cause his name to become a mockery in his mother-land. It would carry him on its refluent wave to Peru. It would cause him there to be hailed almost as a god—to pass under triumphal arches, amid singing priests, dancing Indians and prostrate people, while the thunder of cannon shook the peaks of the high Andes, and the bells of the cities rang aloud with joy. It would force him into exile again at last, and cause him to die of a broken heart.

But that would not be the end. Caracas, that dressed in festal white for his triumphs, would receive him in robes of black for his burial, and entomb him in glory, and set his statue among the heroes of the world.

In that vow on the Sacred Mount there was begun a new era in the world.

He was now alone in the world, without father, mother, wife or child. He was something of a philosopher. Fresh from the dramatic efforts of the French people to establish a system of republican government, he saw in the young republic of the United States the model for the future of his native land, and for all the Spanish American states of the viceroy. The people of his own country, awakened in part by the suggestions of Miranda, were alive to the cause of liberty. He went to Caracas and joined the revolutionary movements. He took part in the uprising of the people in April, 1810. He received an officer's commission from the Council of State (the junta), and was authorized, with Luis Lepez Mendes, to go to Great Britain to purchase arms for the protection of the revolutionary government. He returned with a cargo of arms in 1811.

Bolivar brought Miranda with him. The events that followed the association of Bolivar and Miranda are among the most affecting and inexplicable in human history. Bolivar had been advised by the supreme junta of Caracas not to bring the schemes of Miranda into the new movement, nor to consult with him about it. But he found Miranda in London, a lonely old man, a patriot with his own dream of the liberty of Venezuela. Bolivar could not refrain from seeking to cheer Miranda's heart by informing him of the progress of events. It was the seed sown by Miranda that was growing. Bolivar generously went to him, invited him to return to Venezuela, and offered him the hospitality of his own house. Bolivar did not do secretly what he held to be an act of justice to a brother patriot. His own return to Caracas would be hailed as a triumph. He would enter the city amid acclamations. He determined that Miranda should ride beside him on the occasion. The people rejoiced when they saw Miranda. It thrilled them to see the old, virtuous, self-sacrificing patriot riding beside young Simon Bolivar.

Ovations to Miranda followed the chief's return. He was looked upon now as a genius, schooled in all the arts of war. His unsuccessful effort in 1806 was now regarded as a splendid achievement. The event of the 19th of April had glorified it. It was, in the light of this event, a trumpet-call to liberty, a summons to victory.

Another great movement for South America was now at hand. The people were gathering in electoral colleges to elect representatives to a congress in Caracas. This congress would deal with the question of independence. The electoral college of Caracas was the first assembly to exercise the principles of executive government in the Andes. To this congress Miranda was elected a deputy by the Pao of Barcelona. He was made lieutenant-general of the Army of the Provinces. He was now at the height of his influence, everywhere hailed as the apostle of liberty, as the man who had perceived the future in a vision. His position at this time shows how perilous is great opportunity.

Events are hurrying. The day of independence is at hand. Caracas stands white in the high plateau of the Andes, amid her green mountain wall of cacti, the peaks gleaming above her, the purple waters shining beneath her. The venerable Miranda is her hero, and young Bolivar among her men of promise. The independence which would make Venezuela a sister of the great republic of the North was the desire of all hearts, the vision of all eyes.

At this happy period, who could have looked upon the city and have forecast the events of the year to follow?

The grand event that led to South American independence took place in Caracas on April 19, 1810. That day was the beginning of Andean liberty. At this period of transition, when there was no general government on the Peninsula, but conflicting authorities, whom should the American colonies obey—Charles, Ferdinand, the royal juntas or the new régime? Why should they not elect juntas of their own, to do their will, and thus be independent? The junta could elect the rulers whom the people favored.

In electing such a junta Caracas led the way. Napoleon was indeed to place Ferdinand on the throne of Spain again, and the latter was to rule over Spain and her provinces with an autocratic will; but after the election of the junta at Caracas, a decree had gone forth by which absolutism in the Andes would never be permanently reestablished.

The proclamation of the independence of Caracas through the junta was brought about by a series of dramatic events. Liberty was in the air, but Emparan, the captain-general of the country, governed the people in the name of the crown of Spain. Three parties arose in Venezuela: those who adhered to the fortunes of King Ferdinand; the imperialists, or Bonapartists; and those who would establish an independent government, corresponding in spirit to the Sons of Liberty in the early days of the American Revolution. These sons of independence we may term the patriots. Of them Don Simon Bolivar was a leader.

On April 18, 1810, Wednesday of Holy Week, there arrived at Caracas commissioners to announce that a regency had been formed at Cadiz, to which the Venezuelans were counseled to be loyal. Don Simon Bolivar spoke the word which turned this event into an inspiration to the patriotic cause. "This power," he said, "which fluctuates in such a manner on the Peninsula, and does not secure itself, *invites us to establish the junta of Caracas, and be governed by ourselves.*" He had sounded the trumpet-note of liberty on the Andes. On the morning of April 19, 1810, the corporation of the city assembled in the church, according to the custom, to assist in the celebration of

Holy Thursday. They invited the governor, Emparan, to meet with them. Emparan was by nature a tyrant. He declared that he governed Caracas by the power of his own will. He ignored the counsels of the corporation. Emparan met the corporation on that holy day. He there heard broached the suggestion of a junta of Caracas. In the suggestion he perceived independence and the end of his own power. He was filled with rage. "I will talk with you after the divine offices in the church," said he to the city council, haughtily. He left the council-hall and went out. Whither had he gone? Would he order their arrest? They awaited the event with suspense and apprehension. What would this last royal governor of Spain do? Return to the council? That would be to break with Spain. Order the arrest of the patriots? That would leave him between two hostile powers. Either event might end his own power. It was an hour of suspense, an hour of human destiny. The governor represented the regency; the city council represented self-government; and a Napoleon was on the throne of Spain. But it was the hour of opportunity, and the patriots so regarded it. At the door of the cathedral were the grenadiers. The patriots stayed in their chamber awaiting events. Emparan entered the cathedral. A patriot met him there. "Return to the council," said the latter, laying his hand on his arm. Emparan obeyed the touch. He reëntered the council-room. The council had resolved on independence, and he was no longer governor. Spain in America was tottering to its fall. The forming of a supreme junta was now proposed to him. He perceived his loss of power, and made no opposition. Encouraged by his silence, the corporation was about to make him the president of the junta when a thrilling incident occurred. There was in Caracas an ardent patriot by the name of José Cortes

Madariga, a native of Chili, and a deacon of the cathedral. He was at confession when he was told what was happening. As if inspired by Providence, he rushed from the church to the council-room, and presented himself like a prophet before the patriots. He said: "I appear before you as a deputy of the clergy. Beware what you do at this hour. You are blind if you again put yourself at the mercy of the representative of Spain. Imperil not your fair prospect of sovereignty—of self-government for a people who should be free." He pictured the condition of political affairs in the Spanish peninsula, and then, with a godlike resolution, added: "I demand the deposition of your governor, in the name of the public good. Yes, I demand it in the name of justice, of my country, and of liberty!"

The words that he spoke were decisive; they were an unwritten law. Emparan fled to the balcony, and summoned the people to hear him speak. Madariga followed him. "Venezuelans," said the governor, "are you content with my administration?" Madariga, standing behind him, made signs to the people to answer "No." A shout rose: "No; we want you not!" The last royal governor saw his doom. "Then I do not want you!" he said. The revolution in spirit was accomplished.

That day the junta of Caracas was proclaimed. It was an independent power. It might choose its own rulers. It voted not to recognize the regency of Cadiz, and announced that Venezuela, in virtue of its natural and political rights, would proceed to the formation of a government of its own, and would exercise authority in the name of Ferdinand VII.

The council decreed the banishment of Emparan, but voted to pay his expenses to the United States. Not a gun had been fired. The revolution was an accomplished fact.

CHAPTER V.

THE INDEPENDENCE, 1811—THE EVENT OF JULY 4—THE DECLARATION.

THAT was a thrilling hour when, on July 4, 1811, Don Simon Bolivar arose in the Patriotic Society of Caracas. Great political movements have frequently begun in clubs. The social revolution in France found its voice in La Montagne. The South American liberties were born in the Patriotic Club in London, of which Miranda was the inspiring spirit. The Patriotic Society of Caracas arose out of the necessities of the hour. It led public opinion, and developed the sentiment of liberty and independence.

The provinces had elected a congress. The deputies of the people met at Caracas. The one question that excited all minds was, Shall the Congress sever the province from Spain, and proclaim to the world its independence? The air was electric with patriotism, but there were conservative minds amid the popular enthusiasm for liberty. Such were jealous of the influence of the Patriotic Society. To them the society was a congress of counsel, whose opinions the legislative body followed as a matter of form. In this society these cautious minds saw the methods of the French Revolution.

On July 4, 1811, a very important meeting of the Patriotic Society was held. The declaration had been made that the society was but another congress, without powers, and that its influence tended to schism. To rectify this mistake, young Bolivar rose, and poured forth his ardent and decisive sentiments in fiery words: "Patriots, there are not two congresses, one of opinion, and one of action. The times demand both bodies. Those who feel the necessity of the union of all hearts for liberty can make no schism. Patriots, what we desire is the union of all hearts and minds to inspire us in the achievement of our liberty. The hour has come. Yesterday to repose in the arms of apathy was a disgrace; to-day it is treason. The voice of the people must be heard. The Sovereign Congress assembles; it discusses what should be done in this crisis. What does it say? That we should commence the new order of things in a confederation. Are we not already confederated against foreign tyranny? That we should await the result of the policy of Spain. Await? What is it to us, my countrymen, whether Spain sells her slaves to Bonaparte, or keeps them to do her bidding, if we ourselves are determined to be free? What matters it, O my countrymen? Such sentiments as these are the sorrowful results of our chains. They tell us that vast projects should be developed calmly. Calmly? Are not three hundred years of servitude a sufficient preparation for decisive action? Calmly? Are three hundred years of like tyranny needed to make us men? Our Patriotic Society respects as it should the august Congress of the new nation; but that Congress should remember that our Society responds to the public heart, and is the focus of enlightenment in the revolutionary cause. Patriots, let us lay, without fear, the foundation-stone of South American liberty. To falter is to fall. Venezuelans, I move that a committee be appointed from this body to carry these sentiments to the Sovereign Congress!"

The speech, like that of Patrick Henry amid like events, was decisive. The next day the sun of the Andes shone on a republic, and not on a slave-pen of Spain.

A deputy followed Bolivar, and in the spirit of the thrilling exhortation, "Let us lay the foundation-stone of South American liberty," moved that the "motion of Don Simon Bolivar be adopted." The society carried the motion with the fervor of the growing inspiration, and Dr. Miguel Pena was instructed to write the petition to the Sovereign Congress, expressing the views of Bolivar.

The petition was read in the legislative body on July 4, the eve of the memorable day of Venezuela and of the meridional world. It was a hammer-stroke. The privileged group of the Patriotic Society had recorded an opinion that was unwritten law.

It was July 5, 1811. As the light poured over the purple Caribbean Sea and the green Andes, the people hailed the rising sun as the beginning of a new era. Congress this day would record the patriotic declaration of the 4th. Congress assembled, presumably in the Federal Palace. The president of the Congress faced the future boldly, and in a clear and heroic voice said to the excited deputies: "We have now arrived at the hour most opportune to treat the question of absolute independence. The question should be discussed immediately." The galleries thundered with applause. Deputies sprang to their feet to support the motion. "Shall the motion to make Venezuela free be adopted?" "Motion!"

What events of three hundred years of servitude in South America lay behind that motion, trembling in the air, in that bright room lit by the sun of the Andes! The provinces of South America had been but prisons of Spain. The mita had hardly been more oppressive upon them than the Spanish king had been to his own people of the

Peninsula. Charles IV. once said, on returning a petition of the people of Mérida for a school: "I do not consider learning proper in America." The Peninsular kings held all Americans in their provinces to be slaves, denied them the right to think, and accounted any independent expression of thought as treason.

Larrazabal, in a clear and masterly manner, makes a summary of the most conspicuous of these grievances: the printing and even the sale of books of any kind without the sanction of the Council of the West Indies were prohibited; the reading of Robertson's popular history of America was forbidden under the penalty of death; a publisher of desirable works, presumably without the license of the West India Council, was condemned to wear the chains of the dungeons of Cartagena; the newspaper press had no independent voice; South American commerce with foreign countries was carefully guarded; no vessel was allowed to sail the Spanish Main without a license from the foreign court; the South Americans were not allowed to make any contract with foreigners, either to sell or to buy, without the approval of the Spanish courts; no one was allowed to visit America without the royal permission, under the penalty of death; in 1706 the Royal Audiencia of Peru published a law that no Indian should be allowed to have stores or to trade, for the reason that such industries put the native population on a social level with Spanish merchants.

But not only were Americans forbidden to trade with foreign nations; they were forbidden to engage in traffic between the provinces. The tyrant's hand was laid also upon the products of the fields. Here was prohibited the planting of vines and olives, there the sowing of flax; in one place the export of wines, almonds and raisins, in another place the building of mills. The Spanish grandee

STREET SCENE IN CARACAS, VENEZUELA, SHOWING CAPITOL ON THE LEFT.

controlled everything in the interests of the throne of the Peninsula.

The church was as intolerant as the government. It has been quite common for Protestant writers to depict in vivid colors this form of intolerance, themselves forgetting the ecclesiastical bigotry and crimes of the days of Calvin in Geneva and of Mather in New England. There are, however, few chapters of horrors in the world's history that can equal that of the Spanish Inquisition of Mexico, Cartagena and Peru. It would be a painful task to depict the tortures inflicted upon helpless people by it for obeying the laws which God has written in every soul. Apart from these merciless tortures, into which entered the spirit that animates the bull-fight, and which gratified the most inhuman and unchristian instincts, the general purpose of the ecclesiastical rule was to forbid any freedom of thought or of personal rights.

Few South Americans ever rose to public office. Out of one hundred and sixty viceroys, only four were not Spanish. Of minor offices a similar statement would be true.

The taxed tea, the stamped paper, and like injustices that led to the Revolution in North America were light matters indeed when compared with what the colonies of the palm-lands suffered from three centuries of Spanish rule. The cause of Samuel Adams was a just one, but that of Bolivar was a necessity to the existence of any personal liberty.

The motion that voiced the resolution of the Patriotic Society of July 4 was made in the Sovereign Congress of Venezuela, and was adopted. Venezuela had followed the example of Switzerland, of Holland, of the United States of North America, and was free.

Jefferson's sublime preamble to the Declaration of Independence, beginning, "When in the course of human events," and declaring that "all men are created free and equal," is matched by the words with which the new declaration begins. We quote this powerful state paper in part, following the translation of Larrazabal:

"In the name of the all-powerful God:

"We, the representatives of the United Provinces of Caracas, Cumaná, Varinas, Margarita, Barcelona, Mérida and Truxillo, forming the American Federation of Venezuela, in the south continent, in Congress assembled, considering the full and absolute possession of our rights, which we recovered justly and legally, from the 19th of April, 1810, in consequence of the occurrences in Bayona, and the occupation of the Spanish throne by conquest, and the succession of a new dynasty, constituted without our consent, are desirous, before we make use of the rights of which we have been deprived by force for more than three ages, but now restored to us by the political order of human events, to make known to the world the reasons that have emanated from these same occurrences, and which authorize us to the free use we are about to make of our sovereignty.

"We do not wish, nevertheless, to begin by alleging the rights, inherent in every conquered country, to recover its state of property and independence; we generously forget the long series of ills, injuries and privations, which the sad right of conquest has caused to all the descendants of the discoverers, conquerors and settlers of these countries, plunged into a worse state by the very same cause that ought to have favored them; and, drawing a veil over the three hundred years of Spanish domain in America, we will now only present to view the authentic and well-known facts which ought to have wrested from one world the right over the other, by the disorder and conquest that have already dissolved the Spanish nation.

"Always deaf to the cries of justice on our part, the governments of Spain have endeavored to discredit all our efforts, by declaring as criminal, and stamping with infamy, and rewarding with the scaffold and confiscation every attempt which, at different periods, some Americans have made for the felicity of their country; as was that which lately our own security dictated to us, that we might not be drawn into a state of disorder which we foresaw, and hurried to that horrid fate which we are about to remove forever from before us. By means of atrocious policy, they have succeeded in making our brethren insensible to our misfortunes; in arming them against us; in erasing from their bosoms the sweet impressions of friendship, of consanguinity, and converting into enemies a part of our own great family.

"At a time that we, faithful to our promise, were sacrificing our security and civil dignity not to abandon the rights which we generously presented to Ferdinand of Bourbon, we have seen that, to the relations of force which bound him to the Emperor of the French, he has added the ties of blood and friendship, in consequence of which even the governments of Spain have already declared their resolution to acknowledge him conditionally.

"In this mournful alternative, we have remained three years in a state of political indecision and ambiguity, so fatal and dangerous that this alone would suffice to authorize the resolution which the faith of our promises and bonds of fraternity had caused us to defer till necessity was obliged to go beyond what we at first proposed, impelled by the hostile and unnatural conduct of the governments of Spain, which have disburdened us from our conditional oath, by which circumstance we are called to the august representation we now exercise.

"But we, who glory in grounding our proceedings on

better principles, and not wishing to establish our felicity on the misfortunes of our fellow-beings, do consider and declare as friends, companions of our fate, and participators of our felicity, those who, united to us by the ties of blood, language and religion, have suffered the same evils in the anterior order of things, provided they acknowledge our *absolute independence* of the same, and of any other foreign power whatever; that they aid to sustain it with their lives, fortunes and sentiments; declaring and acknowledging them (as well as any other nation), in war, enemies; in peace, friends, brothers and compatriots.

"In consequence of all these solid, public and incontestable reasons of policy, which so powerfully urge the necessity of recovering our national dignity, restored to us by the order of events; and in compliance with the imprescriptible rights enjoyed by nations to destroy every pact, agreement or association which does not answer the purpose for which governments were established, we believe that we cannot, and ought not, preserve the bonds which hitherto have kept us united to the governments of Spain; and that, like all other nations of the world, we are free, and authorized not to depend on any other authority than our own, and to take among the powers of the earth the place of equality which the Supreme Being of nature assigned to us, and to which we are called by the succession of human events, and urged by our own good and utility.

"Notwithstanding we are aware of the difficulties that attend, and the obligations imposed upon us, by the rank we are about to take in the political order of the world, as well as the powerful influence of forms and habitudes to which unfortunately we have been accustomed, we, at the same time, know that shameful submission to them, when we can throw them off, would be still more ignominious to us, and more fatal to our posterity, than our long and

INNER COURT OF THE CAPITOL, CARACAS, VENEZUELA.

painful slavery; and that it now becomes an indispensable duty to provide for our own preservation, security and felicity, by essentially varying all the forms of our former constitution.

"In consequence whereof, considering, by the reasons thus alleged, that we have satisfied the respect which we owe to the opinion of the human race and the dignity of other nations, in the number of whom we are about to enter, and on whose communication and friendship we rely:

"We, the representatives of the United Provinces of Venezuela, calling on the Supreme Being to witness the justice of our proceedings and the rectitude of our intentions, do implore his divine and celestial help; and ratifying, at the moment in which we are born to the dignity which his providence restores to us, the desire we have of living and dying free, and of believing and defending the Holy Catholic and Apostolic Religion of Jesus Christ; we, therefore, in the name and by the will and authority which we hold for the virtuous people of Venezuela, do declare solemnly to the world that its United Provinces are, and ought to be from this day, by act and right, *free, sovereign and independent states;* and that they are absolved from every submission and dependence on the throne of Spain, or on those who do or may call themselves its agents and representatives; and that a free and independent state, thus constituted, has full power to take that form of government which may be conformable to the general wish of the people; to declare war, make peace, form alliances, regulate treaties of commerce, limits and navigation, and to do and transact every act in like manner as other free and independent states. And that this our solemn declaration may be held valid, firm and durable, we hereby mutually bind each province to the other, and pledge our lives, fortunes, and the sacred tie of our national honor.

"Done in the Federal Palace of Caracas, signed by our own hands, sealed with the Great Provincial Seal of the Confederation, and countersigned by the Secretary of Congress, this fifth day of July, 1811, the first of our independence."

On the same, the ever-memorable 5th of July, the Congress adopted the tricolor flag of Miranda as the emblem of the new liberty.

The next day the sun of liberty rose on the Maritime Andes, and upon a people who had begun the emancipation of the meridional world.

The sublime words with which the first declaration of independence of a South American province opens and closes breathe the high patriotism of the Continental Congress of North America. They have a tone of reverence, a sense of the Divine Providence, and a faith in the Supreme Ruler of the cause. They read like a prophet's inspiration. Only a sense of the grandeur and magnitude of the event could have inspired them.

CHAPTER VI

THE EARTHQUAKE AT CARACAS—AN HEROIC EPISODE —MONTEVERDE—THE UNLOCKED DOOR—THE FAILURE OF MIRANDA

TO use a figure in the Manifesto of Caracas, Venezuela had arisen from the dust and cast off her chains. But the Sovereign Congress and its generals had to deal with an ignorant and superstitious people. Some of the priests were patriots, and had the spirit of the great Mexican emancipator Hidalgo; but, as a rule, they followed the fortunes of the deposed monarch Ferdinand VII.

The people, as previously stated, were superstitious. Of the danger lying in that direction young Bolivar received warning. "If any misfortune should suddenly fall upon the people, it would be attributed to God, as a judgment upon the people for proclaiming the independence," was the voice of apprehension. Bolivar felt its force.

In beautiful Caracas all was prosperous and tranquil; there were no sickness, no calamities, no alarming revolts. The first days of freedom came and went in unexampled serenity. There was dissent as to what had been done; there were disturbances in one of the provinces; but the new republic, as a whole, seemed starting out on a march of security, prosperity and peace. The patriots, notwithstanding, felt the force of the warning, "If there should come a calamity!"

Venezuela now prepared a federal constitution, and assigned to Miranda the command of her army. Thus he whom Bolivar, in his magnanimity, had induced to return to his native city of Caracas, and who had entered that city by Bolivar's side, amid the acclamations of the people, and found a place in his home, was now in a position to realize the dreams that had haunted his imagination for years.

The constitution was a glorious document. It was devoted to justice, to equal rights. It gave to man his birthright; to him who would make for himself a home and a name, a field of labor; and to him who toiled, his dues. It sounded the call to welfare and wealth, to honor, and not titled vanity. Personal liberty was granted to all. The enjoyment of property was made universal. No one could be despoiled of the labors of his hands. Torture was abolished. The Holy Inquisition was suppressed. Titles of nobility were abrogated. The slave-trade was condemned. The new era was to begin in the brotherhood of man.

At this time there arrived at Porto Rico an ambitious and cruel adventurer by the name of Domingo Monteverde, a native of Orotava in Teneriffe. He was a man of little education, a seeker after fame. He earnestly espoused the cause of Ferdinand VII. in America. He attained the position of field-marshal in the royal army. He landed in Venezuela, invaded Carora, and there defeated the patriots. He resolved to make himself the leader of the cause of Ferdinand VII. against the insurgent provinces.

The first year of the independence was passing. It was spring in the Andes. The Easter festival was approaching, when the joyous bells would ring out. Holy Thursday, the 26th of March, arrived. There was a vaporous stillness in the air, on the earth, and over the sea. The sun shone as in a veil of shadow; the birds screamed in the air, and lifted their wings uneasily. The heat was intolerable. Noonday brought a calm that was oppressive, with a sky brilliant and transparent. Drops of rain fell, but there was no visible cloud in the sky. ,In the silence and fiery light something seemed to be impending. In the middle of the afternoon, despite the heat, and the strange drops of rain, and the oppressive atmosphere, the churches were thronged with people. Four o'clock was the vesper hour. The following day would be Good Friday; it was almost the close of the penitential days of Lent. At seven minutes past four, when the solemn services in the church were beginning, the earth seemed to reel. There was a fearful crash, followed by a deep sound as of thunder. It came not from the sky, but from the caverns below. The people started up. What was happening? Where? They felt their feet unsteady. The earth was trembling, and in the tremor buildings were crumbling, melting away, as, it were. Pillars and towers afforded no protection. They were not dashed down; they crumbled.

The people ran hither and thither, calling on Heaven for mercy. The beasts sought the caves. Birds screamed affrighted in the air. Many were buried beneath the ruins. Some ten thousand people perished. "Caracas," says Humboldt, "sleeps in her own grave." Not only Caracas crumbled and made a tomb for her people, but La Guayra, Mérida and other towns were destroyed. The town of San Felipe totally disappeared. Its houses, public buildings and inhabitants were never seen again.

The people who survived fled to the fields, and wandered about, lamenting and praying. No one knew who of his family or friends was left him. In a moment all

had been changed. The people who fled looked up to the sky and down upon the heap that had been their beautiful city.

Where was Simon Bolivar amid these terrible and exciting scenes? He was among the survivors. Did he recall the warning, "If any misfortune should happen"? There are in all history few incidents more sublime than the conduct and the words of the fiery and undaunted patriot in the early evening of that dreadful day.

We will describe the event in the words of Diaz, who was not friendly to Bolivar, and who misinterpreted his sublime and unparalleled exclamation.

"To that inexplicable noise," says Diaz, "followed the silence of death. The groans of the dying arose from the Church of San Jacinto. I surmounted the ruins of the church, and entered the interior. On the highest spot I met Don Simon Bolivar. He was in his shirt-sleeves, engaged in the search for the living who could be rescued. Terror and desperation were depicted on his countenance. He recognized me, and addressed to me the following impious and extravagant words: '*If nature opposes herself, we will wrestle with her, and compel her to obey.*'"

The words were neither "impious" nor "extravagant." They were the cry of a soul whose sense of justice the earthquake could not stifle. Bolivar knew that the earthquake was but a natural event, and one that had no moral significance.

While his soul thus rose in a grand exhibition of the omnipotence of spiritual power, the Plaza was wild with cries for mercy. Many of the priests took advantage of the horror of the hour. Believing as they did that Ferdinand VII. was the Lord's anointed, they believed the convulsion to be a manifestation of the divine displeasure against the events of the 4th and 5th of July of the year

BOLIVAR AT THE EARTHQUAKE OF CARACAS.

that had passed. The ignorant people, knowing not what to do or what to believe, were influenced by these priests. They began to lose faith in their leaders. The glory of the independence became a lost luster before Caracas had celebrated the first anniversary of her freedom.

This was a dark hour for Miranda. Six hundred patriot soldiers had perished in the barracks at Caracas. Six hundred more, who were on their way to San Felipe, had been swallowed with the town. Twelve hundred patriots during a review at Barquisimeto, and two columns who were on the march, had disappeared from the sight of the sun.

Monteverde perceived his opportunity and availed himself of it. He had a triumphal march, bearing as he did the banner of Ferdinand. He swept nearly everything before him from Coro to Caracas. He took possession of Barquisimeto, where an ecclesiastic, by preaching from the ruins, had prepared the people for his coming. Monteverde's army grew; his armaments increased. He was checked temporarily, but he entered San Carlos in triumph, and sacked the city.

On April 4 another earthquake filled the country with new alarms. The royalists were strengthened by the terror it awakened.

The government was now at La Victoria. Miranda, who had been made generalissimo, went to Caracas. He there met Bolivar, to whom he gave the order: "Go immediately to Puerto Cabello, and take command of the fortress." The fortress was a prison, and was filled with prisoners of war. Bolivar desired a different appointment—one that would take him into the open field. He, however, obeyed the command.

On May 1 Miranda marched out of the ruined city of Caracas against Monteverde, and entered upon a most disastrous campaign. He had under his command twelve thousand men. His antagonist was but an adventurer with a small force, but the people had lost heart through superstition. Public sentiment had turned in Monteverde's favor. Miranda's troops began to lose faith in the cause. The general's heart became doubtful of final victory. He had only begun his march against the enemy when a sound as of battle was heard in the air. He ordered his army to halt. The sound proceeded from an eruption of the volcano San Vicente. The march was resumed, it seemed, under an evil star. His men began to desert him. A whole company of men under Pedro Ponce, a Spaniard, went over to the enemy. Depression of spirit fell upon Miranda. He lost faith in his soldiers. He lived in suspense. He knew not what to do. He ceased to advance; he retreated. This retreat depressed still further the spirits of his followers. He took up quarters at Maracay, and announced that his campaign would henceforth be defensive. The declaration was dispiriting. He had made for himself an army without hearts. In this state of mind he retreated to La Victoria. Here he was surprised by Monteverde, whom he repulsed. He did not follow up his advantage. This caused him to fall under the displeasure and criticism of his troops.

At La Victoria Miranda received a message from Bolivar. "Puerto Cabello," it said, "is threatened, and there is no force here to defend it." But Miranda made no attempt to reinforce the fortress, which contained military stores.

On the 30th of June a terrible disaster to the republican cause occurred at Puerto Cabello. A temporary commander of the prison set the prisoners at liberty, formed of them, with deserters, a force of royalists, and raised the Spanish flag. The fortress commanded the harbor and the city. It turned its guns on both, and compelled both to surrender.

Bolivar had but a small force now left to him. He attempted the defense of the city with forty men. Even these in part deserted him. The news came flying to the port that the victorious Monteverde was marching toward the city. There was nothing for Bolivar to do but to surrender or fly. He secured a brig, and sailed to La Guayra. This was on the 5th of July, just one year from the glorious day on which had been proclaimed to the world the independence of Venezuela.

Miranda's nerves were now more unstrung than ever. Every one seemed to distrust him. In this time of distress a new terror seized the people. An army of liberated slaves from the provinces was marching upon Caracas.

In the thickening clouds of misfortunes—the earthquake, the volcanic flames, the victories of Monteverde, the failure of the hearts of the soldiers, the loss of Puerto Cabello—there came to the shaken and irresolute Miranda one Don Antonio Fernandez de Leon, Marquis de Casa Leon, a reputed patriot from Caracas. "You see the situation of affairs," he said to Miranda—"shattered Caracas threatened with invasion, the fort of Puerto Cabello in the hands of the enemy, the people disheartened by the misfortunes of the earthquake. It is useless for us to oppose the royal arms. The time has come to end this war among brothers by an honorable peace."

Peace! It would bring to an end the achievements of the republic. It would bring Miranda under suspicion of treason. Miranda pondered. He hesitated. These minutes were the turning-point of his life. Casa Leon followed up his advice. "As for you, I will supply you with the means of living in a foreign country." But what would life in any country be under the suspicions that would fall upon him after such a surrender? The old man remained thoughtful. The spell of his melancholy was evidently upon him. It was a spectacle pitiable to behold. "I will myself," said Casa Leon, "go to General Monteverde and arrange all the terms. You must decide at once; the moments are flying." A great conflict was going on in Miranda's weakened mind. "I am willing," he said at last. Fatal words! He never saw a happy moment again.

Miranda seems to have looked upon Bolivar as a traitor for the loss of Puerto Cabello. Bolivar believed Miranda to be a traitor from the hour that he heard that Miranda had consented to make a treaty with Monteverde. Both were mistaken. It was now only a little more than a year and a half since the two, amid the vivas of the people, entered Caracas together (December, 1810). At that time they were ardent friends, the young man and the old.

Monteverde wrote to Miranda, proffering terms of peace. Miranda sent the letter to Congress, then in session at La Victoria. Congress gave to Miranda the authority to treat with the Spanish general. As a result, a treaty was concluded July 29, 1812, in which it was stipulated, among other things: "That the constitution presented by the Cortes to the Spaniards should be accepted by Venezuela. That no person should be prosecuted for his political opinions."

Thus the republic was for the time destroyed, and Caracas, the theater of thrilling events, fell again under the domain of Spain.

On July 30, 1812, Miranda arrived at La Guayra, a fallen man. He was criticized by all the patriots. He was as one who had shattered the fabrics of his visions with his own hands. He found at La Guayra a company of patriots, and among them Simon Bolivar. The question arose among these patriots, Would it not be for the inter-

STREET SCENE IN LA GUAYRA, VENEZUELA.

est of the new treaty to hold Miranda here? The old man arrived in the afternoon, fatigued by the intense heat. The ship was waiting for him. The patriots invited him to stay to supper, and to remain on shore overnight. "No," said the captain of the ship to Miranda; "it is for your interest to go on board to-night." "You are too tired to go on board the vessel now. The land-breeze will not arise until morning," said the patriots. "I will spend the night on shore," said Miranda, whose wits seem to have gone. The captain of the ship shook his head. The supper was prepared. At the table sat Bolivar, with other patriotic leaders, among them Colonel Manuel Maria Casas, the military commandant, at whose house he was entertained.

In the house was a closet that could not be locked. Colonel Casas ordered that a bed be prepared for the old man in that closet. Miranda retired early. The patriots sat down to consider the consequence to the treaty should they allow him to depart. They decided that it would be for the interest of the country to arrest him. General H. L. v. Ducoudray-Holstein, who was an enemy to Bolivar, thus describes the pitiable scene of the early morning, in the closet that could not be locked:

"Miranda was arrested in the following manner. Having ascertained that the general was sound asleep, the three leaders, after a short consultation, determined to seize him that night, and give him up to the Spanish commandant Monteverde. Casas, as military commandant at La Guayra, ordered a strong detachment from the principal guard. This detachment he commanded to surround his own house in perfect silence, to suffer no one to pass, and to kill any one who attempted to escape. Not a word was said of Miranda. When all was ready, Peña, Casas and Bolivar, at two o'clock in the morning, with four armed soldiers, entered the unlocked room of General

Miranda. He was in a profound sleep. They seized his sword and pistols, which he had placed before him. They then awakened him, and abruptly told him to rise and dress quickly, and follow them. Miranda, in surprise, asked them why they awakened him at such an early hour, it being not yet daylight. Instead of answering the question, they told him he was a traitor, who deserved to be hanged.

"Miranda, unable to resist, dressed himself, and was forced to follow. They escorted him to the fort called San Carlos, at some distance from La Guayra, and situated upon a strong hill, where he arrived, exhausted from fatigue and chagrin. Having borne all the invectives they chose to load him with on the road, which he was obliged to walk, as soon as they were come to the fort they ordered him to be put in irons, and notwithstanding his pathetic and fervent expostulations, he was locked in one of the darkest dungeons, and treated like the vilest criminal.

"The three chiefs returned, with their guard, to La Guayra, and the same night despatched an express with a letter to the Spanish general Monteverde, informing him of the arrest of Miranda. This commander was surprised at the intelligence. Instead of ordering the immediate release of Miranda, and so preserving inviolate the faith of his own treaty, he received the news with his accustomed indifference and apathy, and took no step in favor of Miranda, or against him.

"The day after Miranda's arrest, a Spanish column arrived in the fort of San Carlos, to relieve the independents. Its commander was surprised to find Miranda in irons, and sent him immediately, with an escort, back to La Guayra, where he was again shut up in a dark, mephitic prison in one of the walls of this place, where he remained in irons during several months. The Spanish commandant

Don Francisco Xavier Cerveres, who had relieved the patriot commander Casas, gave orders to send Miranda back to Porto Rico. He was thence transported to Cadiz, where he remained in irons, in the fort of La Caraca, for some years, and perished.

"Such was the miserable end of General Miranda. Without entering into any political controversy, without inquiring whether Miranda was a traitor to his country (which well-informed men affirm not to have been the case), history will demand what right Dr. Miguel Peña, Don Maria Casas and Simon Bolivar had to arrest their former chief and superior. That they did so without order, information or participation of the Spanish general-in-chief Domingo Monteverde, is an undoubted fact."

Larrazabal thus describes Miranda's arrest:

"Bolivar was at La Guayra when the generalissimo arrived at that port. It was about seven o'clock of the evening of the 30th of July.

"Afterward many of the officers arrived, flying from the persecution they justly feared; and it was divulged (which unfortunately was true) that Miranda had concealed his voyage, and that, in Caracas, he had told them that they could retire to their homes, abandoning them to the most cruel suspense. The irregularity and uncertainty with which the capitulation was passed through, the confused dissolution of the army, and the ignorance of the terms of the agreement, gave sufficient ground to judge wrongly of the acts of the dictator, and to make them suspicious of him; and the exaltation of their minds counseled them toward taking the violent measures which their mutual unhappy fate justified.

"Immediately after the arrival of the generalissimo at La Guayra, Captain Haynes came on land. Miranda, wearied by his fatigues and the heat of the day, was reposing. Afterward he seated himself at the table, being present Manuel Maria Casas, military commander, who had accompanied him, the Dr. Miguel Peña, civil and political governor, the Dr. Pedro Gual, and others. While at the table, it was talked of that Miranda should remain on the land for that night, *it being too late already for him to embark.* Haynes insisted, saying that on board the commodities were plentiful enough for the general. Notwithstanding this, as nothing needed such a ridiculous precipitation, Miranda consented to remain until the following morning. Haynes left, visibly disgusted.

"That same night secretly assembled the Dr. Miguel Peña, Manuel Maria Casas, the Colonels Simon Bolivar, Juan Paz del Castillo, José Mires and José Cortes; the Commandants Tomas Montilla, Rafael Chatillon, Miguel Carabano, Rafael Castillo, José Landaeta, who commanded the garrison, and Juan José Valdez, sergeant-major of the Plaza. They spoke of the conduct of the generalissimo, who was remiss in his duties, abandoning the defense of his country when all predicted victory; that he had submitted them shamefully to the chains and revenge of Spain. They blamed his conduct, and resented the insulting replies which at table he had given to the Dr. Gual and to the Colonel Castillo, when, in a friendly manner, they asked explanations upon the treaty of capitulation. . . . It is unnecessary to say that Bolivar surpassed them all in his warmth, because he who had spoken to the Minister Wellesley of independence in 1810, and who in Rome, in advance of all purposes and hopes, swore for it on the Monte Sacro in 1805, could ill brook the disastrous idea of a new slavery.

"Indignant, then, at the treasons (as they named them) of Miranda, they deliberated to detain him, because they judged that, once on board, he would not ratify the capitulation, leaving the patriots strongly compromised, and the only hope of a less unhappy fate disappearing. They wished to oblige him to sanction with his signature that important document, which was the safeguard of their lives and property. The pressure of the moment, in an affair of such transcendental importance, did not permit them to reflect clearly and calmly, because, if Miranda had not ratified the agreement, of what value was the signature of Miranda to Monteverde, being given in a prison, where he was placed by his own friends and subordinates? This consideration was evident; but they were irritated, and did not understand anything within the limits of reason. . . . It was all, at the time, surprise and consternation. At the bottom of all these were errors, inconsistencies, abandon. With Bolivar, Montilla and their ardent companions, all was passion. Passion dictated their resolutions.

> "'Male cuncta ministrat
> Impetus.'
> (STATIUS, *Thebaid*, x.)

"For the execution of that project, which should result so lamentably, without contributing in any manner to the bettering of the country, the services were combined as follows: Casas (in whose house was accommodated the old man, sleeping in an unlocked room) should place himself at the head of the troops in the castle of Colorado; Valdez should surround the house in which Miranda slept with a body of men; Bolivar, Chatillon and Montilla should take possession of his person, either willingly or by force; Mires was to receive and guard him in the *castillo*. All was executed as was disposed; and at three o'clock in the morning of the 31st of July, Miranda was a prisoner.

"He was plunged in a profound sleep when he was

awakened by those charged to capture him. '*Is it not too early?*' he inquired, thinking that he was called up to embark. His astonishment was unspeakable when he found he was a prisoner. Thoughtful and resigned, he silently followed his conductors, without proffering any complaint or resistance."

Unhappy Miranda! The rest of his life was passed in dungeons, prisons and chains. They took him to Puerto Cabello, thence to Porto Rico, and thence to Cadiz, Spain.

"I have seen the nobleman," said a British officer, "tied to a wall, with a chain about his neck, neither more nor less than a dog."

Death came to relieve him of his melancholy and miseries on the morning of July 14, 1816. He was not a traitor; he was a man who failed to fulfil his ideals. Amid the hurry of events he had been misjudged, and amid the same swiftly shifting scenes Bolivar himself had sought to act for the good of the whole people.

Had Miranda, with his twelve thousand patriots, marched directly against the small forces of the adventurer Monteverde, he could have destroyed them and made the republic secure. He could easily have cut off the Spanish general from retreat. But he took the wrong steps at the critical moment. He hesitated, when decision would have been victory. Had he gone on board the ship at La Guayra his end might have been less tragic. There are men who lose inspiration and faith in the hour of the opportunity that they themselves have made, and this seems to have been the case with Miranda.

But the good that men have done is a harvest that can never be forgotten. Truly said Simon Bolivar, years afterward, in his hour of triumph: "*The seed of liberty yields its just fruit. If there is anything which is never lost, it is the blood which is shed for a just cause.*" We cannot believe Bolivar to have been insincere when he said this, or when, in the following words, he revealed the motives which governed him: "My only ambition is the freedom of my fellow-citizens. My love of the independence of South America has caused me to make different sacrifices, sometimes in peace, sometimes in war. I shall never refuse these sacrifices, because he who abandons all to be useful to his country loses nothing, but gains all he consecrates."

In his day Bolivar was South America. His heart, thoughts and deeds were her pulse-beat and her destiny. In order that the reader may follow in detail the events of his life, I give a résumé of them:

The oath at Monte Sacro, Rome, 1805.
Visits the United States, 1809.
Joins the revolutionary movement, 1810.
Goes to England to purchase arms.
Returns, 1811.
Advocates the independence of Venezuela, 1811.
Enters the services, on the staff of General Miranda, 1811.
Arrests Miranda, 1812.
Goes to Curaçao as a refugee.
Enlists refugees at Cartagena, accompanied by Manuel Castillo.
Rekindles the revolution in Venezuela.
Commissioned as general by New Granada.
Issues his proclamation of *guerra á muerte*, 1813.
Enters Caracas in a car of triumph drawn by the daughters of the nobles, 1814.
Defeated at Boves.
Escapes to Cumaná.
Lays siege to Cartagena.
Flees from the country.
Goes to Kingston.
Escapes assassination there.
Gathers a force at Port au Prince.

Secures four negro battalions from President Pétion.
Returns to the islands of the coast.
Is appointed commander-in-chief of the forces of New Granada.
Emancipates the slaves by proclamation, June 1, 1816.
Is defeated at Ocumare.
Is again supplied with arms by the President of Hayti.
Defeats Morillo, February 16, 1817.
Condemns the negro general Piar to death for treason.
Gathers an army of nine thousand men.
Goes to Angostura.
Meets Santander of New Granada, who advises a New Granada campaign.
Organizes a congress at Angostura.
Gathers an army of fourteen thousand men.
Crosses the Cordilleras.
Gains the victory of Boyacá, August 7, 1819.
Returns victorious to Venezuela.
Proclaims the Republic of Colombia, December 17, 1819.
Gains the decisive victory of Carabobo, June 24, 1821.
Elected President of Colombia, 1821.
Determines to liberate all South America.
Wins the battle of Pichincha, through the aid of Sucre.
Enters Quito, June, 1822.
In response to San Martin he marches to Peru.
Gains the victory of Ayacucho, Peru, December 9, 1824.
Declared Protector of Peru.
Escapes assassination at Bogotá, September 25, 1828.
Condemned for ambitious designs by the Congress of Caracas, November 25, 1829.
Sends his final resignation as President to Congress, April 27, 1830.
Goes into exile.
Dies December 17, 1830.

CHAPTER VII

THE COLONIAL SYSTEM—WHAT LATIN AMERICA SUF-
FERED—THE SPANISH VICEROYALTIES—THE MANI-
FESTO OF ARGENTINA—THE EXPULSION OF THE JEWS
FROM SPAIN—THE PERSECUTIONS OF THE NATIVE
AMERICAN RACES—CUBA—THE CREOLES

TO enter into the spirit of the story of liberty in the Andean republics and in Cuba, one must have a view of the causes of the struggles for emancipation. The history of these struggles may be summed up in the words of Voltaire: "Cruelty leads to independence."

The colonial system of Spain in South and Central America and on the Spanish Main was one of selfishness, cruelty and tyranny. Only Spaniards were allowed to trade with the Spanish colonial ports. Hence arose buccaneers and pirates to claim the rights of the sea. For a long period ships engaged in trade with those ports were allowed to sail only from Cadiz. A company of Spanish merchants and grandees, organized under the name of the Philippine Company, once purchased of the government the sole right to trade with the Indies and to govern the trade. The viceroy himself could not interfere with its rights. The company compelled the colonists to sell to it the products of the country at its own price, and it reaped a profit of three hundred per cent. To oppose in any form this tyranny of the sea was death.

The colonial system did not recognize local human rights. Under it it was treason for a man to assert his freedom or to seek the free field of nature for his labor. The earth existed for the Spanish throne.

The mita was a cause of the darkest crimes in the long period of the viceroys. Those who sought to escape from hard labor as slaves of the system were tortured most cruelly. By the mita, free people, usually Indians, were compelled to labor for the state in the mines, or in any work of public profit or improvement. In the beginning this involuntary servitude was not wholly without compensation. It was under the mita that the native races were diminished in numbers and almost disappeared in many parts of the viceroyalties, notably so in parts of Peru.

From this system of tyranny the native Indian and the poor creole could only appeal to those who would at once regard them with suspicion, or to arms. For generations they struggled against their fate, only to be crushed, tortured and slain. The local government, the church, except a few patriot priests of eternal honor, and the Spanish throne were against them.

Education was denied. Instead of a beneficent system of free instruction, such as Pestalozzi gave to Switzerland and Prussia, the young were trained by the bull-fight. The trumpet-call of the old Moorish brutality, and not the school-bell, echoed from the Andes. The *plaza del toro* was the agora and the school-room object-lessons. The picadors and the matadors were the heroes of the day.

Take the educational condition of Porto Rico, one of the fairest of the Antilles. The island has a population of 480,267 white people, 248,690 of mixed races, and 77,751 negroes. The taxes of these poor people for a recent tax year were $4,374,874. Much of this money goes toward the support of high-salaried foreign officials, who live in luxury. The number of officers living upon the Porto Ricans is about 35,000. Yet out of 480,267 white inhabitants, only 96,867 could read and write.

Go to Quito, which under the Incas rose into such splendor and freedom that its history reads like an Oriental dream. Its empire swept from the fiery arch of the equator to the silver desert of Atacama. Within its mountain walls, with their crystal peaks, rose palaces gleaming with the gems of the Esmeraldas and the earth-covered treasures of the Andes. The people were happy and free. The Sun was their father in this world, and in the next their souls would ascend to the Incas, who dwelt with the Ineffable. Spain, with her mita, made a Sahara of this land. Her laws forbade every right and privilege that did not yield a revenue to a throne thousands of miles away. The colonist planted, but not for himself; he reaped, but the harvest was not his. If he murmured, he was answered by the lash. To have an opinion of his own was treason. To assert his birthright of liberty was death.

But what was the compensation to the world for this system of slavery? Go ask the dons at the bull-fights. Churches, indeed, arose where ancient temples fell, but the spirit of the Mount of Beatitudes was almost as much absent from them as from the altars of Persepolis, Babylon, Nineveh. Good priests, indeed, there were, by whom truth was preached; but those who raised their voices for humanity fell under the tyrannous insanity that too often follows material success. The land became a slave-pen, and tyranny triumphed.

Go to San Carlos after the victory of Carabobo. The Spanish general Calzada, as soon as he had taken possession of the beautiful town, caused more than two hundred persons to be murdered, sparing neither the aged nor the infants. A patriotic priest of San Carlos, named Carlos

Quintana, was seized. His ears were cut off; he was flayed alive, and his own bleeding skin was held up before his dying eyes; he was then beheaded. The village was reduced to ashes.

Go to Cartagena, that old city with yellow walls, slumbering in the dreamy days, by the listless harbor of the purple sea. The walls sixty feet thick, into which went the unrequited toil of a generation of slaves; the sunken sea-walls that stayed the invader; the castle-like monasteries and convents on the hills, where the golden lamps light the shadows of solitudes; the old broken church, with a torture-bed of the Inquisition still used as a grating for one of its lower windows—all reveal the soul of a system that is dead. The surrounding country, with its cool palm-gardens and its always blooming flowers, is one of the most beautiful in all the world, but there ignorance wanders in rags.

One may think that history exaggerates such scenes of injustice and cruelty, and their withering influences. Read the manifesto addressed to all the nations of the earth by the Constituent Congress of the United Provinces of South America, respecting the treatment and cruelties they received from the Spaniards. It was the precursor of the Argentine Declaration of Independence, which was issued from Buenos Ayres on October 25, 1817. Never was there such an arraignment of any civilized nation as that of this manifesto. Every fact it mentions is abundantly verified and is absolutely true.

MANIFESTO

"Addressed to all Nations of the Earth by the General Constituent Congress of the United Provinces of South America, respecting the treatment and cruelties they have experienced from the Spaniards, and which have given rise to the Declaration of Independence.

"Honor is a distinction which mortals esteem more than their own existence, and they are bound to defend it above all earthly benefits, however great and sublime they may be. The United Provinces of the river Plata have been accused by the Spanish government, before other nations, of rebellion and perfidy; and as such, also, has been denounced the memorable Act of Emancipation, proclaimed by the National Congress in Tucuman on July 9, 1816, by imputing to it ideas of anarchy, and a wish to introduce into other countries seditious principles, at the very time the said provinces were soliciting the friendship of these same nations, and the acknowledgment of this memorable act, for the purpose of forming one among them. The first and among the most sacred of the duties imposed on the National Congress is to wipe away so foul a stigma, and defend the cause of their country, by displaying the cruelties and motives which led them to the Declaration of Independence. This, indeed, is not to be considered as an act of submission, which may attribute to any other nation of the earth the power of disposing of a fate which has already cost America torrents of blood and all kinds of sacrifices and bitter privations; it is rather an important consideration we owe to our outraged honor, and the decorum due to other nations.

"We waive all investigations respecting the rights of conquest, papal grants, and other titles on which Spaniards have usually founded and upheld their dominion. We do not seek to recur to principles which might give rise to problematical discussions, and revive points of argument which have had defenders on both sides. We appeal to facts, which form a painful contrast to our forbearance with the oppression and cruelty of Spaniards. We will exhibit a frightful abyss which Spain was opening under our feet, and into which these provinces were about to be precipitated, if they had not interposed the safeguard of their own emancipation. We will, in short, exhibit reasons which no rational man can disregard, unless he could find sufficient pleas to persuade a country forever to renounce all idea of its own felicity, and, in preference, adopt a system of ruin, opprobrium and forbearance. Let us place before the eyes of the world this picture, one which it will be impossible to behold without being profoundly moved by the same sentiments as those by which we are ourselves actuated.

"From the moment when the Spaniards possessed themselves of these countries, they preferred the system of securing their dominion by extermination, destruction and degradation. The plans of this extensive mischief were forthwith carried into effect, and have been continued without any intermission during the space of three hundred years. They began by assassinating the monarchs of Peru, and they afterward did the same with the other chieftains and distinguished men who came in their way. The inhabitants of the country, anxious to restrain such ferocious intrusion, under the great disadvantage of their arms became the victims of fire and sword, and were compelled to leave their settlements a prey to the devouring flames, which were everywhere applied without pity or distinction.

"The Spaniards then placed a barrier to the population of the country. They prohibited, under laws the most rigorous, the ingress of foreigners, and in every possible respect limited that of even Spaniards themselves, although in times more recent the emigration of criminal and immoral men, outcasts, was encouraged, of men such as it was expedient to expel from the Peninsula. Neither our vast though beautiful deserts, formed by the extermination of the natives; the advantages Spain would have derived from the cultivation of regions as immense as they are fertile; the incitement of mines, the richest and most abundant on earth; the stimulus of innumerable productions, partly till then unknown, but all estimable for their value and variety, and capable of encouraging and carrying agriculture and commerce to their highest pitch of opulence; in short, not even the wanton wickedness of retaining these choice countries plunged into the most abject misery, were any of them motives sufficiently powerful to change the dark and inauspicious principles of the cabinet of Madrid. Hundreds of leagues do we still behold, unsettled and uncultivated, in the space intervening from one city to another. Entire towns have, in some places, disappeared, either buried in the ruins of mines, or their inhabitants destroyed by the compulsive and poisonous labor of working them; nor have the cries of all Peru, nor the energetic remonstrances of the most zealous ministers, been capable of reforming this exterminating system of forced labor, carried on within the bowels of the earth.

"The art of working the mines, among us beheld with apathy and neglect, has been unattended with those improvements which have distinguished the enlightened age in which we live, and diminished the attendant casualties; hence opulent mines, worked in the most clumsy and improvident manner, have sunk in and been overwhelmed, either through the undermining of the mineral ridges, or the rush of waters which have totally inundated them. Other rare and estimable productions of the country are still confounded with nature and neglected by the government, and if, among us, any enlightened observer has attempted to point out their advantages, he has been reprehended by the court, and forced to silence, owing to the competition that might arise to a few artisans of the mother-country.

"The teaching of science was forbidden us, and we were allowed to study only the Latin grammar, ancient philosophy, theology, civil and canonical jurisprudence. Viceroy Joaquin del Pino took the greatest umbrage at the Buenos Ayres Board of Trade because it presumed to bear the expenses of a nautical school. In compliance with the orders transmitted from court, it was closed. An injunction, besides, was laid upon us that our youths should not be sent to Paris to become professors of chemistry, with a view of teaching this science among their own countrymen.

Commerce has at all times been an exclusive monopoly in the hands of the traders of Spain and the consignees they sent over to America. The public offices were reserved for Spaniards, and notwithstanding, by the laws, these were equally open to Americans, we seldom attained them, and when we did, it was by satiating the avarice of the court through the sacrifice of immense treasures. Among one hundred and sixty viceroys who have governed in America, four natives of the country alone are numbered; and of six hundred and two captains-general and governors, with the exception of fourteen, all have been Spaniards. The same proportionally happened in the other offices of importance. Scarcely, indeed, had the Americans an opportunity of alternating with Spaniards in situations the most subaltern.

"Everything was so arranged by Spain that the degradation of the natives should prevail in America. It did not enter into her views that wise men should be formed, fearful that minds and talents would be created capable of promoting the interests of their country, and causing civilization, manners, and those excellent capabilities with which the Colombian children are gifted, to make a rapid progress. She unceasingly diminished our population, apprehensive that some day or other it might be in a state to rise against a dominion sustained only by a few hands to whom the keeping of detached and extensive regions was intrusted. She carried on an exclusive trade because she supposed opulence would make us proud and inclined to free ourselves from outrage. She denied to us the advancement of industry in order that we might be divested of the means of rising out of misery and poverty; and we were excluded from offices of trust in order that Peninsulars only might hold influence in the country, and form the necessary habits and inclinations, with a view of leaving us in such a state of dependence as to be unable to think or act, unless according to Spanish forms.

"Such was the system firmly and steadily upheld by the viceroys, each one of whom bore the state and arrogance of a vizier. Their power was sufficient to crush any one who had the misfortune to displease them. However great their outrages, they were to be borne with resignation, for by their satellites and flatterers their frown was superstitiously compared to the anger of God. Complaints addressed to the throne were either lost in the extended interval of those thousands of leagues it was necessary to cross, or buried in the offices at home by the relatives or patrons of men wielding viceregal power. This system, so far from having been softened, has been strengthened, so that all hopes that even time would produce this effect were totally lost. We held neither direct nor indirect influence in our own legislation; this was instituted in Spain. Nor were we allowed the right of sending over persons who might point out what was fit and suitable, empowered to assist at its enactment, as the cities of Spain were authorized to do. Neither had we any influence over the administration of government, which might, in some measure, have tempered the rigor of such laws as were in force. We were aware that no other resource was left to us than patience, and that for him who was not resigned to endure all, even capital punishment was not sufficient, since, for cases of this kind, torments new and of unheard-of cruelty had been invented, such as made nature shudder.

"Neither so great nor so repeated were the hardships which roused the provinces of Holland when they took up arms to free themselves from the yoke of Spain, nor those of Portugal to effect the same purpose. Less were the hardships which placed the Swiss under the direction of William Tell, and in open opposition to the German emperor; less those which determined the United States of North America to resist the imposts forced upon them by a British king; less, in short, the powerful motives which have urged other countries, not separated by nature from the parent state, to cast off an iron yoke and consult their own felicity."

Of the conduct of Spain toward her colonies, on the return of Ferdinand to the throne, this manifesto gives the following description:

"Posterity will be astonished at the ferocity exercised against us by men interested in the preservation of Spanish power in America; and that rashness and folly with which they have sought to punish demonstrations the most evident of fidelity and love, will ever be matter of the greatest surprise. The name of Ferdinand de Bourbon preceded all the decrees of our government, and was at the head of all its public acts. The Spanish flag waved on our vessels and served to animate our soldiers. The provinces, seeing themselves in a bereft state through the overthrow of the national government, owing to the want of another legitimate and respectable one substituted in its stead, and the conquest of nearly the whole of the mother-country, raised up a watch-tower, as it were, within themselves, to attend to their own security and self-preservation, reserving themselves for the captive monarch, in case he recovered his freedom. This measure was in imitation of the public conduct of Spain, and called forth by the declaration made to America that she was an integral part of the monarchy, and in rights equal with the former; and it had, moreover, been resorted to in Montevideo, through the advice of the Spaniards themselves. We offered to continue pecuniary succors and voluntary donations in order to prosecute the war, and we a thousand times published the soundness of our intentions and the sincerity of our wishes. Great Britain, at that time so well deserving of Spain, interposed her mediation and good offices in order that we might not be treated in so harsh and cruel a manner. But the Spanish ministers, blinded by their sanguinary caprice, spurned the mediation, and issued rigorous orders to all their generals to push the war, and to inflict heavier punishments. On every side scaffolds were raised, and recourse was had to every invention for spreading consternation and dismay.

"From that moment they endeavored to divide us by all the means in their power, in order that we might exterminate each other. They propagated against us atrocious calumnies, attributing to us the design of destroying our sacred religion, of setting aside all morality, and establishing licentiousness of manners. They carried on a war of religion against us, devising many and various plots to agitate and alarm the consciences of the people, by causing the Spanish bishops to issue edicts of ecclesiastical censure and interdiction among the faithful, to publish excommunications, and, by means of some ignorant confessors, to sow fanatical doctrines in the tribunal of penance. By the aid of such religious discords, they have sown dissension in families, produced quarrels between parents and their children, torn asunder the bonds which united man and wife, scattered implacable enmity and rancor among brothers formerly the most affectionate, and even placed nature herself in a state of hostility and variance.

"They have adopted the system of killing men indiscriminately, in order to diminish our numbers. On their entry into towns, they have seized non-combatants, hurried them in groups to the squares, and there shot them one by one. The cities of Chuquisaca and Cochabamba have more than once been the theaters of these ferocious acts.

" They have mixed our captive prisoners among their own troops, carrying off our officers in irons to secluded dungeons, where, during the period of a year, it was impossible for them to retain their health. Others they have left to die of hunger and misery in the prisons, and many they have compelled to toil in public works. In a boasting manner they have shot the bearers of our flags of truce, and committed the basest horrors upon military chiefs and other principal persons who had already surrendered themselves, notwithstanding the humanity we have always displayed toward prisoners taken from them. In proof of this assertion, we can quote the cases of Deputy Matos from Potosí, Captain-General Pumacagua, General Angulo and his brother, Commandant Munecas, and other leaders, shot in cold blood many days after they had been made prisoners.

" In the town of Valle-Grande they enjoyed the brutal

pleasure of cutting off the ears of the inhabitants, and sent off a basket filled with these presents to their headquarters. They afterward burned the town, set fire to thirty other populous ones belonging to Peru, and took delight in shutting up persons in their own houses before the flames were applied to them, in order that they might there be burned to death.

"They have not only been cruel and implacable in murdering, but they have also divested themselves of all morality and public decency, by whipping old religious persons in the open squares, and also women, bound to a cannon, causing them previously to be stripped and exposed to shame and derision.

"For all these kinds of punishments they established an inquisitorial system. They have seized the persons of several peaceable citizens and conveyed them beyond seas, there to be judged for supposed crimes. Many they have sent to execution without any form of trial whatever.

"They have destroyed our vessels, plundered our coasts, butchered their defenseless inhabitants, without even sparing superannuated priests; and, by order of General Pezuela, they burned the church belonging to the town of Puna, and put to the sword old men, women and children, the only inhabitants therein found. They have excited atrocious conspiracies among the Spaniards domiciliated in our cities, and forced us into the painful alternative of imposing capital punishment on the fathers of numerous families.

"They have compelled our brethren and children to take up arms against us, and, forming armies out of the inhabitants of the country, under the command of their own officers, they have forced them into battle with our troops. They have stirred up domestic plots and conspiracies, by corrupting with money, and by means of all kinds of machinations, the peaceful inhabitants of the country, in order to involve us in dreadful anarchy, and then to attack us in a weak and divided state.

"In a most shameful and infamous manner they have failed to fulfil every capitulation we have, on repeated occasions, concluded with them, even at a time when we have had them under our own swords. They caused four thousand men, after they had surrendered, again to take up arms, together with General Tristan, at the action of Salta, to whom General Belgrano generously granted terms of capitulation on the field of battle, and more generously complied with them, trusting to their word and honor.

"They have invented a new species of horrid warfare, by poisoning the waters and aliments, as they did when conquered in La Paz by General Pinelo; and in return for the kind manner in which the latter treated them, after surrendering at discretion, they resorted to the barbarous stratagem of blowing up the soldiers' quarters, which they had previously undermined. They have had the baseness to tamper with our generals and governors, by availing themselves of and abusing the sacred privilege of flags of truce, exciting them to act traitorously toward us, for this purpose making written overtures to them. They have declared that the laws of war observed among civilized nations ought not to be practised among us; and their general Pezuela, after the battle of Ayouma, in order to avoid any compromise or understanding, had the arrogance to answer General Belgrano that with insurgents it was impossible to enter into treaties.

"Such has been the conduct of Spaniards toward us since the restoration of Ferdinand de Bourbon to the throne of his ancestors. We then believed that the termination of so many sufferings and disasters had arrived.

We had supposed that a king schooled by the lessons of adversity would not be indifferent to the desolation of his people, and we sent over a commissioner to him in order to acquaint him with our situation. We could not for a moment conceive that he would fail to meet our wishes as a benign prince, nor could we doubt that our requests would interest him in a manner corresponding to that gratitude and goodness which the courtiers of Spain had extolled to the skies. But a new and unknown species of ingratitude was reserved for America, surpassing all the examples found in the histories of the greatest tyrants.

"Given in the Hall of Congress, Buenos Ayres, this twenty-fifth day of October, eighteen hundred and seventeen.

"DR. PEDRO IGNÁCIO DE CASTRO Y BARROS,
                                                President.
"DR. JOSÉ EUGÉNIO DE ELIAS,
                                                Secretary."

The cruel policy of Spain did not begin in her colonies. The sufferings of the Jews in Spain are one of the most terrible chapters in human history. The defenseless Hebrews were driven from their homes. They were deprived not only of their estates, but of their means of support. The women and children wandered homeless and foodless. Many of these people, after their expulsion, became the victims of the Inquisition, and fed the fires of the auto da fé. The crown profited by the confiscated property. During the eighteen years of Torquemada's ministry more than ten thousand Jews were burned alive. The expulsion of the Jews was the beginning of the fall of Spain.

In Cuba, the glory of the Spanish Main, the colonial

system was reasserted in 1825, under the name of "Royal Order." This order placed the absolute power in the hands of the captain-general, and gave to this officer " the whole extent of authority *which is granted to the governors of besieged towns.*" Cuba may be said to have been under martial law from that date. Since 1825 there was no legislative assembly in Cuba, except that of the revolutionists. Since 1836 it has not had any real representation in the Cortes. There have been no popular assemblies, no juntas, no elections, no juries to protect individual rights. The press and the public amusements have been under censorship. Patriots were subject to banishment without charge, trial or record. There was, indeed, a Real Audiencia, but it obeyed the will of the governor.

No native Cuban could hold any office of honor or emolument. The army was composed almost wholly of Spaniards. No man in Cuba might entertain a stranger in any time of public peril overnight, without permission of the magistrate. No one might carry weapons of defense.

But though the people were not allowed to exercise their rights, they were heavily taxed. To be taxed seems to have been, in the eyes of their taskmasters, the only purpose of their existence. Cuba paid the expenses of the government of her tyrants, and sent enormous revenues to Spain. What Cuba was from 1825 to 1898 represents the ancient colonial system of the whole Spanish empire in the South. The Peninsular king was the state. His empires existed for him and his. He was to be regarded as the elect of God, and could do no wrong.

The Spanish rule of slavery and robbery in Cuba began in 1511, more than a hundred years before the sailing of the *Mayflower*. Within half a century after the discovery, Spanish cruelty almost extinguished the innocent native population. Negro slavery followed this great injustice. Havana became a port of the slave-trade, which was carried on for the enrichment of Spain, whose monarchs never regarded Cuba as an integral part of their empire. Half a million slaves were brought to Cuba as late as the early part of the present century. The cruelty with which these slaves were treated led to the fearful insurrections of 1844 and 1868.

An effort for the independence of Cuba was made in the middle of this century. The isle of June, the ever-beautiful isle, began to feel the influence of the republics with which it was surrounded. The men doomed to toil for the luxury of a foreign court became restless to be free.

Puerto Principe, a central province four hundred and fifty miles from Havana, contained a population favorable to the development of liberty. It became the starting-place of the insurrection. Its soil is rich and productive, and it is flanked by noble mountains on either hand.

Here was an inland city of the same name as the province, which was remote from political cabals. The inhabitants were virtuous, upright and strong. They breathed the air of liberty and felt the strength of the hills. They came to abhor oppression. They were the Puritans of Cuba. They saw what the island might be under the rule of democracy, liberty and a free conscience. But the garrote, the dungeon and the sword held their growing patriotism in check. Suddenly twelve of their noble citizens were arrested for participating in revolutionary movements. The city, then of some one hundred thousand souls, was thrown into intense excitement. The flag of independence was unfurled on July 4, 1852, in the groves where the people assembled. The battle of Puerto Principe, which followed the movement, was a victory for the Cuban patriots, and the country arose in arms. The battles of Coscorro, Las Tunas, Najassa, San Miguel and Cerro followed.

Soon General Lopez, from Key West, with a force of patriots, appeared on the coast to aid the Cubans. He repulsed the Spanish.

The war opened with a scene of barbarism. Fifty-two American citizens, who had gone out from the invading expedition in four launches, were captured by a Spanish man-of-war, and were condemned to death. The captives were brought to Havana on August 16, and were executed the same day. They were compelled to kneel with their backs to the executioners, in view of some twenty thousand spectators. After being shot, their bodies were dragged by the feet, by negroes, and then left to the fury of the mob, who stripped them of most of their clothes, and bore them through the public streets, crying out like demons. The barbarous manner of the execution of these patriotic adventurers filled America with indignation. Public meetings were held there to express the popular feeling.

The whole Spanish force was now directed against General Lopez. He was defeated and wounded. He was run down by bloodhounds, captured and executed. His last words were,'" Adieu, dear Cuba!"

Some thirty-five years ago the *Virginius*, a ship that was secretly in the service of the Cuban patriots, but not proved to have been so until long after her capture, was seized by the Spanish cruiser *Tornada*, not far from Jamaica. She was sailing under the United States flag, and had United States papers. Her officers and men were taken to Santiago de Cuba, and were shot a day or two after their capture. The captain of the *Virginius* was named Fry. His farewell to his men was most affecting. Some of the wounded adventurers had their heads blown off in a savage way, and the bodies of all were given over to the chain-gang. The slaughter of these men without any reference of the case to consular powers for the decision of international tribunals was barbarism, and was accomplished in a barbarous manner. If the men had forfeited their lives, it should have been proved before their execution.

The revolution of 1868–78 developed the same injustice and cruelty on the part of the Spanish. The principal Cuban grievance at this time was that the Spaniards drained the island of between forty and fifty per cent. of the annual income, and left the people poor and uncared for. They were simply slaves of a foreign power, that robbed them of the fruits of their labors. Spain promised to redress this and the other grievances. The rebels, reposing confidence in Spain's honor, laid down their arms. Spain betrayed that confidence.

This failure of Spain to keep her promise caused the present rebellion. At first Marshal Campos was sent to Cuba. He was recalled, and Weyler was sent. Weyler inaugurated the policy of the *trocha*, or the confinement of the Cubans in certain limits. He caused them to be concentrated within the plowed furrows around fortified places, to starve in a land of plenty.

On January 8, 1898, General Lee, consul-general of the United States at Havana, made the following report to his government:

"SIR: I have the honor to state, as a matter of public interest, that the 'reconcentrado order' of General Weyler, formerly governor-general of this island, transformed about four hundred thousand self-supporting people, principally women and children, into a multitude to be sustained by the contributions of others, or die of starvation or of fevers resulting from a low physical condition, and being massed in large bodies, without change of clothing and without food. Their homes were burned, their fields and plant-beds destroyed, and their live stock driven away or killed.

"I estimate that probably two hundred thousand of the rural population in the provinces of Pinar del Rio, Havana, Matanzas and Santa Clara have died of starvation or from resultant causes; and the deaths of whole families almost simultaneously, or within a few days of each other, and mothers praying for their children to be relieved of their horrible suffering by death, are not the least of the many pitiable scenes which were ever present."

The sufferings of the reconcentrados awakened the sympathy of humanity. Spain yielded to the awakened sentiment of the Christian nations, and removed Weyler. After nearly four hundred years of injustice in Cuba, her power in the most beautiful land that eyes ever beheld had been overthrown.

The church in this long period of injustice has too often stood by the throne, and yet out of it have come patriot priests like Hidalgo in Mexico, Beltran of the Army of the Andes, and some of the heroes of the independence of Peru. These patriot priests have followed the principles of Las Casas, one of the most noble philanthropists that ever honored the cause of true Christianity. He was a Dominican monk. To him it was noble to be noble, without any fear of punishment or hope of reward. Las Casas was born in Seville in 1474. He made himself the defender of the rights of the native people in America, and boldly declared that any war waged against these people, or any robbery of them or injustice toward them, because they were regarded as "infidels," was wrong. He announced that Christianity was sufficient for their conversion, and he brought under its influence a most warlike nation in Guatemala by the simple preaching of the gospel. His success in thus winning a nation awakened the admiration of Pope Paul III., who was led to issue a sentence of excommunication against any "who should reduce these Indians to slavery, or rob them of their goods." Las Casas brought a golden age to Guatemala, as Quetzalcohuatl, the legendary St. Thomas, had to the ancient Mexicans.

We have seen in the fate of Atahualpa and of the two Tupactmarus what the native races were called upon to endure in the persons of their chiefs. Gonzalo Pizarro was of the same spirit as his brother. He tortured the Indians to make them reveal places of hidden treasures. For the same reason he burned some of them, and caused others to be torn to pieces by bloodhounds trained to feed on human flesh. De Soto, whose heart was schooled in these Peruvian barbarities, pursued the same course wherever he went. He landed at Tampa with horses mounted with gold, but with bloodhounds trained to tear to pieces the native inhabitants who should oppose his march or seek to hide from him their treasures. He robbed the caciques, or native kings or chiefs, not only of their goods, but of the beautiful women of their families.

The torture of Guatemotzin, the nephew of Montezuma II. and the last of the Aztecs, illustrates the same spirit of cruelty. He had been promised protection by Cortez. But in the fall of the City of Mexico less gold was found there than the conquerors had expected, and the captive monarch was suspected of having hidden the royal treasure. On being taken captive, he had said to Cortez: "I have done all I could to defend my people. I am reduced to this state. Better despatch me with your poniard and end my life now." "Fear not," replied Cortez. "You have defended your capital bravely, and shall be treated with honor. A Spaniard knows how to respect the valor of an enemy." In the rage of the Spaniards at not finding a great hoard of treasure in the fallen city, he was put to torture. According to the historic monument, his feet were placed over a slow fire. He bore the torture in stoical silence.

The cacique of Tacuba was tortured with him. He confessed to a knowledge of hidden treasure. They released him to find it. But he could discover none. "My only motive for confessing," he said, "was the hope that I might die on the road to the place that I named."

The cruelty of the Spanish rulers fell also upon the creoles, or the descendants of European immigrants who were born in America. Most of those in Latin America were of Spanish descent, and were proud of their ancestry and of the glory of Spain. They believed in the divine right of kings, and thought that the throne of Spain could do no wrong. They at first believed that the will of heaven was in Spain's triumphal march over the seas and sierras. For two centuries they bore all with patience. They were deprived of their rights, were heavily taxed, were compelled to toil and do the will of the viceroy for the glory of Spain.

The struggles for independence brought out all the cruel selfishness and intolerance of the Spanish national character. Larrazabal, whom we have much quoted, gives us some descriptions of the inhumanity of the war in Venezuela. General Boves, the Spanish commander there, swore that he would exterminate the whole American race. In 1814, and later, the Spanish army there entered into his spirit. When he was victorious Boves would say that he had gained, and when he was defeated he would say that he had gained, as in either case his purpose was the destruction of the American race.

Field-Marshal Don Francisco Montalvo reported to the

minister of war in Spain, in 1814, as follows: "Don José Tomas Boves and those who follow him do not distinguish between delinquents and innocents. All such die for the crime of being born in America."

Larrazabal says of the massacre of Aragua: "Children were murdered on the very breasts of their mothers. The same knife divided the heads of both." Again: "They were flayed alive, and then thrown into poisonous and pestilential swamps."

It was such crimes that led Simon Bolivar to issue his ever-to-be-regretted proclamation of war to the death. The land smoked with burning houses; the highways were strewn with bodies of the dead. The young, the old, the mother, the daughter, all perished, and the land where Boves marched became a desolation. Honor counted for nothing, virtue for nothing, in those days when the smoke of villages turned the sun into darkness and when rivers became streams of blood.

In Peru the tragedy went on for centuries. After the first Pizarro came Carbajal, a monster so cruel that he was believed to have had a "familiar," or to have been possessed of an evil spirit. He was guilty of the death of hundreds of political offenders, whom he delighted to torture, and to jeer at when dying. At the age of eighty-four he himself was condemned to death. He was thrown into a basket and carried to execution amid jeers as heartless as those he had been accustomed to heap upon others.

The colonial system of Spain has crumbled, as all injustice must, by the law of its own gravitation. To Spain the last of her colonial empires is lost; the Pearl of the Antilles follows the example of Lima, the Pearl of the Pacific. Cuba ends the long empire of injustice, and sets her banner in the line of the republics of the Sun.

A better age is at hand. The gates of the twentieth century are opening, and through them are to pass the armies of the schools. The days of the bull-fights are gone. The times of persecution, in any form, are already a part of the darkness of the past. Liberty gives to man his birthright. The end of liberty is justice, and the end of justice is peace. The deeds of Hernando Cortez, of Pedro de Alvarado, of Francisco Pizarro and of Philip II. will never again be enacted on the American continent.

CHAPTER VIII

THE LIBERATING ARMY OF THE NORTH — THE TRIUMPH OF BOLIVAR — THE BATTLE OF ARAURE — PÉTION — PIAR — BOLIVAR ELECTED PRESIDENT — THE MARCH OVER THE CORDILLERAS — THE BATTLE OF BOYACÁ — ANGOSTURA — COLOMBIA

LET us repeat. There were three great struggles for liberty in South America—that of the north under Bolivar, that of the south under San Martin, and that of the center under Sucre. Bolivar led the movement of the north.

When Miranda lay down in the closet he had a new vision. He hoped to go to New Granada and unite his fortunes with the liberal government there, and, old as he was, make a new struggle for South American liberty.

Strangely enough, the last dream of the unhappy Miranda was to be fulfilled in Bolivar, who had become his enemy. Bolivar took up the work of liberation that Miranda had left uncompleted. He felt that this was his mission, that in fulfilling it he was being led by a divinity. From the hour when he took the hand of Rodriguez on Monte Sacro, and swore to devote his life to the liberties of his country, he felt that to accomplish that task was his destiny. We must ever judge his purpose by this oath. If he committed sins, they brought their punishment, as all sins do. They made his life less successful than it might have been. But in nearly every proclamation that he issued he recognized the Divine Being that his heart wished to follow. He made himself the altar of liberty, and at last laid himself upon it.

He came to Venezuela to achieve the liberties of the people. He began this achievement as a soldier of Miranda. He failed and fled. He came back again by the way of New Granada. He entered Caracas in triumph. His cause seemed to fail, but it had made progress. He again became an exile. He returned by the way of republican New Granada. Again he entered Caracas in triumph. The cause had advanced. But he failed a second time, and sought refuge in the island of Jamaica. Again he returned. He became the hero of Boyacá and Carabobo. He united the republics of New Granada and Venezuela. He swept over the snowy Cordilleras, and added Ecuador to the growing empire. He entered the magical atmosphere of Peru, and there laid the foundations of the republic. He was dictator, president, the inspiration of emancipation and liberty. After every success and seeming failure the cause of freedom in the Andes advanced. Then he surrendered all to the cause, and died of a broken heart; but his influence in the world still grew. The inspiration that filled the heart of the young traveler at Monte Sacro will never cease to influence his countrymen.

To return to his early history, a new theater awaits him now. He is to win back the liberties of Venezuela, but through New Granada.

Beautiful New Granada! It bears the name that was the pride of Spain, of the historic and scenic province of the Sierra Nevada and the Guadalquivir. Spain crowned this viceroyalty with her choicest name. She might well do so. The Andes have a loftier brow here than the mountains in enthralling Andalusia, and the Magdalena moves on a more majestic way to the Caribbean than does the Guadalquivir to the Mediterranean. Cartagena, like another Cadiz, here arose on the margin of the purple sea. Spain lavished millions upon its walls. She even built walls under the sea. The city in its ruin, with the monasteries and convents crowning its green hills, with its yellow walls sixty feet thick,—walls that cost so much that an old legend reports that the King of Spain expected to see them rising over the sea,—with its ancient church, with its quintas, its gardens of palms, its wildernesses of all floral delights, is still a picture of Spain in the New World. The republic now has an area of some 513,000 square miles, and a population of three millions, of whom nearly one half are of European origin. Its highest plateaus rise 14,000 feet. Its mountain-crown has an altitude of 18,200 feet. From this sublime range, Nevada de Tolma, on the frontier of Ecuador, the Magdalena flows.

The ancient city of Santa Fé de Bogotá stands above the Magdalena, on a plateau 8690 feet high. It is approached from the Caribbean by steamboats on the river, and by mules from the shore. The Cordilleras are white with snow, and the valleys are green with verdure. The products of all climates may be cultivated here.

The republic has ever had a liberal heart. Its people are given to literary and scientific culture, and this inspiration has found a field in a thousand schools.

New Granada was erected into a viceroyalty of Spain in 1718. When Napoleon set aside Ferdinand VII., and put his own brother Joseph on the throne of Spain, a republican sentiment began to develop in New Granada, and the people formed a government of their own. It united with Venezuela and Ecuador to form a northern republic under Bolivar, but became independent of the union in 1858, under the name of the United States of Colombia.

History now follows the course of the life of Bolivar, whom the patriotic clubs were already hailing as the Liberator. We have seen no more interesting account of this period of Bolivar's life than is contained in a review of the "Historia de la Revolucion de la República de Colombia, por José Manuel Restrepo, Secretario del Interior del Poder Ejecutivo de la misma Republica," by the Hon. Caleb Cushing. It appeared in the " North American Review" for January, 1829. It pictures not only the military movements of Bolivar, but the animus and methods of the great leader.

After the disaster at Puerto Cabello, Bolivar retired to New Granada, and his life from this date is portrayed in a single paragraph by Mr. Cushing: "The government of Cartagena, little anticipating the brilliant fortune which awaited Bolivar, appointed him to the command of the little station Barranca, within the district committed to the adventurer Labatut, and, of course, regularly under his orders. But the active spirit of Bolivar prevented his remaining contented in the obscurity of a subordinate command, and led him to undertake of his own authority a movement of that bold conception and vigorous, rapid execution which afterward became the great characteristic of his military genius, and he rose to be the trusted leader of the armies of the independence."

Young Bolivar found a shelter in Cartagena, the stronghold of republicanism. He met there a patriot leader who was marching upon Santa Marta. He offered to enlist under him as a private. Bolivar's patriotism at this time found expression in a declaration the sincerity of which cannot be doubted, and which merits immortality: "*I disregarded rank and distinction, because I aspired to a more honorable destiny—to shed my blood for the liberty of my country!"*

The first movement of Bolivar was the key-note of the march which ended in Lima, the "City of the Kings." The Spaniards held the Magdalena, and the Magdalena must be free. His movements were so bold and swift as to take the enemy at a disadvantage. He accomplished his purpose, and won the approval of the republic. His name in New Granada became a star. The state made him a general. His army grew, owing to his magnetism. Having freed the Magdalena and gained other successes, he resolved to march into the interior. The Spaniards, who boasted that they would not respect a flag of truce, were compelled to flee before him. He won victory after victory, and on August 6, 1813, entered the city of Caracas in triumph, amid the vivas of the multitude.

Larrazabal vividly describes the triumphal entry of the Liberator into his native city. " Long live the Liberator! Long live New Granada! Long live the savior of Vènezuela!" was shouted by a concourse of more than thirty thousand people. Says Larrazabal: " A multitude of beautiful young women, dressed in white and bearing crowns of laurel, pushed their way through the crowds to take hold of the bridle of his horse. Bolivar dismounted, and was almost overpowered by the crowns cast upon him. The people wept for joy."

On December 3, 1813, the patriots encamped on the plain of Araure. They numbered thirty-five hundred men. The battle that followed was a furious one. The fate of the day was decided by a sudden and unexpected movement directed by the Liberator. The enemy was routed, and fled, leaving in the hands of the patriots one thousand muskets, ten field-pieces, four flags and three thousand prisoners.

Larrazabal relates an incident of this contest which shows the spirit of true heroes who have been vanquished. Few stories of the victories of the vanquished are more thrilling or better illustrate the unconquerable power of purpose. "At the battle of Araure, memorable feat of arms, in which the most intrepid valor was crowned with the most signal victory, all the soldiers, officers and chiefs made themselves worthy of admiration; but there was a battalion which was particularly distinguished by the conferring of the title of 'Conquerors of Araure,' and to which Bolivar presented a flag. What was the motive of such an honorable distinction? We remember that at Barquisimeto the sound alone of the signal of retreat, executed by a drummer, placed our infantry in irreparable disorder, the extraordinary efforts of the general-in-chief and his brave officers not being sufficient to remedy it. Of the relics preserved another battalion was formed at San Carlos. Bolivar, who had been extremely irritated by the unpardonable conduct of the infantry, gave it the title of 'Battalion without Name,' and did not allow it a flag until it should win it on the battle-field. The 'Battalion without Name,' mortified by this degrading treatment, determined to gain a famous name, and to take flags from the enemy. At Araure it composed the center. Eight minutes had not transpired from the time they opened their fire when they already had possession of a flag, throwing themselves with heroic intrepidity upon the triple Spanish line of formidable artillery, infantry and cavalry. Bolivar, who beheld them perform these prodigies of valor, named the battalion 'Conquerors of Araure,' and on the day following the victory, in a review, he presented them a flag, saying: 'Soldiers, your bravery yesterday on the field of battle has gained a name for your corps, and in the midst of the fire, when I beheld you triumphing, I proclaimed you "Conquerors of Araure." You have taken flags from the enemy who at one moment was victorious; you have gained the celebrated one called the "Invincible Numancia." Carry, soldiers, this flag of the republic. I am certain that you will always follow it with glory. . . .'

"The battalion received the flag from the hands of the Liberator with a concert of joy and enthusiasm, giving vivas to the genius of victory."

Boves now entered the field for Spain, with the purpose of killing every patriot he could find, and striking terror to all hearts by torture, fire and merciless deeds. The patriot cause for a while grew; but eventually Boves, with Spanish recruits, defeated Bolivar at La Puerta, and the great expectation of Venezuela remained unrealized.

Bolivar returned to New Granada, organized a new army, and continued' the war upon the coast. The war became a political contest with his rival Castillo. He now found himself in a difficult position, owing to political entanglements. He seems to have acted unwisely. He was forced to conclude a treaty, relinquished the command of the army to General Palacios, and sailed for Jamaica, May 8, 1815. But, notwithstanding these disasters, his faith in the cause was not lost. He was ready to enter the field again when the gate of opportunity should open.

An unsuccessful attempt to assassinate him was made at Jamaica. A negro was engaged to do the deed. On the night appointed another man chanced to sleep in Bolivar's bed, and received the dagger-thrust intended for the Liberator.

Bolivar, restless and ill at ease, now went to Aux-Cayes. He found sympathy there in the negro republic. He began to organize a new expedition for the emancipation of Venezuela. He desired to return there and again place himself at the head of the patriots who were struggling to maintain the cause of independence.

Bolivar furnishes one of the most notable examples of persistency of purpose in all history. If one opportunity failed, he waited for a greater one. At this time, when so much seemed lost, his vision of what America might be grew more and more clear. "I desire," he said, "to see in America the greatest nation in the world, famed less for its extension and riches than for its glory and liberty. America can sustain seventeen nations. The states from the Isthmus of Panama to Guatemala shall form an association. This magnificent position between the two great oceans shall be in turn the emporium of the world. Its canals shall shorten the distances of the earth. How grand would it be if the Isthmus of Panama could be to us what Corinth was to the Greeks! God grant that we may some day have the fortune of convening there an august congress of the representatives of the republics, kingdoms and empires to discuss the all-important interests of peace and war with the nations of the world!"

Bolivar now met the immortal apostle of liberty, Alexandre Pétion, President of Hayti. This man, whose name is forever beloved by the negro race, was born at Port au Prince in 1770. He was well educated. He had lived in France at the period of the rise of Napoleon. On returning to Hayti he had entered with a true and noble sympathy into the cause of his race. After the overthrow of Toussaint L'Ouverture he entered into the plans of Dessalines in the demand for the independence of his country. He became the idol of the Haytians. He was elected President, and later was reëlected. On the achievement of liberty in Hayti he believed that the mission of his life was accomplished.

When Bolivar and Pétion met, the latter was affected

to tears, and said: "Que le bon Dieu vous bénir dans toutes vos entreprises!" He rendered Bolivar all the aid in his power toward the fitting out of the expedition for the recovery of Venezuela. The Liberator speaks thus of this man: "His first quality was kindness, and kindness is that human virtue that does most honor to a man." "I shall always pay my tribute to that great man," said Pétion of Bolivar. "I feel toward him as toward the noble minds of antiquity." He saw in Bolivar a man who could advance the interests of his own race. "When your expedition shall land in Venezuela," he said to Bolivar, "free the slaves. For how can you found a republic where slavery exists?"

Bolivar himself had the same thought and purpose. On landing in Venezuela he freed his own slaves, and issued a proclamation giving freedom to the slaves of the country.

He devoted the resources of his own property to this new expedition. He collected some six ships, and an army of one hundred and fifty exiles. With these he set forth, for the third time, for the emancipation of Venezuela. He landed at Margarita. Here he captured two Spanish vessels, and was hailed by the people as chief. He issued a proclamation announcing the third period of the republic. He penetrated into the interior, his army gathering force. His name was an inspiration. He returned to Hayti to organize a new expedition among the islanders. He saw that the new liberation must come in part from the islands. The republic of Hayti had forced upon the amiable Pétion, by acclamation, the title of "Chief for life." The latter entered again into the cause of Bolivar, but under the limitations of international law. Bolivar organized a new force, and again landed at Margarita, and there again issued a proclamation to the Venezuelan patriots, calling upon them to convene a congress at Margarita: "Venezuelans, name your deputies to Congress. The island of Margarita is completely free. In it your assemblies shall be respected and defended by a people who are heroes in virtue, in valor and in patriotism. Assemble on this sacred soil, organize, open your sessions. The first act of your functions may be the acceptance of my resignation. Margarita, December 28, 1816."

On January 1, 1817, Bolivar landed at Barcelona, never again to be driven from the country. This time he was to organize a movement that should give liberty to the New World. His great opportunity had now come. The country was ripe for a new struggle for emancipation. The people were driven to desperation by the barbarity of the Spanish rule.

Though now but the leader of small bodies of men, he wrote to General Palacios on January 2, 1817: "The troops of Urdaneta have joined those of Zaraza. When this army shall have the arms it needs, and joins our forces, there will be formed a mass of ten thousand men. We shall be able to march to Santa Fé and Peru, and liberate those provinces from the yoke of the tyrants that oppress them."

The patriots in most places were disposed to hail Bolivar as their chief, and to seek his will and direction. His position at Barcelona was a perilous one. Mariño, the patriot general of the south, who saw Bolivar's danger, brought to him twelve hundred men. "I have come to embrace the Liberator of the liberator," said Mariño's principal general, on meeting Bolivar.

The liberating army now marched into the interior by the way of the Orinoco, where a part of the patriot forces were contending, near Angostura. Left with but a small protection, Barcelona was besieged by the Spanish general Aldama, and was compelled to surrender. The Spaniards massacred nearly seven hundred soldiers, more than three hundred old men, women and children, and fifty invalids in the hospital. The cruelties of this slaughter are indescribable.

The clouds darkened again about Bolivar. Barcelona was ruined. Mariño withdrew dissatisfied. Morillo, the Spanish general, had returned from the kingdom of Santa Fé resolved on the total extermination of the patriots. Piar, a signally successful general, conspired against Bolivar.

Thus the cause of independence in Venezuela had lived amid many vicissitudes. Bolivar may have made mistakes, but the patriots believed in his patriotism. He had returned to Venezuela without substantial authority, but the patriot cause had again turned to him for leadership. As soon as he returned the patriots felt that they were again a republic. The Spanish army under Morillo was yet powerful, but the desire of the people was for liberty, and Simon Bolivar was looked upon as the man providentially appointed to lead their cause.

Manuel Carlos Piar, a soldier of Curaçao, West Indies, was born in 1782. His youth was spent in hardship. He engaged in trade with Venezuela, and there came to meet the patriot Miranda. He entered the patriot army of Venezuela as a lieutenant. Although a soldier under Mariño, he engaged in a conspiracy against him and Bolivar. After the Spanish successes he left the country for the islands. Bolivar forgave his treachery. In 1816 he joined the expedition of Bolivar from Hayti, and was made a major-general of the invading army. He gained a great victory at San Felix, April, 1817. He again entered into a conspiracy against Bolivar, and sought to overthrow him and supplant him. He was condemned to death by a court martial, and was shot at Angostura, October 16, 1817.

Bolivar has been censured for the death of Piar, but he sought to save him from both treachery and death. He remembered San Felix, and exercised a great magnanimity toward this brilliant but vain and ambitious man, who had twice become his enemy.

The Liberator, on the day following the death of Piar, issued a proclamation:

"SOLDIERS: Yesterday was a day of pain for my heart. General Piar was executed for his crimes of high treason, conspiracy and desertion. A just and legal tribunal pronounced the sentence against that unfortunate citizen, who, intoxicated by the favors of fortune, and to satiate his ambition, attempted to ruin the country. General Piar really had done important services to the republic, and although the course of his conduct had always been mutinous, his services were bountifully rewarded by the government of Venezuela.

" Nothing was left to be desired by a chief who had obtained the highest grades of the army. The second authority of the republic, which was vacant by the dissidence of General Mariño, was to be conferred on him before his rebellion; but he aspired to the supreme command, and formed a purpose the most atrocious that can be conceived. Not only had Piar intended civil war, but also anarchy, and the most inhuman sacrifice of his own companions and brethren.

" Soldiers! You know it. Equality, liberty and independence are our motto. Has not humanity recovered her rights by our laws? Have not our arms broken the chains of the slaves? Has not the hateful difference of classes and colors been abolished forever? Have not the national moneys been ordered to be divided among you? Do not fortune and glory await you? Are not your

merits abundantly rewarded, or at least justly? What, then, did General Piar want for you? Are you not equal, free, independent, happy and honored? Could Piar obtain for you greater wealth? No, no, no. The tomb was being opened by Piar with his own hands, to bury in it the life, the wealth, the honor of the brave defenders of the liberty of Venezuela, their children, wives and fathers. . . .

"Soldiers! Heaven watches for your well-being, and the government, which is your father, is vigilant in your behalf. Your chief, who is your companion in arms, who is always at your head, and has participated in your perils and privations, as also in your victories, confides in you; rely then on him, sure that he loves you more than if even he were your father or your son.

"SIMON BOLIVAR.
"HEADQUARTERS OF ANGOSTURA,
"October 17, 1817."

These words reveal the spirit of Bolivar. We cannot doubt Bolivar's sincerity. The execution of Piar caused him as much suffering as that of Major André caused Washington.

Bolivar now convened a Council of State at Angostura. He there organized a government, gave himself to the creation of a new republican sentiment, and formed a new army.

The Council of State at Angostura provided for the election of a Congress. The representatives of the people to this Congress met there on January 1, of the eventful year 1819. Bolivar was elected President with dictatorial power.

What should be the next movement in this long contest? "Fabius was prudent, I am impetuous," said Bolivar, on being compelled, after the Congress of Angostura, to adopt the Fabian policy of wearing out an enemy by delay.

The contest with the Spanish general Morillo, on the plains, had moved slowly, and Bolivar was not constituted for a campaign whose end was exhaustion. He said at Angostura: "Granadians, Venezuela with me marches to liberate you, as you with me marched to liberate Venezuela. The sun shall not complete its annual period without beholding raised in all your territory the altars of liberty."

There seemed to come to Bolivar a new and sudden inspiration. He decided to cross the Granadian Andes, the mountain heights of winter and storm and desert, depose the viceroy, and restore to Granada her lost liberties. He would then reconquer Venezuela.

The war in Venezuela stopped, or consisted only of movements to wear out the power of Morillo. Bolivar looked up to the rainy Andes, shadowed with clouds. He gave the first order to his army to begin the ascent of the Cordilleras, an order that caused even some of the llaneros to shrink and to desert. Those who watched the movement said with wonder, "Whither go they?"

The march through the desert altitudes, in winter weather, with the half-naked troops of the plains, was arduous and perilous. The fiery faith of Bolivar in the power of the human will here found its most magnificent expression. His soul rose superior to all difficulties. In the clouded plains of the heights he led a dying army, but the men followed him.

On the 25th of May he issued a manifesto of the liberty of Granada. On the 22d of June he left the plains of Casanare. He ascended the heights almost without food and shelter. His cavalry in part vanished where it seemed that only the mules could live.

He descended and met the Granadian army, which hailed him like one bringing an army from the skies. He said to these heroes of liberty: "In your midst you now have an army of friends and benefactors, and the God of suffering humanity will grant victory to our redeeming arms."

On the 25th of July he met the Spanish general Barreiro in the open field. Bolivar had left behind no way of retreat. He led his troops in person. His voice was a trumpet-tone. He was victorious against a disciplined army. The Spaniards lost five hundred men, and left their flags, muskets and ammunition in the hands of the patriots.

Granada rose to receive the liberating army, which grew by reinforcements. What this army had suffered and endured for the cause became an inspiration. The invading army followed Barreiro in his retreat, and came to Boyacá. Here it compelled Barreiro again to try the fortunes of war. Barreiro had three thousand men, Bolivar two thousand, but the latter had the spirit of freedom, and every man was as two. To Anzoatequi, a personal friend of Bolivar, who loved the latter as a brother and reverenced him almost as a god, was intrusted the direction of this great battle. He inspired the men with his own spirit. He surrounded body after body of the enemy, until the cavalry began to fly. The army broke, and Barreiro found it impossible to rally it. He himself became lost as if in a whirlwind, and was taken prisoner. The officers were nearly all made prisoners, together with sixteen hundred soldiers, their artillery and arms. The friend of Bolivar slept that night on the field of battle under the moon and stars. Bolivar marched to Bogotá in triumph, and entered the astonished city, from which the viceroy had fled.

He issued a manifesto which is a history, and rings in harmony with the event that it celebrated:

"HEADQUARTERS OF SANTA FÉ, August 14, 1819.

"*Simon Bolivar, President of the Republic, Captain-General of the Armies of Venezuela and New Granada, etc., to his Excellency the Vice-President of the Republic:*

"From the moment that I conceived the project of advancing my marches to the interior of this kingdom, I knew that an alarming fear would put in action all the resources of the Spanish authorities. In effect, this idea, based on the experience of my observations, was more confirmed when, in the states which were under the power of the viceroy Don Juan Samano, I found that a superior force, well organized and disciplined, was the wall against which it was intended that the brave liberating army should perish.

"I calculated, notwithstanding, that the abundance of evils with which these people had been and still were afflicted should have prepared their minds to embrace with pleasure their heroic defenders. And, in truth, scarcely had I taken the first steps on this side of the mountains which divide the plains from the hilly country bounding the province of Casanare, when I heard resound before me the blessings of some men who awaited my arms with all the enthusiasm of liberty, as a remedy for the calamities and misfortunes which had carried them to the last degree of exasperation.

"An experienced chief, at the head of an army of four or five thousand men, is the first thing which presents itself to me on the battle-field. The General Don José Maria Barreiro, charged with its direction, drains all his resources. The discipline of his troops, his fine organization, the advantageous position he occupied, and the abundance of resources he had opportunely prepared for himself, caused me to believe that this enterprise was only proper to the intrepidity and bravery of the republican arms.

"The battle of Boyacá, the complete victory which I have just obtained, has decided the fate of these inhabitants, and after having destroyed the army of the king I have flown to this capital."

Bolivar, now master of the two republics, returned to Venezuela with the purpose of uniting them and forming the one republic of Colombia.

The return of Bolivar to Angostura is thus dramatically described by Larrazabal: "On the day of his arrival at Angostura Baralt affirms that Bolivar appeared in the Hall of Congress. This is untrue. On the 11th he did not leave the house, receiving there the compliments of his friends; the 12th he passed in seclusion, if not from sickness, at least suffering the fatigues of continued travel; the 13th, in virtue of an official notice, from the minister of the interior to the secretary of the Congress, announcing that the Liberator, President of the republic, would proceed *personally* to present to the National Assembly the homage of the victories obtained under his command in New Granada, and the unanimous wish of those people for political reunion with Venezuela, an extraordinary session was appointed at twelve o'clock of the following day; and as there were no ceremonies prepared for the reception of the Liberator, the Congress busied itself on the morning of the 14th in considering what should be observed in such an act.

"At midday of the 14th the Congress was convened,

and the president, at that time Senator Zea, appointed a committee which, preceded by a military band, should proceed to congratulate his Excellency, and accompany him to the Hall of the Sessions.

"Three cannon announced the march of Bolivar from his house. On entering the square before the Congress he was saluted with twenty-one rounds.

"The Congress in a body went out to receive him outside the railing, and the president, by a singular demonstration, ceded him the chief seat, and said to him: 'Your Excellency has the floor. Congress awaits and desires to hear you.' Bolivar made a profound bow to the assembly, and said: 'On entering this august place my first feeling is that of gratitude for the infinite honor which Congress has thought proper to confer upon me, allowing me to return to occupy this chair, which scarcely a year ago I ceded to the president of the representatives of the people. When, undeservedly and against my strongest feelings, I was invested with the executive power at the beginning of this year, I represented to the sovereign body that my profession, my character and my talents were incompatible with the functions of the magistrate; thus, separated from these duties, I left their performance to the vice-president, and only took upon myself the charge of directing the war. I afterward marched against the Army of the West, at whose head was General Morillo. At the approach of winter General Morillo abandoned the plain of Araure, and I judged that the liberty of New Granada would produce more advantages to the republic than the completion of that of Venezuela.

"'It would be lengthy to detail to the Congress the efforts made by the troops of the liberating army. The winter on the inundated plains, the frozen summits of the Andes, the sudden change of climate, a warlike army thrice our superior, and in possession of the best military localities of South America, and many other obstacles we had to surmount at Paya, Gameza, Vargas, Boyacá and Popayan, to liberate in less than three months twelve provinces of New Granada.

"'I recommend to the national sovereignty the merit of these great services on the part of my intrepid companions in arms, who, with an unexampled constancy, underwent mortal privations, and, with a valor unequaled in the annals of Venezuela, conquered and captured the army of the king.

"'But it is not only to the liberating army that we owe the advantages acquired. The people of New Granada have shown themselves worthy of being free. Their efficacious coöperation repaired our losses and increased our forces. This generous people have offered all their property and their lives on the altars of the country. Their desire for the union of their provinces to the provinces of Venezuela is also unanimous. The Granadians are thoroughly convinced of the immense advantage which will result to one and the other people by the creation of a new republic composed of these two nations. The reunion of New Granada and Venezuela is the only object which I have entertained since my first battle. It is the vote of the citizens of both countries, and it is the guaranty of the liberty of South America.

"'Legislators! The moment of giving a fixed and eternal base to our republic has arrived. To decree this great social act, and to establish the principles upon which will be founded this vast republic, belong to your wisdom. Proclaim it to the world, and my services will be amply rewarded.'

"When the Liberator pronounced this sentence, the Señor Zea stood up, full of inspiration and patriotism, and said:

'Imagination, sirs, does not reach that which the hero of Venezuela has done since he left this august Congress installed. The undertaking of crossing the Andes with an army fatigued by so long and painful a campaign—this daring undertàking, during the rigor of the rainy season and hurricanes, appeared so extraordinary that the enemy believed it to be a *military delirium*. Nature being conquered, further opposition was met with in an army three times more numerous, well provided, posted on that frontier, and always fighting in advantageous positions,— Gameza, Vargas, Bonza, Boyacá,—under the orders of a general as able as he was experienced. But all yields to the rapid and terrible impetus of the soldiers of the independence. Scarcely can victory keep up with the victor, and in less than three months the principal and main portion of New Granada has been freed by these same troops, whose complete destruction was held by the viceroy of Santa Fé to be sure and inevitable.

"'And what man sensible of the sublime and great, what country capable of appreciating lofty names, will not pay to the name of Bolivar the tribute of enthusiasm due to so much audacity and to such superhuman prodigies? To have carried the lightning of the arms and the vengeance of Venezuela from the shores of the Atlantic to those of the Pacific; to have hoisted the standard of liberty upon the Andes of the east and west; to have snatched away twelve provinces from the Inquisition and tyranny; to have caused to reëcho from the burning plains of Casanare to the frozen summits of the mountains of Ecuador, an extension of forty thousand square leagues, the heroic cry of *liberty or death*, which each time the people repeat with fresh energy and more intrepid resolution—will it not be admired? And the genius to whom this is due, will he not obtain the reward he expects? What! shall he not attain the union of the people whom he has freed and is still freeing? If Quito, Santa Fé and Venezuela are joined in one sole republic, who can calculate the power and prosperity corresponding to such an immense mass? May heaven bless this union, whose consolidation is the object of all my vigilance and the most ardent desire of my heart.'

"The Liberator replied to the discourse of Zea, attributing the glory of the redemption of New Granada to the valor and intrepidity of the troops, to the sublime enthusiasm of the people, and to the ability and heroism of the chiefs, among whom he distinguished the English colonel Rook and the general of division, Anzoatequi. He also made an honorable commemoration of the distinguished patriotism of the secular and regular clergy of New Granada, who were convinced that the independence of America would extend the empire of religion and would give it new brilliance and splendor."

The motion creating the Republic of Colombia was approved by Congress on December 17, 1819. The president of the Congress announced, "The Republic of Colombia is constituted!" To the presidency of this new republic General Simon Bolivar was unanimously elected.

CHAPTER IX

THE BATTLE OF CARABOBO—PAEZ—THE LIBERTY OF
THE NORTH—THE MAGNANIMITY OF BOLIVAR

EARLY in the year 1821 an armistice had been proclaimed. Morillo had gone to Havana, leaving the army under the command of General La Torre. On March 10, 1821, Bolivar informed General La Torre that hostilities were about to be resumed. Bolivar was now at the head of a splendid army. His forces, gathered in Venezuela, amounted to fifteen thousand men. Among these were the fiery llaneros and two thousand European troops.

The Spaniards had taken position at Carabobo, a village on the high Andes, near the beautiful city of Valencia, a sister city of Caracas. The port of Valencia is Puerto Cabello.

On June 24 a part of the Colombian army, eight thousand strong, appeared before the enemy. Bolivar believed that the future of liberty in South America depended upon this battle. He moved cautiously. He called a council of war and advised care in so great a peril. One of his trusty guides heard what he had said. The guide came up to him and said in a low tone: " I know a footpath by means of which a body of men could move unseen and turn the Spaniards' right." Bolivar knew the man well. What he had suggested was the need of the hour.

"General Paez," Bolivar said, "follow the guide!" Paez went forth, followed by strong columns of cavalry. That order won the battle of Carabobo.

The path over which the faithful guide led the division was almost impassable. The foot-soldiers were obliged to tear up their clothing in order to make bandages for their bleeding feet. The battalions suddenly appeared in the forest to the right of their astonished enemy. The cavalry impetuously charged. The Spanish were thrown into confusion, and General La Torre lost his presence of mind. General Paez threw his forces upon the disconcerted enemy, who fled on every hand. General La Torre and the remnant of his army shut themselves up in Puerto Cabello.

The hero of Carabobo was José Antonio Paez, a llanero who rose to the highest offices in the republic. He was born in the province of Barinas, June 13, 1790. He was practically the President of Venezuela for some seventeen years, after that country separated from Colombia. To this man, in the height of his popularity and power, the Congress presented a golden sword, and the title of "Illustrious Citizen."

At the age of seventeen he was intrusted with some money, when he was waylaid in a wild region by four robbers. One of these robbers he slew on the spot. He escaped, fled to the plains of Barinas, and found employment among the shepherds and cattle-dealers.

The Spanish forces offered him a place of honor, but he was unwilling to bear arms against the patriot cause. He fled over the mountains, and in 1810 joined the patriot troops. He became a cavalry leader, and inflicted severe blows on the Spanish forces. For services in the field he was honored by Granada, and when Francisco Santander, the commander of the Granadian army, resigned, Paez became the military chief of the mountaineers.

In 1817 Paez gave his sword to the cause of Bolivar. In 1819 he was made a major-general. He organized an army, won the decisive victory of Carabobo, and was raised to the rank of general-in-chief.

When Venezuela became dissatisfied with the federal union and declared her independence of it, Paez was elected President. He retained his power, either by his own reëlection or by the election of men of his choice, for some seventeen years. It was during his administration of affairs that the body of Simon Bolivar was removed to Caracas, and that city paid the dead hero the honors that she had twice bestowed upon him when living.

Paez passed his old age in the United States, dying in New York city in 1873. After his death his remains were removed to his native land.

He was very severely criticized for the influence which he exercised in dismembering the Colombian republic. His political life made for him ardent friends and bitter enemies.

The battle of Boyacá was a decisive event, but its results were completed in the field of the north by the victory of Carabobo, which ended the Spanish power in the new Republic of Colombia.

The triumph of Carabobo brought out the true nobility of Bolivar. He had once given an order of war to the death. It was called forth amid terrible circumstances. Bolivar thus describes those circumstances in a manifesto issued at the time:

"Yes, Americans, the hateful and cruel Spaniards have introduced desolation in the midst of the innocent and peaceful people of the Columbian hemisphere. The war to the death which these Spaniards wage has forced them to abandon their native country, which they have not known how to preserve, and have ignominiously lost. Fugitives and wanderers, like the enemies of the Saviour God, they behold themselves cast away from all parts, and persecuted by all men. Europe expels them, America repels them. Their vices in both worlds have loaded them with the malediction of all humankind. All parts of the globe are tinged with the innocent blood which the ferocious Spaniards have caused to flow. All of them are stained with the crimes which they have committed, not for the love of glory, but in the search of a vile metal, which is their supreme god. The executioners, who have entitled themselves our enemies, have most outrageously violated the rights of people and of nations at Quito, La Paz, Mexico, Caracas, and recently at Popayan. They sacrificed our virtuous brethren in their dungeons in the cities of Quito and La Paz; they beheaded thousands of our prisoners in Mexico; they buried alive, in the cells and floating prisons of Puerto Cabello and La Guayra, our fathers, children, and friends of Venezuela; they have immolated the president and commandant of Popayan, with all their companions of misfortunes; and lastly, O God! almost in our presence they have committed a most horrid slaughter at Barinas, of our prisoners of war and our peaceful countrymen of that capital. . . . But these victims shall be revenged, these assassins exterminated. Our kindness is now quenched, and as our oppressors force us into a mortal war, they shall disappear from America, and our land shall be purged of the monsters who infest it. Our hatred will be implacable, and the war shall be to death. "SIMON BOLIVAR.

"HEADQUARTERS OF MÉRIDA, June 8, 1813."

The critics of Bolivar have made free use of this manifesto. This policy, however, was but temporary. It was in another spirit that he began the campaigns that ended in Carabobo and in Peru. When beginning them he said:

"Soldiers! I hope that you will have humanity and compassion even for your most bitter enemies. Be the mediators between the vanquished and your victorious arms, and show yourselves as great in generosity as you are in victory!

"LIBERATING HEADQUARTERS, BARINAS, April 17, 1821."

As noble are the words of another manifesto, issued at this period, when complete victory rose clearly in view: "Colombians! This war shall not be a war of death, nor even of rigor; it shall be a sanctified crusade. We shall fight to disarm, not to exterminate, our enemy!"

Such words as these express Bolivar's sentiments. He made mistakes, but at heart he was generous, merciful and true. He lived in the hope of all that was best for humanity. He desired influence, but only to use it for the good of all mankind.

On the 29th of June General Bolivar again entered Caracas in triumph. There were no arches, no strewings of flowers nor ringing of bells. The city was as one of the dead. There was hardly a white inhabitant in the deserted streets. The houses were empty. There were pitiful beggars and dead bodies everywhere. Some negroes cried, "Vive Colombia!" then all was silent save the wails of the famishing.

But the north was free, and another movement for liberty, under a leader as noble, was going on in the south. The two leaders would soon be marching toward each other, one from the south, one from the north. The high Andes was soon to witness the final triumph of the cause of each.

To that movement we will now turn.

WASHINGTON PLAZA, CARACAS, VENEZUELA.

CHAPTER X

ARGENTINA—THE LIBERATING ARMY OF THE SOUTH

"WHAT good airs are here!" exclaimed a Spanish sailor on landing on the shores of the pampas, in the age of the explorers. His exclamation, "*Buenos ayres!*" according to the popular tradition, gave the name to the littoral part of that country which became the viceroyalty of Buenos Ayres, and is now the Argentine Republic. The Spanish viceroyalty of Buenos Ayres occupied a wide territory. On the separation of the country from Spain this territory came to form, after some changes, the republics of Argentina, Bolivia, Paraguay and the Banda Oriental del Uruguay. It covered an area as large as central and western Europe, and its resources and fertility are such that it might sustain a European population. Here the sea, the air, the sky, wear a purple hue; the flag of Argentina is purple; and that color so prevails that the country has been called "the purple empire that England lost."

Argentina is the land of the pampas. The sterile plains of Patagonia are on one side, and the Gran Chaco, like a world's museum of natural history, on the other. Over it on the west looms the high Andes, rising in Aconcagua to a height of more than twenty thousand feet. Of the Cordilleras, whose long, lofty lines of white glimmer above the pampas, Mr. Darwin says: "The highest peaks appear to consist of active, or more commonly dormant, volcanoes, such as Tupungato, Maypo and Aconcagua, which latter stands twenty-three thousand feet above the level of the sea. This grand range has suffered both the most violent dislocations, and slow, though powerful, upward and downward movements in a mass. I know not whether the spectacle of its immense valleys, with mountain masses of once liquefied and intrusive rocks now barred and intersected, or whether the view of the plains, composed of shingle and sediment hence derived, which stretch to the borders of the Atlantic Ocean, is better adapted to excite our astonishment at the amount of wear and tear that these mountains have undergone."

On one side the Argentine, Patagonia has the climate of Norway and Sweden. On the other side is the perpetual glow of the tropics. In the middle is the subdued and ethereal mildness of southern France and of Italy. Its agricultural productions, therefore, are diversified and almost boundless.

The wars between England and Spain first broke the authority of the viceroys. In June, 1806, General Beresford landed on the Rio de la Plata, or river Plate, with a body of English troops, and took possession of the city of Buenos Ayres. Sobremonto, the Spanish viceroy, fled to Cordova, where General Liniers gathered an army. He defeated Beresford, who surrendered to him in the summer of the same year. In February, 1807, Sir Samuel Auchmuty stormed the city of Montevideo and captured it. In 1808 the English, under General Whitelock, again endeavored to take possession of Buenos Ayres. The inhabitants made a resistance which was of such a heroic character as to have been a favorite subject of romance and song. The houses of old Buenos Ayres were built with large windows, protected by strong iron railings, open to the street. For the purpose of defense this made the city a great fortress. The low, flat roofs were also favorable for repelling an invasion. The English army experienced heavy losses and capitulated.

The resistance to the English invasion inspired the people of the country with a sense of their own valor and strength. The overturning of the throne of Spain by Napoleon gave them the opportunity for self-government. They refused to acknowledge the authority of Joseph Bonaparte, whom Napoleon had placed on the throne of Spain.

In 1809 Cisneros was made viceroy by the junta of Seville, in the name of the deposed Spanish king, Ferdinand VII. On May 25, 1810, with the consent of the viceroy, a council was formed, which was called the Provisional Government of the Provinces of the Rio de la Plata. This council was the beginning of Argentine independence. An attempt was made by the loyal subjects of King Ferdinand to make the viceroy president of the council. It failed, and Cisneros retired to Montevideo.

In 1813, on the 31st of January, a congress assembled at Buenos Ayres, and elected Posadas Dictator of the republic.

The people of Uruguay were still favorable to the cause of Ferdinand. The city of Montevideo was attacked by the republicans from Buenos Ayres in 1814, and after a siege captured.

The party of independence grew in Argentina, and became a powerful organization on both sides of the river Plate.

On March 25, 1816, a new congress of deputies, elected

by the Argentine people, met at Tucuman. Pueyrredon
was elected President of the republic, and on July 9 the
independence of Argentina was formally declared, with
Buenos Ayres as the seat of government.

But the union of the whole country was not secured.
Paraguay, Uruguay and what is now Bolivia, after many
changes of political fortunes, established independent
governments. Buenos Ayres, from her commanding
position, excited the jealousy of a part of the Argentine
Republic. The independence of the country from Spain
had been proclaimed, and it was rapidly progressing toward freedom.

At the period when the cause of South American
independence in Argentina most needed a directing
mind, civil and military, there landed on her shores a
young hero of fame, one born on her own soil, and who
was destined to be known as the greatest of creoles—
José de San Martin. He was born on February 25,
1778, in Yapeyú, Missiones. He was the fourth son of
the lieutenant-governor of the department of Yapeyú.
When he was eight years of age he was taken to Spain,
where he became a pupil in the Seminary of Nobles at
Madrid. At the age of twelve he was a cadet in white
and blue. Before he had reached the age of twenty we
find him in Africa fighting against the Moors. Though
a lover of peace, he was educated to war, and though he
became a champion of republican principles, he was trained
in the armies of royalty.

Strangely enough, this young creole, like Bolivar, met
Miranda, then the ardent apostle of South American liberty,
in Europe, and fell under his influence. He was one of
those young men to whom Miranda disclosed the restless
secret of his political dream. Miranda had established in
London the Gran Reunion Americana for the emancipa-

tion of South America from foreign dominion, and was engaged in forming like societies on the Continent.

Bolivar was to liberate half of the South American continent; San Martin was to free the other half from foreign dominion. The two followers of Miranda were to meet under the glowing arch of the equator, and there clasp hands for the first time.

The life-thought of San Martin was one of the noblest that has ever inspired the human breast:

> Thou must be that which thou ought'st to be,
> And without that thou shalt be nothing.

His life fulfilled this principle. There was a moral grandeur in his character that places him in the rank of Pericles, Cincinnatus, the Gracchi, and other great leaders of the world. What this man's faults and errors were we do not know, unless the distribution of medals to the Order of the Sun in Peru, which act was called unrepublican, be one. It has been said that he held a too conservative view of the capability of men for self-government. Be this as it may, he gave his sword to the best interests of the human race, lived stainlessly, and when he could best serve the cause of humanity by retirement and poverty, he went into exile. Chili voted to him ten thousand ounces of gold, but he refused it, and gave it over to the public good.

On May 25, 1810, the Argentine government passed into the hands of the representatives of the people. A junta first exercised the power. This was succeeded by a triumvirate. This represented no party, but sought only the welfare of the people. A national congress proclaimed republican principles. All of these bodies acted in the name of the deposed King Ferdinand.

San Martin, on his arrival at Buenos Ayres, began a military reform. He was soon called to succeed the eminent patriot Belgrano in the command of the army. His political influence grew. The name of the King of Spain disappeared from public affairs. The Inquisition was abolished, and the flag of blue and white took the place of the colors of the Peninsula.

San Martin assumed the command of the army. He now determined to liberate Chili and Peru. The way to Lima from Buenos Ayres had been by the mountain-passes of Upper Peru.

To create an army and to cross the Andes now became the first effort of San Martin. With this army he would descend, as it were, from the sky, and meet the Spanish power as the condor strikes his prey. He would begin that march that would not end until he met the patriots of the north at the equator. Such was the plan of San Martin.

The work began at Mendoza, at the foot of the Andes. Here the army of liberation began to assemble. From this point the march which would free South America should begin. He decided that the highway of his army should not be by the road to Upper Peru. He would cross the Andes by the Uspallata Pass, nearly thirteen thousand feet high, would liberate Chili, and pass to Lower Peru. The plan was so bold that he guarded it as a secret. He resigned his place as commander of the Army of the North to his friend General Alvear, and accepted the appointment of governor of Cuzco. Here an army of rugged patriots, mountaineers and plainsmen, could be slowly formed, men of lofty courage, who would dare to scale the pinnacles of the Andes and die for liberty on any field.

On August 10, 1814, he became governor of Cuzco, and

from that time his eye was fixed upon the Andes, whose forbidding heights towered over him in the sun. He saw the way to victory there, in the line of the flight of the condor. Would his daring thought ever turn into deeds? The purpose of Bolivar amid the ruins of Caracas was equaled by that of San Martin.

CHAPTER XI

CUZCO—THE BANNER OF THE SUN

THE province of Cuzco lies under the high Andes. It is inhabited by brave and liberty-loving mountaineers. The way to Upper Peru lay through its hills. The region is "beautiful, glorious and sublime." The snows melt and flow down from the colossal mountain-wall, and form crystal lakes. To drink of their pure, clear water is to live. The hills roll like billows of land into the quiet sea of the plain. The condor wheels in the sky as on a motionless wing, a creature that typifies his own native wilds amid the peaks of the air. Mendoza, San Juan and San Luis were then parts of the province. There were some forty thousand inhabitants in the province. They were a hard-working, clear-thinking people, of large sympathies and of sterling moral worth.

Here was the road to Chili over the Cordilleras, and also that from Chili to Buenos Ayres over the pampas. Here bullock-carts lumbered along the unfenced roads. Here came and went pack-mules with fruits, flour and wine.

San Martin was named governor of Cuzco in 1814. He lived in republican simplicity. He refused to occupy the handsome house offered him by the *cabildo* (town-meeting or folkmoot) of Mendoza, and he returned one half of his salary in the interests of public economy. He

THE BANNER OF THE SUN.

accepted the position of general in the army only on the condition that he should resign it when the service was no longer a necessity.

Chili had gained her liberties, but only to lose them again. To free Chili would be, in his opinion, to win the cause of liberty for South America. To that cause San Martin now gave his heart. To lead an army over the Andes was his ambition. Such an army must be one of no ordinary men. The virtuous laborers of Cuzco were men who possessed uncommon strength of body and soul. San Martin began to organize such an army, and to arouse the people to a sense of their opportunity. Unpaid volunteers responded to his call. The ladies of Mendoza, headed by his own wife, cast their jewels into the public treasury for the patriotic cause.

He was a stern disciplinarian, yet his heart was full of mercy. One day an officer came to him. "I have done wrong. I have lost, in a game, money that was intrusted to me for the regiment." San Martin saw that the soul of the man had worth, else he would not have made the confession. "How much have you lost?" The officer named the amount. San Martin handed to him the sum in gold coin. "Pay the money back with this," he said, "but keep the transaction secret. If I ever hear that you have told of it you shall be shot."

In 1815 the republicans met with disasters in Upper Peru and in Colombia. One day when San Martin was dining with his officers he offered a toast: "To the first shot fired beyond the Andes against the tyrants of Chili!" The toast expressed the one purpose of his soul, the reconquest of Chili for the cause of universal liberty.

Over Chili Abascal was viceroy, and Osorio there led the Spanish army. Abascal ruled with an iron hand, without justice or mercy. The people cried in secret for deliverance. The leader of the Chilian patriots was Manuel Rodriguez. He secretly organized volunteers, who were to await an opportunity to rise.

In 1816 San Martin, under the sanction of the Tucuman Congress, began to form the Army of the Andes. The expenses of the army were in part sustained by patriotic subscriptions. Some who could not give money gave labor.

The Benjamin Franklin of this period of preparation, when the genius of effective organization was a most important factor, was Luis Beltran, a mendicant friar. He was one of those patriotic priests who, from the time of the reaction against the cruelty of Spain in Lima to the awakening of Mexico under Hidalgo, repudiated the orders of their superiors. This man, strange as it may seem, became the Vulcan of the new army, and was assigned to the charge of the forges and the mechanical works. He was a native of Mendoza. He had joined the patriots in Chili, and had served as an artilleryman there. After the defeat of the patriots he returned to Cuzco "with a bag of tools of his own making on his shoulders."

He became a chaplain in the new Army of the Andes. His nobility as a patriot and his genius as a mechanic were recognized by San Martin. The latter commanded him to establish an arsenal, an extraordinary assignment to a chaplain. Friar Beltran found himself at the head of a military school of three hundred workmen, whom he taught to cast cannon, shot and shell, and to melt down church bells for the new march of liberty. He unfrocked himself in 1816, and put on the uniform of an officer of the artillery. "He became," says Mitre, "the Archimedes of the Army of the Andes."

The new year, 1817, had come to Mendoza. A new light was kindling on the peaks. The 17th of January was a high holiday in the beautiful town. The Army of the Andes, before it was to begin its march over the Andes, was to pass in review before San Martin. The women of Mendoza were to present to the army a flag which they had made. The flag bore the emblem of the Sun. The town of Mendoza was filled with banners. The army marched in amid the firing of cannon and the rolling of drums. The flag of the Sun was committed by the patriotic ladies into the hands of San Martin. The general mounted a platform in the great square, and waving the flag, amid a thrill of enthusiasm, exclaimed: "Behold the first flag of independence which has been blessed in America!" A shout of *"Vive la patria!"* rent the air. "Soldiers, swear to maintain it, as I now do!" Twenty-five guns saluted the flag. Mitre says this flag was raised for "the redemption of the half of South America which passed the Cordilleras. It waved in triumph along the Pacific coast, floated over the foundations of two new republics, aided in the liberation of another, and after sixty years served as the funeral pall to the body of the hero who had delivered it to the care of the immortal Army of the Andes."

Martin Güemes, the Gaucho horseman of the plains, who had made for himself a name in the re-conquest of Buenos Ayres, had protected the first patriot army on the invasion of Alta Peru. He now became a power. His wild horsemen breathed the spirit of liberty. They had inhaled it from the air of the plains, under the gleaming peaks. They knew how to cover and shield and prepare the way for the vanguard of an army in the sierra.

Güemes found his field at Salta, a province of the patriots under the mountain-wall. Salta at this time was a part of Jujuy, among the spurs of the Andes which border the ranges of Upper Peru. Through it was the highway from the plains to the mountains, from the tropical to the temperate zone. It was an agricultural province. The people were a rugged race. They were brave, and lovers of freedom. The blow of these mountaineers was a hammer-stroke. They flew, as it were, on their trained horses, and, as they came and went with the speed of the wind, landed their shots with unerring aim.

Güemes and his Gauchos became a terror to the royalists. They guarded the mountain ways, and their swift movements were like thunderbolts from the mountain clouds.

Güemes, for his intrepid movements and daring adventures in the patriot cause, was assigned places of honor by San Martin, and became the Gaucho or cavalry hero of the spurs of the Andes. He was made governor of Salta, and held the office from May, 1815, to May, 1820. His death was tragic. In 1821, while he was absent from the city, Salta was surprised and captured by the royalists. He returned home at night, not knowing that the place was in the enemy's hands. He rode into the public square and was met with a volley of shot. He was severely wounded, but rode away bleeding and dying. He died some days after this last swift ride of death. His deeds were long celebrated by the Gaucho minstrels, as the wandering musicians of the plains were called.

CHAPTER XII

THE BATTLE OF MAYPO—CHILI—PERU—THE MEETING OF THE TWO LIBERATORS—ABNEGATION AND MORAL HEROISM OF SAN MARTIN

THE five great battles that decided South American independence were Boyacá, Maypo, Carabobo, Pichincha and Ayacucho. Of these Boyacá and Maypo are the most famous. Of these two Maypo is that which has more interested the world. It was a battle won by the power of the human will; it was fought according to the laws of military science and amid the most stupendous mountain scenery; its thunders, like an earthquake, shattered the Spanish power in South America. The scene of the battle, with its mountain towers, was not only one of the most majestic in the world, but the meeting and clash of the two armies were attended by thrilling events. Here liberty and despotism measured their forces, and the old civilization of the foreign kings went down. It was fought on April 5, 1818. The royal army numbered fifty-five hundred men, and was led by Osorio. The army of the patriots was nearly as large. It was filled with the spirit of victory, which it caught from its general, who was as constant to his purpose under reverses as in the hours following victory.

From Santiago there runs a succession of white hills,

called Lorna Blanca, overlooking desert lands, and overlooked by the majestic range of mountains out of which rises Aconcagua. On one crest of this Lorna, at a place that commanded the roads to the passes of the Maypo and to Santiago, the patriot army was encamped. In front of it rose another ridge, which was occupied by the royalist army.

The patriot army was placed in three divisions: one, under the command of Las Heras, on the right; the second, under Lavarado, on the left; and in the rear the reserve, commanded by Quintana. The infantry was commanded by Belcarce, while San Martin himself commanded the cavalry.

Below the Lorna ran the Maypo, with its mountain waters and its forests. As the first light of the morning illumined the mountains, San Martin rode to the edge of the Lorna to survey the movements of the royal army. It began to occupy the high ground in front of the patriot army. As San Martin had feared that it might take a position near the road to Valparaiso for the purpose of retreat, he said to his officers: "I take the sun to witness that the day is ours!" As he spoke, there swept over the desert, river and white crests of the Andes the beams of the cloudless sun. As the men beheld it they saw the banner of the Sun. The event seemed prophetic. At ten o'clock the eventful march of the patriot army began. "A half-hour will decide the fate of Chili," said San Martin.

The royalist general Osorio made a movement to the west to protect the road of retreat to Valparaiso, a road that he would soon need. The white crest of the Lorna was filled with his glittering infantry. His cannon were brought into position. There was a brief silence in the hills, and then San Martin gave the order to the infantry to advance.

After the preliminary attacks San Martin ordered an oblique movement so as to fall upon the flank of the Spanish infantry. This was done with the greatest impetuosity, and was supported by the reserves. The royal infantry stood firm. The Chilian cavalry had driven back the royal cavalry, and it now turned to the support of this oblique movement of the left. The onset was overwhelming. Osorio gave orders to retreat, and himself fled to a farm-house, leaving Ordenez in command. The royal army made a stand at the place called the farm-house of Espejo, but its spirit was lost. The patriots closely pursued it, flushed with the certainty of complete victory. The royalists sought refuge in the vineyards from terrible onslaughts.

The thunder of the carnage ceased. Ordenez asked for an interview with Las Heras. He surrendered his sword. Osorio fled toward Valparaiso. The victory was complete. The royalist army lost 1000 men killed, 150 officers and 2000 men prisoners. Its guns, flags and equipments all fell into the hands of the patriots. The army of liberation lost 1000 men in killed and wounded. Osorio reached the coast with fourteen men.

Victory crowned the banner of the Sun. The independence of Chili was won. The words of San Martin, spoken as the sun shone over the white crests of the Andes in the early morning, "I take the sun to witness that the day is ours!" were prophetic.

The couriers rushed down the Andes to Mendoza with the news of the victory. They bore it across the pampas to Buenos Ayres, to fill that city with joy.

Argentina and Chili were free. The triumphal march of liberty must now be toward Peru. For this final achievement of the army of the liberation the way must be made by the sea. Five days after the battle of Maypo, San Martin crossed the mountains to lay before the government of Buenos Ayres a plan for the liberation of Peru. The Dictator of Argentina, Don Juan Martin de Pueyrredon, sustained the plan of San Martin, which was a naval expedition from Valparaiso. San Martin returned to Chili and assembled a new army for the liberation of Peru. A large part of the soldiers for this expedition were citizens of the Argentine Republic. Sixty-two of the officers were Europeans, and Lieutenant Charles Eldridge, Captain Henry Ross and Captain Daniel L. N. Carson were from the United States.

The Spanish viceroy of Peru had an army of about twenty thousand men.

The patriot fleet was commanded by Lord Cochrane, a British admiral, who arrived at Valparaiso in November, 1818. After two ineffectual attempts to reduce Callao, the fleet again sailed for Peru with San Martin's army, August, 1820. Lord Cochrane's first victory was the cutting out of the *Esmeralda*, under the guns of Callao, on the night of the 5th of November.

The viceroy, La Serna, retired with his forces to Cuzco. San Martin entered Lima. Peru proclaimed her independence on July 28, 1821. San Martin was appointed the Protector of the state.

There are two anecdotes related by General Mitre, the first constitutional President of Argentina, in his " History of San Martin," that reveal the character of that hero.

On the morning march along the Lorna, Marshal Brayer forced himself upon San Martin. " I am suffering from my old wound. I want your permission to retire at once to the baths of Colma." " Marshal, a half-hour will decide the fate of Chili. The enemy is in sight. The baths are thirteen leagues away. Your place is here." " But the old wound is in such a condition that I cannot go on." " Señor," said San Martin, " the lowest drummer in the army has more honor than you." He sent word to Belcarce, the commander of the infantry: "Announce to the army that Marshal Brayer is cashiered for conduct unworthy of an officer!" The order was a moral death.

The other anecdote is this: Of the abundant trophies of victory San Martin kept for himself only one. It was a portfolio which contained the secret letters of the fugitive Osorio. These letters revealed those who were true and those who were false to the patriotic cause. He must open these letters for the sake of the cause. He sat down under the shade of a tree and read the contents of the portfolio. Some of the letters, indeed, disclosed secret disloyalty to Chili. After reading them he dropped them one by one into the fire. He never disclosed their contents. They were not his, except for the purpose of protecting the cause. He was seeking no personal revenge, but only the welfare of mankind.

Captain Basil Hall met San Martin in Lima, and he left in his journal some pen-pictures of the hero of Maypo. Says Captain Hall: "On the 25th of June I had an interview with General San Martin on board a little schooner anchored in Callao roads. . . . There was little at first sight in his appearance to engage attention, but when he rose and began to speak, his great superiority over every other person I had seen in South America was sufficiently apparent. He received us in a very homely style, on the deck of his vessel, dressed in a surtout coat and a large fur cap, seated at a table made of a few loose planks laid along the top of two empty casks.

". . . Several persons came on board privately from Lima to discuss the state of affairs, upon which occasion his views and feelings were distinctly stated. I saw nothing in his conduct afterward to cast a doubt upon the sincerity with which he then spoke. 'The contest in

Peru,' he said, 'was not of an ordinary description; not a war of conquest and glory, but entirely of opinion. It was a war of new and liberal principles against prejudice, bigotry and tyranny. People ask why I do not march to Lima at once; so I might, and instantly would, were it suitable to my views, which it is not. I do not want military renown. I have no ambition to be conqueror of Peru. I want solely to liberate the country from oppression. Of what use would Lima be to me if the inhabitants were hostile in political sentiment? How could the cause of independence be advanced by my holding Lima, or even the whole country, in military possession? Far different are my views. I wish to have all thinking men with me, and do not choose to advance a step beyond the march of public opinion. . . . I have been gaining day by day fresh allies in the hearts of the people, the only certain allies in such a war.'"

These anecdotes reveal the motives and character of San Martin.

In 1822 there occurred at Guayaquil one of the most notable events in human history, namely, the meeting of the two liberators, Bolivar and San Martin. The conduct of San Martin at this memorable meeting reveals his true greatness. Modern history has few examples that are comparable to it, and none that surpasses it.

Bolivar was now "arbiter of the destiny of South America." San Martin recognized this fact. He perceived, moreover, that Bolivar could now àccomplish the liberation of the whole country better without than with his assistance. Was San Martin, after creating the Army of the Andes and leading the army of emancipation to Peru, willing to subordinate his personal interests to the cause of liberty? Did the hero of the Andes rise to the high demands of an occasion like this?

Bolivar came to Guayaquil with some fifteen hundred men. He entered the city under arches of triumph. On the 25th of July San Martin arrived by sea on the ship *Macedonia*. He landed and passed through files of soldiers to the house where the Liberator of the north was awaiting him. The two heroes met for the first time. They embraced, and entered the house arm in arm, and were left alone. What occurred no one can tell, but it was an hour of abnegation to San Martin. During it he resolved to leave South America and go into exile for the good of the cause of the liberties of the Andes.

A great ball was given to the two heroes. It was preceded by a banquet. Bolivar loved festive and joyous scenes. San Martin wished to avoid them. He was a serene, philosophical man. Accustomed to great events amid sublime scenery, banquets and balls seemed trivial to him. But he proposed a toast on this occasion. It was: "To the speedy end of the war; to the organization of the different republics; and to the health of the Liberator of Colombia!"

After leaving Guayaquil San Martin expressed this opinion of Bolivar: "He is the most extraordinary character of South America, one of those to whom difficulties only add strength."

On his return to Peru San Martin wrote to Bolivar: "My decision is irrevocable. I have convened the Congress of Peru; the day after its meeting I shall leave for Chili, believing that my presence is the only obstacle that keeps you from coming to Peru with your army."

The final declaration of the abdication of San Martin is worthy to be written in letters of gold: "The presence of a fortunate general in the country which he has conquered is detrimental to the state. I have achieved the independence of Peru. I cease to be a public man!"

He to whom had been offered ten thousand ounces of gold now took some three thousand dollars, crossed the Andes, and with his daughter Mercedes went to Europe, and lived there in poverty and neglect for nearly thirty years.

When the republics that he had liberated at last recalled his true greatness, they brought his body to Argentina, and crowned the dead hero. The tomb of San Martin forms a part of the cathedral of Buenos Ayres, and is one of the most beautiful in the western world.

Truly says General Mitre: " History records not in her pages an act of self-abnegation executed with more conscientiousness and greater modesty."

" I desire that my heart shall rest in Buenos Ayres," said San Martin. His heart is forever embalmed in the hearts of the people of Buenos Ayres.

MAUSOLEUM OF SAN MARTIN, IN BUENOS AYRES.

CHAPTER XIII

AVACUCHO, THE DECISIVE BATTLE OF SOUTH AMERICA—ITS DRAMATIC AND THRILLING EVENTS—BOLIVIA—THE TRIUMPHAL ENTRANCE OF BOLIVAR INTO POTOSÍ

THE decisive battle of South American liberty was that of Ayacucho. The Army of the North found its decisive fields at Boyacá and Carabobo; the Army of the South at Maypo. The united and central army of Upper Peru, commanded by General Sucre, completed at Ayacucho the work of Bolivar in the north and of San Martin in the south. The royalist forces in this battle were led by the viceroy of Peru, La Serna. He was overthrown. With his defeat the Spanish power in South America was brought to an end.

The events leading up to this decisive victory are among the most dramatic and thrilling in history. In 1823 General Bolivar, leaving the presidency of the newly founded Republic of Colombia to Vice-President Santander, at Bogotá, embarked at Guayaquil for Peru. His purpose was to complete the work of South American independence. He landed in Callao on September 1, 1823, and was received with acclamations. Shortly after, he entered Lima amid the joy of the people. He recruited the Peruvian army, and marched from Lima in the second week of November. His principal generals in this campaign were the chivalrous Sucre and the heroic English soldier William Miller.

There were patriots of many lands in this new army of liberation. Some of them had fought at Maypó and Boyacá; some had followed the eagles of France under Napoleon, others the cross of St. George under Wellington. Many had fought under San Martin. General Miller was the chief of staff of the Peruvian army.

There are men who become the souls of great organizations. Such a man was José de Antonio Sucre, whom Bolivar called the "soul of the army." He was born at Cumaná, Venezuela, February 3, 1795. He was a military student of Caracas. While yet a youth he espoused the patriot cause. He was given a position upon the staff of General Miranda. He joined the invading forces under Marino, and in 1814 those of Bolivar. After the temporary defeat of the patriot cause Sucre took refuge in Trinidad. On Bolivar's landing in Venezuela in 1816 Sucre again joined the patriot forces. In 1818 Bolivar commissioned him to secure arms in the West Indies. Sucre pledged his own fortune for the payment of the arms. He returned with nearly ten thousand stands of arms and twelve cannon. Bolivar made him chief of staff. Sucre put his whole soul into the reorganization of the patriot army. He inspired the troops in the victorious invasion of New Granada in 1819. He led the movement south to Quito. In 1821 he landed at Guayaquil to protect the patriot government that had been established there. He marched upon Quito, and on May 24, 1822, won a great battle at Pichincha. This victory ended the Spanish power in Ecuador. The new republic joined the United States of Colombia. Sucre, steadily rising by merit, was made major-general and intendant of the department of Quito.

In 1823 he led a part of the army of Colombia for the liberation of Peru. He refused the chief command of the army, but awaited the arrival of Bolivar in Peru.

Bolivar was made Dictator of Peru. At the beginning of the campaign his force consisted of six thousand Colombians and four thousand Peruvians. The liberating army concentrated at Huaraz, in the ancient land of the Incas. At this place among the high Andes, General Miller, who had done brilliant service on the coast, for the first time met General Bolivar. The day after this meeting General Miller was appointed commandant-general of the Peruvian cavalry, which was composed of intrepid mountaineers. The beautiful valley of Huaraz became the scene of the preparation for the great campaign against the last of the viceroys.

The royalist chiefs had gained advantages since the campaign of San Martin. They hoped in this campaign to overthrow Bolivar, to regain Peru, and to reëstablish the South American viceroyalties. The viceroy entered upon the war in Upper Peru confident of victory. He seemed to think that it was the will of destiny that the viceroys of Spain should be successful, and that the banner of Spain should again wave in triumph over the lands of the Incas.

In the "Life of General Miller" is a description of the review of the patriot army by General Bolivar: "On the 2d of August Bolivar reviewed his forces, nine thousand strong, on the plain between Rancas and Pasco. The troops were well appointed, and made a really brilliant appearance. An energetic address from the Liberator was read to each corps at the same moment, and produced indescribable enthusiasm. Nothing could exceed the excitement felt upon that occasion. Every circumstance tended to impart a most romantic interest to the scene. Near the same spot, four years before, the royalists had been defeated by General Arenales. The view from the table-land, upon which the troops were reviewed, and which is at an elevation of more than twelve thousand feet above the level of the sea, is perhaps the most magnificent in the world. On the west arose the Andes, which had just been surmounted with so much toil. On the east were enormous ramifications of the Cordilleras, stretching toward Brazil. North and south the view was bounded by mountains whose tops were hidden in the clouds. On that plain, surrounded by such sublime scenery, and on the margin of the most magnificent lake of Reyes, the principal source of the Amazon, the mightiest of rivers, were now assembled men from Caracas, Panama, Quito, Lima, Chili and Buenos Ayres; men who had fought at Maypo in Chili, at San Lorenzo on the banks of the Paraná, at Carabobo in Venezuela, and at Pichincha at the foot of the Chimborazo. Amid those devoted Americans were a few foreigners, still firm and faithful to the cause in support of which so many of their countrymen had fallen. Among those few survivors were men who had fought on the banks of the Guadiana and of the Rhine, who had witnessed the conflagration of Moscow and the capitulation of Paris. Such were the men assembled at what might be considered a fresh starting-point in the career of glory. American or European, they were all animated by one sole spirit, that of assuring the political existence of a vast continent. The exhilarating vivas of the troops filled every breast with ardor and prophetic hope."

The two armies had their first encounter at Junin, a battle of the saber and lance, at which no shot was fired. The patriots had the advantage, and Bolivar, seeing that final victory in the field was assured, retired from the army, and gave himself to the demands of state.

The viceroy took command of the army of some thirteen thousand men in the historic province of Cuzco, the scene of the Incarial capital. General Miller and his mountaineers led the van of the patriots. The two armies met on the hills and plain of Ayacucho. The liberating army was drawn up on the plain, and the royalists on the summit of a ridge.

The night before the battle, on the results of which hung the cause of South America and the destiny of Spain in the lands the viceroys had despoiled, was one of the deepest anxiety. The army of the viceroy was much larger than that of the liberators, and it was confident of success.

The morning of December 9, 1824, dawned bright and clear on the stupendous mountain-peaks of the province of Cuzco. There was a mountain chilliness in the first purple light, but when the sun burst forth over the valley, a genial warmth made nature as lovely as in the days of the great Inca festivals. The patriots beheld in the brightness of the day a favorable omen, like that of Maypo.

The royalist army appeared on the hills. The viceroy was at its head. It descended through the craggy ravines with the step of expectant victory.

General Sucre rode along the line of the patriot army. He felt the full responsibility of the hour. He wheeled and faced the army at a central point, and, raising his voice to a trumpet-tone, he said: "Soldiers, on what we do to-day depends the destiny of South America!" He turned his face to the enemy descending the hills. He pointed to the banners of Spain. "Soldiers, another day of glory is to crown your constancy to the cause of liberty!"

Vivas answered the address. The men felt that the day of destiny had indeed arrived. They waited the shock with hearts that beat high for their own cause and the cause of liberty in the world. The Spanish army had reached the plain. "Cordova, advance!" commanded Sucre.

General Cordova leaped from his horse, and placed himself some fifteen yards in front of his division of heroes. He lifted his hat, and exclaimed: *"Adelante, paso de vencedores!"* ("Forward, with the step of conquerors!")

The men advanced. Their hearts were filled with the valor that knows no defeat. They launched themselves upon the Spanish bayonets as though life was naught. The onset was irresistible.

The army of the viceroy was shattered. The viceroy himself was wounded and was taken prisoner. Nothing could stand before the spirit of the patriots. The royalists rushed to the cover of the hills, falling on every side under the fire of the patriot artillery and the charges of the cavalry. Their cause was lost forever.

The battle lasted but one hour. It is the greatest in its valor and results in South American history. In that single hour fourteen hundred royalists were killed and seven hundred wounded. They left their artillery on the field. At sunset the royalist general sued for terms, and entered the tent of Sucre to sign the articles of capitulation.

At midnight General Miller went to see the fallen viceroy. His biographer thus records the memorable interview:

"About midnight he visited the captive viceroy, General La Serna, who had been placed in one of the best of the miserable habitations of Quinua. When Miller entered he found the viceroy sitting on a bench, and leaning against the mud wall of the hut. A feeble glimmering from the wick of a small earthen lamp threw just enough light around to render visible his features, which were shaded by his white hair, still partially clotted with blood from the wound he had received. His person, tall, and at all times dignified, now appeared most venerable and interesting. The attitude, the situation and the scene were precisely those which an historical painter would have chosen to represent the dignity of fallen greatness. Reflecting on the vicissitudes of fortune, it may be imagined with what feelings Miller advanced toward the man who, but a few hours previously, had exercised a kingly power. The viceroy was the first to speak, and holding out his hand, said: '*You*, general, we all know full well. We have always considered you as a personal friend, notwithstanding all the mischief you have done, and the state of alarm in which you have so repeatedly kept us. In spite of my misfortunes, I rejoice to see you.' The viceroy afterward observed that a sentry had been placed, as he supposed by some mistake, in the same room with him, and that in the confusion and hurry of the time his own wound had not even been washed. General Miller immediately ordered the guard outside, and sent for a surgeon. When the wound was dressed, Miller, in tendering his further services, told the viceroy that the only refreshment he had it in his power to offer was a little tea, which he happened to have with him, and which he believed no other person in the army could supply. The viceroy, enfeebled by loss of blood, appeared to revive at the very mention of this beverage. He said: 'It is, indeed, the only thing I could now take. One cup of it would reanimate and keep me from sinking.' When the tea was brought, the venerable viceroy drank it with eagerness, and was perhaps more grateful for this seasonable relief than for any other kindness or favor he had ever received. He expressed his acknowledgments in the warmest terms to Miller, who felt peculiar gratification in having it in his power to pay this small attention to the distinguished prisoner. He had been long before informed that the viceroy had repeatedly declared that, in the event of his (Miller's) being taken prisoner, he should be treated as a brother (*como hermano*), and furnished with ample means to return to his own country, the only condition meant to be imposed upon him."

The patriot army entered Cuzco in triumph on Christmas day, 1824. The battle crowned the plans of Bolivar for the emancipation of South America. He was now at the height of his power, the hero of the continent, and hailed wherever he went as being more a god than a man. Who that saw him in these fortunate days could have believed that his heart would ever be crushed again?

The greatest honors of his life now awaited him. The provinces of Upper Peru had once formed a part of the viceroyalty of Buenos Ayres. The Argentine Republic now relinquished its claim, and left this land of the valleys, of the mountains and the sky to follow its own will, either to incorporate itself with the republic of Peru, or to remain as a part of the republic of Argentina, or to form a separate government, as it chose. The people elected a deliberative assembly. This met at Chuquisaca in 1825, and decided that Upper Peru, the land of the Incas and high Andes, should become a free and independent nation. What should be its name? The gratitude of the people would find expression in one that would associate the name of the new nation with that of the Liberator. The new republic was called Bolivia. The name was hailed with rejoicing by the sisterhood of republics.

The assembly voted a million dollars to General Bolivar as a reward for his services. Bolivar, like San Martin, did not covet money. He gave a large portion of his own private fortune to the patriot cause. He accepted the gift of the new republic only on the condition that the money should be used for the emancipation of slaves in Bolivia.

The Congress of Lima in 1825 elected General Bolivar perpetual Dictator. He now made a journey through the high provinces of the new republics. He was hailed with salvos of artillery, the vivas of the people, the ringing of bells and scattering of flowers. He entered Cuzco in triumph. Such a day had probably never been seen since the festivals of the Incas. His reception at Potosí reads like a poem. When two leagues from the city he met the first of a number of triumphal arches that recorded his deeds and his glory. About these arches were gathered Indians in festal dress, with plumes and ornaments, who danced after the manner of their joyous festivals. The dancers and their chiefs wore medals on which was stamped the head of Bolivar. He was met by the leading citizens on horseback, preceded by the alcaldes with gilded staffs. These were followed by the clergy in festal robes. The *cerro*, or highland, of Potosí is very grand and commanding. As soon as Bolivar came into view of it, the flags of the republics of Peru, Buenos Ayres, Chili and Colombia were, at the same moment, unrolled to the sun. As he entered the town, twenty-one powerful shells were exploded, the report of which was equal to that of "six twenty-four pounders." The bells rang; the windows were draped in silk and festooned with flowers. The balconies were thronged with ladies. The shouts of fifty thousand people rent the air. He came to the government palace. A great arch rose before it. From this two children dressed in white, representing angels, were let down as from the skies, and each pronounced before him poetic orations. In the flower-strewn halls he was crowned with laurels by the ladies of Potosí. A grand Te Deum followed in the church, to which he was conducted amid salvos of artillery. He was seated under a canopy.

General Sucre was with Bolivar on the day of his triumph at Potosí. A constitution was formed for Bolivia, called the "Code Boliviano." Under it General Sucre was elected President. The Code Boliviano was accepted by Peru, under the influence of Bolivar, and under it Bolivar was elected *Presidente vitalicio*.

Bolivar departed for Colombia to enter upon a larger scheme for humanity than had yet engaged the powers of his sympathetic heart and mind, the peace and unity Congress of Panama.

The armies of the north and of the south and the central army were now triumphant. What South America needed was that political education that would bring stability to the republics.

Bolivar perceived it. The Congress of Panama would suggest to the sisterhood of republics their way to the highest destiny.

CHAPTER XIV

THE PANAMA CONGRESS OF 1826—THE UNION AND PEACE OF THE AMERICAN REPUBLICS—THE LAST DAYS OF SIMON BOLIVAR

IN the year 1826 there assembled at Panama an international congress that was a prophecy of the future, a political prevision. It was convened by Simon Bolivar, liberator, conqueror, protector, president, then at the height of his political power. In Bolivar's opinion the time had come for all American republics to form one congress for the protection of the liberties and peace of the republics of the western world.

The congress was in a sense a failure, but it was a suggestion. The twentieth century was in it. The International American Conference of 1890 was an outcome of it.

The nature and purpose of this congress were expressed by Mr. Conas, of the republics of Central America, in these words: "Europe has formed a continental system, and holds a congress whenever questions affecting its interests are to be discussed. America should have a similar system."

The Congress of Panama in 1826 was first planned by Bolivar to secure the union of the Spanish-American republics against Spain. The Monroe Doctrine had placed the United States in an unequivocal position in such matters. The Northern republic was included in the invitation of the Liberator to unite in the congress.

In a paper written in 1815, in exile, called his "Prophetic Letter," Bolivar thus expresses his hopes: "How grand would it be if the Isthmus of Panama could be to us what Corinth was to the Greeks! God grant that we may some day have the fortune of convening there an august congress of the representatives of the republics, kingdoms and empires to discuss the all-important interests of peace and war with the nations of the world!"

He was then President of Colombia. He caused invitations to such a congress to be issued to the governments of the Spanish-American states, and subsequently to the United States. Said Bolivar: "The states from Panama to Guatemala may form a union. The magnificent position of America, situated between the two oceans, will in due time make it the emporium of the universe. Its canals will shorten the distance which separates the nations of the earth."

The general assembly of American republics met at Panama on June 22, 1826. Colombia, Central America, Peru and Mexico were represented at the first meeting. Great Britain sent agents to study the proceedings. The assembly held ten meetings. The result is described in the following resolution which was passed:

"The republics of Colombia, Central America, Peru and the Mexican states do mutually ally and confederate themselves in peace and war in a perpetual compact, the object of which shall be to maintain the sovereignty and independence of the confederated powers against foreign subjection, and to secure the enjoyment of unalterable peace."

A long series of resolutions was adopted. The outcome

of the congress, however, did not meet the expectations of Bolivar.

Let us now turn to the last sad years of this brilliant man.

"The fate of the emancipators of South America," says General Mitre, "is tragical. The first revolutionists of La Paz and of Quito died on the scaffold. Miranda, the apostle of liberty, betrayed by his own people to his enemies, died, alone and naked, in a dungeon. Moreno, the priest of the Argentine revolution, and the teacher of the democratic idea, died at sea, and found a grave in the ocean. Hidalgo, the first popular leader of Mexico, was executed as a criminal. Belgrano, the first champion of Argentine independence, who saved the revolution at Tucuman and Salta, died obscurely, while civil war raged round him. O'Higgins, the hero of Chili, died in exile, as Carrera, his rival, had done before him. Iturbide, the real liberator of Mexico, fell a victim to his own ambition. Montufar, the leader of the revolution in Quito, and his comrade Villavicencio, the promoter of that of Cartagena, were strangled. The first presidents of New Granada, Lozano and Torres, fell sacrifices to the restoration of colonial terrorism. Piar, who found the true base for the insurrection in Colombia, was shot by Bolivar, to whom he had shown the way to victory. Rivadavia, the civil genius of South America, who gave form to her representative institutions, died in exile. Sucre, the conqueror of Ayacucho, was murdered by his own men on a lonely road. Bolivar and San Martin died in banishment."

In January, 1830, Bolivar, accused by his enemies of personal ambition, resigned the presidency for the fifth time. He was reëlected. In Colombia there was a powerful disunion party which he endeavored to overcome. Its principles set at naught the visions and high ambitions of his thrilling life. The disunionists were powerful in the Colombian Congress. They voted to accept his proffered resignation, and to bestow upon him a pension of three thousand dollars a year on the condition that he should reside abroad. The resolution broke his heart. The unity of Colombia and South America seemed to be shattered by it. He sent his final resignation to Congress on April 27, 1830. He left Bogotá and went to Caracas on May 9, with the intention of embarking from Cartagena for England, to go into exile there. Grief and disappointment wore upon him. His health failed. The sword had been too sharp for the scabbard. He went to Santa Marta to visit the bishop there, who was his friend. At Cartagena he had heard of the unhappy death of Sucre. The friends of Bolivar called upon him to put himself at the head of a new movement and restore the union of Colombia. But his malady was fatal. At Santa Marta he breathed the fresh sea-air, and recalled the events of his life from the oath at Rome to the triumphal arches of Potosí. At the *quinta* of San Pedro, seven miles from Santa Marta, came the last pathetic scene. Seated in an arm-chair, and waiting to receive the last rites of the church, he dictated an address to the Colombian people, in which he said: "My wishes are for the happiness of the people. If my death should unite them I will go to the tomb content—yes, to the tomb! The people send me there, but I forgive them."

So died Simon Bolivar, on December 17, 1830, at the age of forty-seven years. He had an ardent nature. Only a great soul could have accomplished what he did. He has been criticized, and not without cause, but he must be numbered among the heroes of civilization, liberty and progress.

Bolivar may not have been a Washington, but the

struggles of his soul to fulfil what is noblest in life appear in his letters and proclamations, in the surrender of his private fortune to the public good, and in the peril to which he exposed his life. He must have a low vision indeed who can only seek in such a life incidents for criticism and detraction. A work written by an officer whom Bolivar had offended and dismissed represents the Liberator as given over to his passions, as living constantly in the practice of dissimulation, as vainglorious, and as seeking the supreme power. Against such accusations are these facts, namely, on the death of his beloved wife the Liberator resolved never to marry again, so that he might devote all his thought to the cause of South American liberty; again and again he placed his resignation of the highest trusts into the hands of the representatives of the people; he declared that if his death would better serve the cause of liberty and unity he was willing to die. It is said that San Martin was less an individual than a mission, and Bolivar was more a cause than a general.

Three notable declarations of Bolivar, all made in his youth, reveal perfectly his character and life: That spoken on Monte Sacro, Rome: "I pledge my life to liberty!" Another spoken at Caracas at the time of the earthquake: "If nature herself opposes us, we will compel her to obey." A third one spoken at Cartagena: "I disregard rank and distinction, because I aspire to a more honorable destiny—to shed my blood for the liberty of my country!"

CHAPTER XV

WILLIAM WHEELWRIGHT AND THE INDUSTRIAL HEROES

THERE are few more beautiful monuments in the cemeteries of the world than that of William Wheelwright in the Recoleta of Buenos Ayres, and as few that commemorate so wonderful a history. A memorial to his memory is also to be found in Valparaiso. He was buried at Newburyport, where a plain monument marks his resting-place.

This man of marvelous achievements was once, when young, a wrecked sailor on the shores of the Rio de la Plata. He is so represented in the Buenos Ayres monument. He entered the vast and undeveloped regions of the pampas as a castaway. He perceived the needs of the immense regions. He rose superior to misfortune and changed the face of the maritime world. As an illustration of the transcendent power of the human will, without other resources than those it can gain, his life is almost unexampled. In the industrial world he ranks with Franklin, and among men of spiritual vision, and almost impossible achievement, with Bolivar and San Martin.

There is a notable sentence in the Hon. Caleb Cushing's introduction to the " Life of Wheelwright." It indirectly pictures the hero of the future, the true leader of the armies of beneficence. Mr. Cushing says: "The contemplation of his life suggests two prominent considerations for South America, namely, that war is not the only department of service which entitles one to a place in history, and that a foreigner, even if he is not a citizen, may sometimes do more to promote a country's welfare than the most distinguished patriot."

Wheelwright saw what South America might become, and attempted to make real the vision. He was considered a visionary. "If that insane Wheelwright calls here again," said an English consul to a servant, "do not admit him." All the world and fate seemed against him, yet his faith rose over all.

He was born in Newburyport, Massachusetts, in 1798. He early became a sailor. When he was but nineteen years of age he commanded a bark bound for Rio de Janeiro. The year 1823 found him in command of the ship *Rising Empire*, when he was wrecked at the mouth of the Rio de la Plata. He arrived in Buenos Ayres empty-handed. The wreck had shown him one of the needs of South America, namely, safe harbors. He became a supercargo on a ship bound around the Horn to Valparaiso. His ambition now was to improve the navigation of South America, and he adopted that country as his home.

He was United States consul at Guayaquil from 1824 to 1829. He improved harbors, and established a line of vessels between Valparaiso and Cobija. He added to this enterprise a line of steamers on the west coast. He sought aid from the United States for his ship schemes, but it was refused. Not daunted by failure, he went to England. He there received a favorable hearing. He organized the Pacific Steam Navigation Company, which has proved a great benefit to England and South America, and also to the civilized world.

The Pacific Steam Navigation Company, in 1876, operated fifty-four steamers and controlled the route through Panama. Wheelwright now dominated the southern sea. The Andes lifted their giant towers above him. Could they also be controlled, harnessed with iron, made highways through the air? He attempted that task. He caused a railroad to be built from Valparaiso to Santiago. It was but the beginning of colossal schemes. He opened the port of Caldera, and built a railway from it to Copiapo. He next planned a railroad from Caldera across the Andes to Rosario. This proved to be the forerunner of the transandine railroad, now nearly completed, one of the most stupendous works ever accomplished by man. In 1863 he obtained the concession for the Grand Argentine Central Railway. In 1872 he completed a railroad thirty miles long, from Buenos Ayres to the harbor of Ensenada. This was connected with the railroad across the pampas.

This man gave to benevolent purposes about six hundred thousand dollars. He died in London, September 26, 1873, at the age of seventy-five. His full-length portrait now adorns the Merchants' Exchange at Valparaiso.

The industrial progress of Peru is largely associated with the enterprises of Henry Meiggs, a man of wonderful achievements and remarkable mistakes. He had a noble heart. The payment of his debts in full, when beyond the reach of his creditors, proves that he was an honest man. With his many mistakes, Henry Meiggs must be numbered among the world's benefactors.

He was born in Catskill, New York, on July 7, 1811. He came to New York when a young man, and engaged in the lumber-trade. He failed in the crisis of 1837, at the age of twenty-six. He recovered from the disaster, and at once established a lumber-yard at Williamsburg, New York. For a while he was prosperous, but in 1842 he again met with reverses, and returned to New York. From there he went to San Francisco with a cargo of lumber, on which he made a large profit. He there saw a new opportunity.

He created a fleet of lumber craft, sloops and schooners, to trade in lumber on the coast. He employed five hundred men in felling trees for a single sawmill on San Francisco Bay. He became rich. His name was a synonym of enterprise. In the second great financial depression, that of 1854, he again failed, and fled from California to South America, leaving debts to the amount of one million dollars. He now sought to recover his fortune and to pay his debts by engaging in enterprises of public improvement in South America. He began building bridges in Chili. In 1858 he became a contractor for the construction of railroads under the Chilian government. He was successful, realizing a profit of one-and-a-half million dollars, and made for himself the reputation of being one of the most successful railroad-builders in the world.

The so-called Oroya Railroad, or the Callao, Lima, and Oroya Railroad, Oroya being the high Andean terminus, is one of the new wonders of the world, and well earned for him a place among the foremost captains of industry. The purpose of this highway through the clouds was to connect the Atlantic and Pacific oceans by rail and steam —by rail over the Cordilleras, and by steam by means of a branch of the Amazon to the Amazon, and thence to the sea. The railroad was to ascend a height nearly the altitude of Mont Blanc. Great gorges would have to be surmounted, rushing streams to be spanned with bridges in what at first seemed to be impossible places, tunnels to be begun by men hanging from ropes over precipices, borings in rocks to be made over the chasms. The implements for work would have to be transported to almost inaccessible heights. Meiggs faced all these difficulties in the spirit of Bolivar: "If nature herself opposes us, we will compel her to obey." The enterprise was begun. It soon overtaxed the financial resources of the Peruvian government.

Meiggs then used his private fortune. The iron road gradually found its way to Oroya, at a height of some fourteen thousand feet. Its connection with the Amazon is but a matter of time.

Henry Meiggs was again a rich man. He devoted a large part of his great wealth to paying his old debts, principal and interest. To recover his influence and to say to the world that he was honest seems to have been his purpose through all his misfortunes.

After the liberators the industrial classes are the true heroes and the real army of liberation in South America. Since the period of her independence of Spain the farmer, the artisan and the schoolmaster have been her benefactors. Out of the war of this army with ignorance, barbarism and the soil, her glory is rising and will continue to rise.

In Argentina is the South American Normal School. It is training a company of teachers to lead the new armies of peace. Just outside of Buenos Ayres rises what is claimed to be the largest roof in the world. Beside the building are many ships, over which fly the flags of the commercial nations. There are many large *estancias*, or ranches, there, on which are flocks and herds, sometimes numbering fifty thousand animals. One of these estancias is owned by Nicholas Lowe. It is situated some fifty or more miles from Buenos Ayres. Mr. Lowe is a Scotchman who has given away a small fortune for educational purposes. He has a flock of more than ten thousand sheep, and took one of the prizes at the World's Columbian Exposition. He is reputed to be wealthy. One of the squares in the town is named for him, and he is regarded in his part of the country as a benefactor. "When I first came to the country," he said, " I was almost empty-handed. My coat was my house. I began work with my own spade." His home is as beautiful as his flocks are numerous and his fields wide. He came to the country to stay in it and to live in it. It is such immigrants as he whose lives are beyond price to South America, and who are playing such an important part in its development.

CHAPTER XVI

THE MONROE DOCTRINE—THE VENEZUELAN BOUNDARY

IN 1814 England acquired from the Dutch about twenty thousand square miles of land in Guiana. This territory, according to the Venezuelan view, had formerly belonged to Spain. It now became a part of the colonial possessions of Great Britain. Later England claimed that the territory extending from the mouth of the river Essequibo to the Orinoco was a part of Dutch Guiana when that territory was ceded by the Dutch to the English in 1814. Venezuela replied that this territory never belonged to Dutch Guiana at all, but that it was Spanish territory, and so became hers when she established her independence.

Between the years 1839 and 1841 Sir Robert H. Schomburgk, without the knowledge of Venezuela at the time, drew a boundary-line for Great Britain, which gave her 60,000 square miles. The territory claimed by the English continued to grow. In 1889 England claimed 76,000 square miles, and later the claim was made for 109,000 square miles.

After the downfall of Napoleon the Holy Alliance of Prussia, Austria and Russia was formed in the interest of absolutism in Europe. South America had thrown off the rule of Spain, and it was feared that this council of the great European powers would restore to Spain her colonies. It then became a question in the United States as to what should be the attitude of the American republics in regard to the interference of European powers in American affairs.

In 1823, when the Allies were considering the affairs of Spain, President Monroe consulted Thomas Jefferson in regard to the new aspect of international affairs. He replied to President Monroe's letters in these strong, clear words: "The question presented by the letters you have sent me is the most momentous which has ever been offered to my contemplation since that of independence. That made us a nation; this sets our compass, and points the course which we are to steer through the ocean of time opening on us. And never could we embark upon it under circumstances more auspicious. Our first and fundamental maxim should be, never to entangle ourselves in the broils of Europe; our second, never to suffer Europe to intermeddle with cisatlantic affairs. America, North and South, has a set of interests distinct from those of Europe, and peculiarly her own. She should therefore have a system of her own, separate and apart from that of Europe. While the last is laboring to become the domicile of despotism, our endeavor should surely be to make our hemisphere that of freedom."

Shortly after, President Monroe announced the principles of a new policy which he thought should govern American diplomacy. It is known as the Monroe Doctrine. "The political system of the allied powers is essentially different in this respect from that of America. We owe it therefore to candor and to the amicable relations existing between the United States and those powers to declare that we should consider any attempt on their part to extend their system to any portion of this hemisphere as dangerous to our peace and safety. With the existing colonies or dependencies of any European power we have not interfered, and shall not interfere. But with the governments who have declared their independence and maintained it, and whose independence we have, on great consideration and on just principles, acknowledged, we could not view any interposition for the purpose of oppressing them, or controlling in any manner their destiny, by any European power, in any other light than as the manifestation of an unfriendly disposition toward the United States.

"Our policy in regard to Europe, which was adopted at an early stage of the wars which have so long agitated that quarter of the globe, nevertheless remains the same, which is not to interfere in the internal concerns of any of its powers; to consider the government *de facto* as legitimate government for us; to cultivate friendly relations with it, and to preserve those relations by a frank, firm and manly policy; meeting in all instances the just claims of every power, submitting to injuries from none. But, in regard to these continents, circumstances are eminently and conspicuously different. It is impossible that the allied powers should extend their political system to any portion of either continent without endangering our peace and happiness; nor can any one believe that our southern brethren, if left to themselves, would adopt it of their own accord. It is equally impossible, therefore, that we should behold such interposition, in any form, with indifference."

President Polk applied the doctrine to Oregon and Yucatan, and President Buchanan to Mexico. President Cleveland did likewise in regard to British enlargement of territory in Venezuela. England's claim to territory larger than all New England had come, in his opinion, to be a matter of territorial interference in America. In his famous message of December 17, 1895, President Cleveland said:

"In my annual message addressed to the Congress on the 3d inst., I called attention to the pending boundary controversy between Great Britain and the republic of Venezuela, and recited the substance of a representation made by this government to her Britannic Majesty's government, suggesting reasons why such dispute should be submitted to arbitration for settlement, and inquiring whether it would be so submitted.

"If a European power, by an extension of its boundaries, takes possession of the territory of one of our neighboring republics against its will and in derogation of its rights, it is difficult to see why, to that extent, such European power does not thereby attempt to extend its system of government to that portion of this continent which is thus taken. This is the precise action which President Monroe declared to be 'dangerous to our peace and safety,' and it can make no difference whether the European system is extended by an advance of frontier or otherwise. . . .

"Assuming, however, that the attitude of Venezuela will remain unchanged, the dispute has reached such a stage as to make it now incumbent upon the United States to take measures to determine with sufficient certainty for its justification what is the true divisional line between the republic of Venezuela and British Guiana. The inquiry to that end should, of course, be conducted carefully and judicially, and due weight should be given to all available evidence, records and facts in support of the claims of both parties.

"In order that such an examination should be prosecuted in a thorough and satisfactory manner, I suggest that Congress make an adequate appropriation for the expenses of a commission, to be appointed by the Executive, which shall make the necessary investigation and report upon the matter with the least possible delay. When such report is made and accepted it will, in my opinion, be the duty of the United States to resist, by every means in its power, as a wilful aggression upon its rights and interests, the appropriation by Great Britain of any lands, or the exercise of governmental jurisdiction over any territory, which, after investigation, we have determined of right belongs to Venezuela.

"In making these recommendations, I am fully alive to the responsibility incurred, and keenly realize all the consequences that may follow.

"I am, nevertheless, firm in my conviction that, while it is a grievous thing to contemplate the two great English-speaking peoples of the world as being otherwise than friendly competitors in the onward march of civilization, and strenuous and worthy rivals in all the arts of peace, there is no calamity which a great nation can invite which equals that which follows a supine submission to wrong and injustice, and the consequent loss of national self-respect and honor, beneath which are shielded and defended a people's safety and greatness."

The necessity of intervention in Cuba in the interests of humanity became obvious in the winter of 1896–97, and brought legislation again face to face with the Monroe Doctrine.

The Senate Committee on Foreign Relations reported on December 21, 1896, a resolution offered by Senator Cameron:

"*Resolved, by the Senate and House of Representatives of the United States of America in Congress assembled*, That the independence of the republic of Cuba be, and the same is hereby, acknowledged by the United States of America.

"*Be it further resolved*, That the United States will use its friendly offices with the government of Spain to bring to a close the war between Spain and the republic of Cuba."

The report accompanying the resolution was regarded as one of the ablest political documents of the last quarter of this century. It reviewed the Monroe Doctrine, and said:

"Into this American system, thus created by Monroe in 1822-23, and embracing then, besides the United States, only Buenos Ayres, Chili, Colombia and Mexico, various other communities have since claimed, and in most cases have received, admission, until it now includes all South America, except the Guianas; all Central America, except the British colony of Honduras; and the two black republics of Spanish Santo Domingo and Hayti in the Antilles.

"No serious question was again raised with any European power in regard to the insurrection or independence of their American possessions until, in 1869, a rebellion broke out in Cuba, and the insurgents, after organizing a government and declaring their independence, claimed recognition from the United States.

"The government of the United States had always regarded Cuba as within the sphere of its most active and serious interest. As early as 1825, when the newly recognized states of Colombia and Mexico were supposed to be preparing an expedition to revolutionize Cuba and Puerto Rico, the United States government interposed its friendly offices with those governments to request their forbearance. The actual condition of Spain seemed to make her retention of Cuba impossible, in which case the United States would have been obliged, for her own safety, to prevent the island from falling into the hands of a stronger power in Europe. That this emergency did not occur may have been partly due to the energy with which Monroe announced 'our right and our power to prevent it,' and his determination to use all the means within his competency 'to guard against and forfend it.'

"This right of intervention in matters relating to the external relations of Cuba, asserted and exercised seventy years ago, has been asserted and exercised at every crisis in which the island has been involved.

"When the Cuban insurgents in 1869 appealed to the United States for recognition, President Grant admitted the justice of the claim, and directed the minister of the United States at Madrid to interpose our good offices with the Spanish government in order to obtain by a friendly arrangement the independence of the island. The story of that intervention is familiar to every member of the Senate, and was made the basis of its resolution last session, requesting the President once more 'to interpose his friendly offices with the Spanish government for the recognition of the independence of Cuba.'

"The resolution then adopted by Congress was perfectly understood to carry with it all the consequences which necessarily would follow the rejection by Spain of friendly offices. On this point the situation needs no further comment. The action taken by Congress in the last session was taken 'on great consideration and on just principles,' on a right of intervention exercised twenty-seven years ago, and after a patient delay unexampled in history.

"The interval of nine months which has elapsed since that action of Congress has proved the necessity of carrying it out to completion. In the words of the President's annual message: 'The stability two years' duration has given to the insurrection; the feasibility of its indefinite prolongation in the nature of things, and as shown by past experience; the utter and imminent ruin of the island unless the present strife is speedily composed,' are, in our opinion, conclusive evidence that ' the inability of Spain to deal successfully with the insurrection has become manifest, and it is demonstrated that the sovereignty is extinct in Cuba for all purposes of its rightful existence; . . . a hopeless struggle for its reëstablishment has degenerated into a strife which means nothing more than the useless sacrifice of human life and the utter destruction of the very subject-matter of the conflict.'

"Although the President appears to have reached a different conclusion from ours, we believe this to be the actual situation of Cuba, and, being unable to see that further delay could lead to any other action than that which the President anticipates, we agree with the conclusion of the message that, in such case, our obligations to the sovereignty of Spain are 'superseded by higher obligations which we can hardly hesitate to recognize and discharge.' Following closely the action of President Monroe, in 1818, Congress has already declared in effect ts opinion that there can be no rational interference except on the basis of independence.

"In 1822, as now, but with more force, it was objected, as we have shown, that the revolted states had no governments to be recognized. Divisions, and even civil war, existed among the insurgents themselves. Among the Cubans no such difficulty is known to exist. In September, 1895, as we know by official documents printed on the spot, the insurgent government was regularly organized, a constitution adopted, a president elected, and, in due course, the various branches of administration set in motion. Since then, so far as we are informed, this government has continued to perform its functions undisturbed. On the military side, as we officially know, they have organized, equipped and maintained in the field sufficient forces to baffle the exertions of two hundred thousand Spanish soldiers. On the civil side they have organized their system of administration in every province; for, as we know officially, they roam at will over at least two thirds of the inland country. Diplomatically they have maintained a regularly accredited representative in the United States for the past year, who has never ceased to ask recognition, and to offer all possible information. There is no reason to suppose that any portion of the Cuban people would be dissatisfied by our recognizing their representative in this country, or that they disagree in the earnest wish for that recognition. The same thing could hardly be said of all the countries recognized by Monroe in 1822. Greece had no such stability when it was recognized by England, Russia and France. Belgium had nothing of the sort when it was recognized by all the powers in 1830. Of the states recognized by the treaty of Berlin in 1878, we need hardly say more than that they were the creatures of intervention.

"The only question that properly remains for Congress to consider is the mode which shall be adopted for the step which Congress is pledged next to take.

"The government of the United States entertains none but the friendliest feelings toward Spain. Its most anxious wish is to avoid even the appearance of an unfriendliness which is wholly foreign to its thought. For more than a hundred years, amid divergent or clashing interests, and under frequent and severe strains, the two governments have succeeded in avoiding collision, and there is no friendly office which Spain could ask which the United States, within the limits of her established principles and policy, would not be glad to extend. In the present instance she is actuated by an earnest wish to avoid the danger of seeming to provoke a conflict.

"The practice of Europe in regard to intervention, as in the instances cited, has been almost invariably harsh and oppressive. The practice of the United States has been almost invariably mild and forbearing. Among the precedents which have been so numerously cited there can be no doubt as to the choice. The most moderate is the best. Among these the attitude taken by President Monroe in 1822 is the only attitude which can properly be regarded as obligatory for a similar situation to-day. The course pursued by the United States in the recognition of Colombia is the only course which Congress can consistently adopt."

In 1898 a squadron of the American navy was at Hong-Kong, China, under Commodore Dewey. He was ordered to proceed to the Philippine Islands and destroy the Spanish fleet in the port of Manila. The order was executed, and resulted in one of the greatest naval victories in American history. The taking of Manila presents a new phase of the Monroe Doctrine. The doctrine that opposed the enlargement of English territory on the Orinoco might, by inference, be interpreted to prevent the New World from seeking expansion in the countries or islands of the Old World. The right of the United States to maintain the principle of the Monroe Doctrine seems a reasonable one, but consistency would require her to maintain a like view and relations in her diplomacy with the powers of the Old World. The maintenance of the principles of the Monroe Doctrine has heretofore seemed to be more valuable to our institutions in the future than any territory that we could secure and hold in the East or in foreign seas. Have changed conditions made necessary a change in this governmental policy?

CHAPTER XVII

BRAZIL

WHAT the Pacific Ocean, lying undisturbed, or moving in long waves that rise and fall in repose, is among waters, that Brazil seems to be among the Latin-American states. She has been the scene of few political tragedies. As a rule, her Indian races have been a quiet and contented people, living under the guidance of rulers that were just. When these races were about to rise against the growing immigration, the Portuguese, who had lived among them, persuaded them to await events. The discovery of the country was claimed by others, but they were persuaded to relinquish their claims in favor of the Portuguese. The many colonies did not often fall into disputes with one another. The captains of the provinces yielded to a governor-general, and the governor-general to a king. When Napoleon displaced thrones, the royal family of Portugal fled to Brazil. The Brazilians were unwilling to have them return. The matter was peacefully adjusted. The constitution was proclaimed by an emperor. He, as emperor, swore to support this constitution. The Brazilians made him emperor for life. This growth of republican sentiments came peacefully. When Dom Pedro I. saw that the people were dissatisfied with him, he abdicated in favor of his son. The people elected the regents for this son. When this son did not come of age at the time they wished, the Congress shortened the time of his minority.

Brazil has been called the "land of diamonds." It has a length of some 2600 British miles, a breadth of 2500 miles, and some 4000 miles of sea-coast. The great river of the lowlands of Brazil, the Amazon, is the monarch of watercourses. With its tributaries it has a free navigation of some 30,000 miles.

All climates are found in this vast empire—the tropical heat in the valleys of the Amazon, the intertropical, and the temperate of the western elevations. The marshy banks of the lowlands are unhealthful, but the climate as a whole is salubrious. With its vigorous coffee-plantations, its india-rubber groves, its cotton, its forests, and its mines of gems, the empire is inexhaustibly rich.

Brazil was discovered in 1499 by Vicente Yañez Pinzon, an explorer in the service of Columbus. He sailed along the coast from the Amazon to the Orinoco, and carried brazil-wood back to Spain.

In 1500 a Portuguese captain, Pedro Alvares Cabral, was commissioned by his king to follow the course of Vasco da Gama. He was driven by winds upon the Brazilian coast. This commander celebrated Easter Sunday on shore, where he erected an altar and uplifted the cross. He took possession of the country in the name of the King of Portugal. He sent back a vessel to Lisbon to proclaim his discovery, while he went on his way to India. He left behind a stone cross to commemorate the event of his visit.

The news of the discovery thrilled Portugal. The king called the Italian explorer Amerigo Vespucci into his service, and sent him with three vessels to explore the country. From him is derived the name of the western world,

America. Vespucci beheld the new land with wonder. He hastened back to Portugal to report what he had seen. He took with him a cargo of brazil-wood, monkeys and parrots. He established a settlement on the coast.

Although Vespucci brought back with him wonderful accounts of the country, he did not bring gold or diamonds. The diamond country had not at that time been discovered. The subjects of Portugal, however, began to go to Brazil for brazil-wood, and to colonize the country. A large Portuguese colony soon began to form there, and out of it grew an empire.

Martin Alfonso de Sousa came to a harbor on the coast on January 1, 1531, and from that circumstance named it Rio de Janeiro, the "River of January." It is one of the finest and most picturesque harbors in the world. He explored the country and made an alliance with the natives. Cotton and sugar-cane were introduced from Madeira. The Portuguese colonies multiplied, flourished and grew.

The city of Rio de Janeiro was founded in 1667 by the Portuguese. Portuguese explorers and noblemen received grants of territory called captaincies. Brazil seemed destined to become the greater Portugal, a great source of that country's revenue, and one of the dependencies of her glory and pride. This, however, was for a time delayed.

Orellana, a Spanish adventurer, had started from Peru, found the Amazon, and sailed down that river. The discovery of the river was claimed by him, and for Spain.

Portugal then found it necessary to appoint a captain-general to protect her territory. Thomé de Sousa was given this office, and in him the viceregal government of Brazil began.

In 1730 the discovery of the diamond-fields was announced to the government, which declared the mines to be *regalia* (royal rights). The white population increased largely and was generally peaceful. There was a contest between the Jesuit missionaries and some of the settlers, but Brazil for a long time had a peaceful history.

In 1807, during the invasion of Portugal by the French, the royal family fled to Brazil for safety. The colony thus became the seat of the throne of the parent country. The return of the royal family to Portugal displeased the Brazilians, as they thereby again became provincial.

Republican ideas, which were filling South America, found ready acceptance in Brazil. In 1822 the independence of Brazil was proclaimed. After many revolutionary changes a constitution was formulated and proclaimed. On March 25, 1824, the emperor swore to support the constitution. By so doing he saved Brazil to the Portuguese throne. The Emperor of Portugal assumed the title of Emperor of Brazil, but abdicated in favor of his son, Dom Pedro I., who, it was expected, would hold the throne for life. Thus Brazil became a republic, with a king of the house of Portugal as its executive officer. The new emperor, however, was favorable to the party of absolutism. He excited opposition, and finally abdicated the throne in favor of his son, Dom Pedro II., then a boy, for whom a regency was formed.

The election of a regent followed. This practically made the government republican. Dom Pedro II. was proclaimed emperor July 23, 1840. With this boy's reign began the prosperous period of the Brazilian monarchy. When the beneficent Dom Pedro II. found that the people desired a republic with an elective head, he abdicated.

CHAPTER XVIII

THE PROGRESS OF ARGENTINA—THE TYRANTS QUIROGA
AND ROSAS—MITRE—THE PERIOD OF PROGRESS

THE Argentine Republic had two struggles for liberty —one with Spain, the other with her own tyrants.

The movements of affairs in Argentina, which through stress and struggle reached the period of splendid achievement under General Mitre, are briefly as follows: Liniers, who was viceroy at the time Joseph Bonaparte was placed on the throne of Spain, was deposed by the adherents of Ferdinand VII., and Cisneros was made viceroy in the name of Ferdinand. On May 25, 1810, a date still celebrated, a provisional government was formed. This was the beginning of the republic. On January 31, 1813, a congress assembled at Buenos Ayres, and Posadas was elected Dictator of the republic. A struggle ensued between the party of independence and that of the royalists. On March 25, 1816, a new congress met at Tucuman, which elected Pueyrredon President of the republic, and declared the separation of the country from Spain. The Congress did not represent all of the ancient viceroyalty. Bolivia, Paraguay and Uruguay became separate republics. The war of liberation under San Martin followed.

On January 23, 1825, the federal states of the present Argentine Republic formulated a national constitution.

Two parties arose in the republic—the Unitarians, who favored a strong central government, after the model of the United States; and the States' Rights Party, or Federalists, who would still hold the old provinces under their local chiefs and laws.

The Banda Oriental of Uruguay was a territory in dispute, but was made independent by the mediation of England in 1827.

In 1825 Rivadavia was elected President of Argentina. He sought to establish a strong central government. He was opposed by the Federalists, who elected Lopez President, and after him Dorrego. There was a fierce contention between the two parties in the days of Quiroga. Rosas became the leader of the Federal party.

After the long period of tyrants began the succession of illustrious presidents who have led Argentina to the front of the new nations of the world.

That a nation which had emancipated itself from Spain should fall into the power of men without heart, without character, without armies, with nothing but the terror that they were able to inspire by a barbarous personality, is one of the events that illustrate how easy is the reaction from enthusiasm, and how unstable are susceptible minds amid changes of fortune.

Juan Facundo Quiroga was born in the province of Rioja in 1790. His parents were shepherds. At school he assaulted the teacher and fled. In 1806 he was sent by his father with merchandise to Chili. He lost the proceeds at the gambling-table. On being reproached by his father he fled again, and collected a band of robbers.

This man, gathering around him a few reckless and adventurous spirits, raided cities, destroyed the liberties of Argentina, and put his own arbitrary and insane will in the place of law. He brought Jujuy, Catamarca, Tucuman, Rioja, San Juan and Mendoza, heroic places associated with the great names and deeds of Belgrano and San Martin, under his influence. He made himself a despot by the force of his irresistible will. The cities as well as the country were at the mercy of this human thunderbolt.

"Most tyrants," says Sarmiento, "are superstitious. Quiroga seems to have been born without fear, though he said he once knew fear when he was watched by the eye of a tiger in a bending tree. He is even said once to have wept when he returned to his old home and saw the ruin that he had brought upon his aged father. But such incidents are but exceptions to his life and conduct. From boyhood he delighted in cruelty, and this nature grew in him until he became like a beast of the forest that has tasted human blood. He gloried in his power over men, and in his power to do injustice.

"He did not believe in God, in any morality or virtue. He had a magnetic will, and to exercise this thrilled him. He was like the hawk when the bush-bird cowers before him. In the line of battle his soldiers trembled with terror, not of the enemy, but of their own chief, who strode behind them brandishing his lance. They fell upon the enemy merely to put something between their eyes and the figure of Quiroga, which haunted them like a phantom."

Quiroga aspired to set up a president who should obey him. He named Dr. José Santos Ortez, ex-governor of San Luis.

Quiroga had one impulse; it was to free Argentina entirely from the rule of Spain. He breathed the air of freedom, and drew men after him like the wind. He had caused the old Spanish cities to fall before him, and wher-

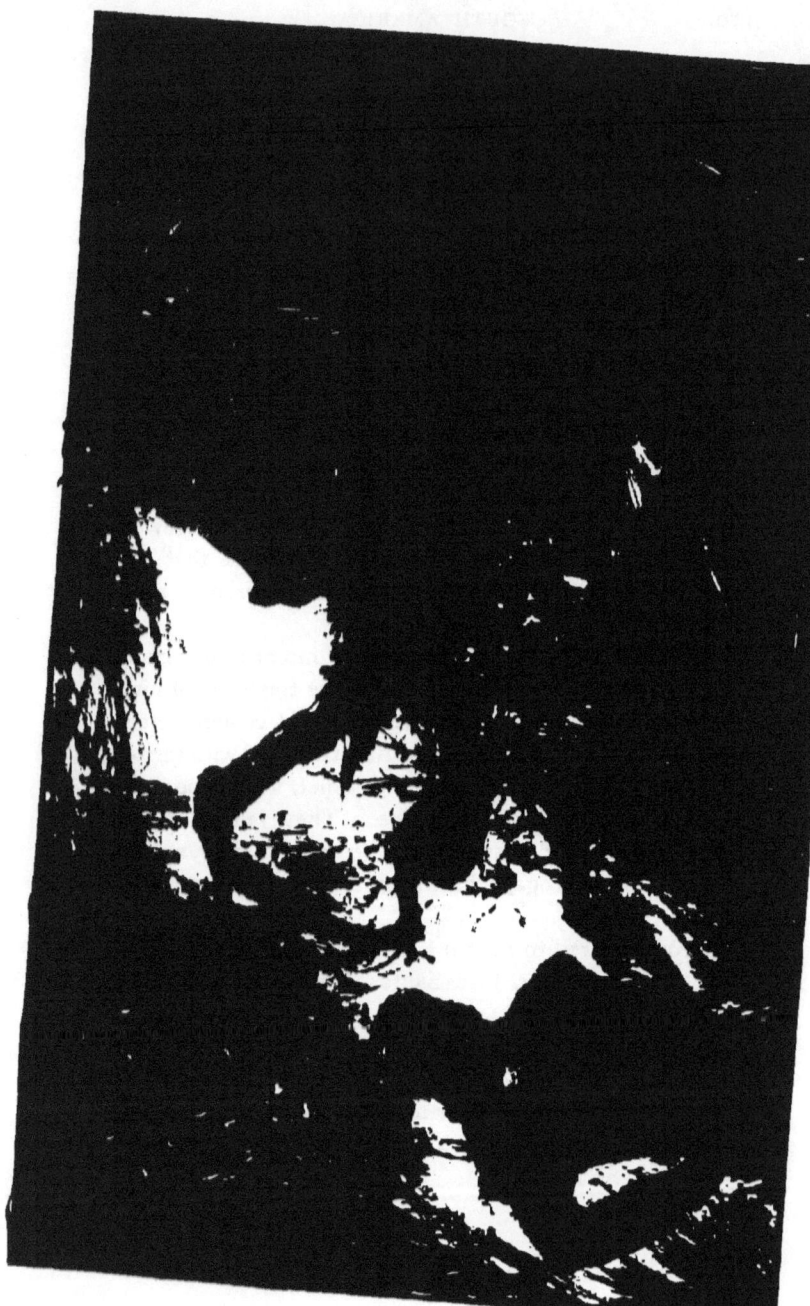

QUIROGA AND THE TIGER.

ever he went he left desolation. He put his own wild will in the place of foreign tyranny.

Sarmiento, in picturing the mad career of the tyrant of the plains, says: "On the Godoy farm in San Juan are shown mud walls of Quiroga's treading. There are others in Fiambala and in Rioja made by him. He himself pointed out others in Mendoza. In that place he had caused twenty-six officers to be shot. What motives induced this man, brought up in a respectable family, to descend to the hireling's work of treading brick?" The question may perhaps be answered by saying that to become a hero of the plainsmen one had at that day to identify one's self with the people.

In the fullness of his power, for men to laugh at him was death. He murdered a girl whom he had promised to marry, and struck dead his own son. "Pax," he said of one of his enemies in the field, "shot six of my officers; I have shot ninety-six of his."

Quiroga talked of the country as though he held its fate in his hand, yet he had no regular army, and was not even the governor of a province. His sword of power was merely the terror which he was able to inspire. The people dared do nothing against his will. He would cut down any opponent without mercy, and without any just cause. No one dared to stay his hand.

He made Rioja the seat of his power. He robbed the country in the name of the government, and sent the treasures to Rioja. It is said that he hid in the woods guns, swords and lances to the number of twelve thousand; that he had sixteen hundred horses in the pastures of Cuzco. He concealed an immense amount of treasures of silver and gold,

Rosas, a man who sprang from the people, was made governor of Buenos Ayres. He, too, was a tyrant. He became a confederate with Quiroga, raised the red flag, and from his campaigns in the interior took the title of the " Hero of the Desert."

The years following the revolution found Argentina and the Banda Oriental largely under the rule of three tyrants —Quiroga, Lopez and Rosas.

Quiroga came to Buenos Ayres unannounced, a man without an army. But in the city of Rosas he soon found himself surrounded by followers, and felt his growing power. He began to speak contemptuously of Rosas, made investments in the public funds, did deeds of personal strength and valor that excited the admiration of the barbarous classes, and boasted that he would one day treat Buenos Ayres as he had done the river provinces.

Rosas resigned the governorship of Buenos Ayres under compulsion, to take up the sword and to follow the example of Quiroga. The year 1834 found two tyrants in the field. One was to destroy the other.

Quiroga was called away from the city of Buenos Ayres to settle divisions that had arisen in the northern provinces. He said to his friends on leaving the port city: " If I succeed, you will see me again; if I fail, farewell forever!" He started forth for the pampas accompanied by Dr. Ortez, whom he had wished to make President.

There comes a time when one's crimes gather upon one's own head, and the man of terror becomes a terror to himself. To Quiroga now came the darkness of apprehension. He felt that he had made an enemy of humanity. He regarded every man as a cunning and merciless assassin. As he rushed over the pampas toward the foot-hills and mountain towns of the Andes, his apprehensions and suspicions grew. " How long since a courier passed? " he asked at every post. "An hour or so," would be the usual answer. "Hurry!" He changed horses rapidly. He was as one who could not wait.

It began to rain on the plains, turning parts of them into lagoons. But he flew on, asking, "When did a courier pass?" He reached Santa Fé after the long ride of terror. His anxieties increased. He seems to have had the conviction that some avenging spirit was pursuing him. On arriving at the post of Pavon he found no horses there. The delay almost crazed him. An evil spirit seemed to possess him. He was not contented except when flying at a deadly pace. When he started out from Santa Fé he exclaimed: "If I can only get beyond the boundary it is enough!" But it was not enough. They arrived at Cordova in the night. He sat in his carriage calling for horses. An officer came to him to invite him to spend the night in the town. "Horses!" answered the chief. "You shall have the hospitality of the place." "Horses!" At midnight he renewed the mad ride. The people were greatly excited at seeing him come and go. There had been a plot formed to assassinate him on his way to the city, but he had escaped it by his haste. He arrived at his point of destination and settled the political difficulties there. Then the madness seemed to return upon him. "To Cordova!" he said to a postilion. This was not the safe way, but he felt it was the one over which fate compelled him to ride. He came to a post-station called Ojo del Agua. A young man came racing out of the woods to give warning to Dr. Ortez, his friend. "A company is stationed near Barranca-Yacco," said the messenger. "It is waiting to fire into the carriage. No one is to escape." The doctor told Quiroga what he had heard. He replied: "The man is not born who can kill Quiroga!" He rode on into the face of death. They came to a post-station. Again they were warned. A company of thirty men was waiting to avenge the crimes of Quiroga. "We must go on—on!" he said. He lay down exhausted. At midnight Dr. Ortez, who had again been warned, aroused him. "We must escape by another way," he said. The chief laughed wildly. "The wrath of Quiroga is more than a match for anything we can meet at Barranca-Yacco," he said. In the gray of the morning the carriage passed on. Dr. Ortez knew that he was following his friend to certain death. But amid his terror Quiroga believed that his methods of the past would render him superior to all his enemies. He was attacked. Men with swords cut down the horses. They stabbed the driver and the courier. "What is this?" cried Quiroga from the coach window. The answer was a ball through his head. He sank. They pierced his body with a sword. He had met the fate that he had made for himself.

The tyrant Rosas followed.

Don Juan Manuel Rosas, who rose to be governor of the Buenos Ayres Confederation, and afterward to be President of the Argentine Confederation, was born at Buenos Ayres, March 30, 1793.

He made the Federal principle the excuse for his rule of blood. About the year 1833 he gained almost absolute power over Argentina, after the methods of Quiroga.

The politics of the country must be understood in order to form a just judgment of the character and conduct of Rosas. Rivadavia, the first President of the republic, endeavored to establish a strong central government. The party which he represented was the Unitarians. The opposing party was known as the Federals. It maintained provincial rights, much after the manner of the old-time South Carolinian idea of State rights in the United States. The Federals aimed to keep each state as independent as possible of the national government. At the end of the first President's term of office his opponents elected Vicente Lopez President, and in 1827 Dorrego, another representative of the Federal plan of government. In 1828 the Unitarians defeated the Federals. Dorrego was shot. Rosas became the leader of the Federal party. He defeated the Unitarians, and inaugurated a reign of terror. He proclaimed himself Dictator, and after many bloody struggles proved himself superior to all of his enemies.

In 1829 he was governor or captain-general of his native province, then in federal union with the provinces. He subdued the Indian revolts, established a tyrannical but stable government, and was elected President of the Argentine Confederation.

Autocrat that he was, intestine revolts subsided under his strong arm. Industrial conditions improved. Commerce revived. Buenos Ayres grew and flourished. The other provinces became jealous of Buenos Ayres. Rosas, to strengthen the river provinces, sought to force Paraguay to unite with the confederation. This policy led to a war with Brazil. Rosas was defeated in the political complications that followed. His rule had been so bloody that it became intolerable, and the states elected General Urquiza President. In a battle at Monte-Caseros, near Buenos Ayres, on February 3, 1852, the forces of Rosas were totally defeated. He fled to England, where he died in exile.

It is hard to estimate the value of a life like that of Rosas. He ruled the country for seventeen years with an iron hand. His strong government represented his own ambition. His utter disregard of the sacredness of human life, his bloody deeds that defied justice, have left him a place among the darkest names of political crimes.

General Mitre may be regarded as the father of the

new republic. Between the years 1810 and 1835 Argentina had known thirty-six political changes. The republic became a unity under Mitre, who, both in and out of public office, for almost a generation was the guardian of her destiny. His principles once sent him into exile, but his influence on progressive Argentina was powerful.

Bartolomé Mitre was born at Buenos Ayres in 1821. Persecuted by Rosas on account of his patriotic writings, he removed to Montevideo, where he became a journalist, and led the country in journalistic enterprises which were made the medias of his progressive opinions. In 1846 he went to Bolivia, and was in the battles of Lalava and Behistre as commander of artillery. He later went to Peru and Chili. In the latter country he awakened enmity by his views in "El Progreso," published at Santiago. He heard of the rising of the Argentines against Rosas, and returned to Argentina. He joined the revolutionary forces under General Urquiza. He commanded the artillery in the decisive battle of Monte-Caseros, February 3, 1852. After the overthrow of Rosas he founded the journal "La Nacion." His influence grew; he was intrusted with high public offices, and appointed to positions of the gravest responsibility. In 1862 he was proclaimed constitutional President for six years. His administration was a glorious industrial period in Argentina. Railroads, telegraph lines and public improvements multiplied, and, like the literary President Sarmiento, he advanced the cause of public education. He led Argentina in the war with Paraguay. His "La Vida de San Martin" is one of the best works for the American reader to select for beginning a study of South American history.

After her second struggle for freedom Buenos Ayres became a commercial city of growing importance, and gathered to herself men who favored the enterprises that

A SCENE IN THE CATTLE-RAISING DISTRICT ON THE PAMPAS OF THE ARGENTINE REPUBLIC.

make such a city prosperous. Societies of the industries and arts multiplied. Literature was cultivated, and stimulated achievement. The English Literary Society, with its extensive library and fine reading-room, became an inspiration to literary culture.

The suburbs of Flores and Belgrano expanded into places famous for the beauty of their villas and gardens. The *recoleta* (cemetery), with its marble homes of the dead, became one of the most beautiful spots on earth. Monuments rose everywhere, each commemorating some illustrious deed.

Three ports instead of one became essential to the trade of the expanding city. Approached from Ensenada, the white domes and tall spires of the city rise in the purple air over the pampas, with a beauty that fills the eye of the traveler with wonder. His admiration grows as the home port, with its city of ships, comes into nearer view. At all hours ships from European ports come and go, and the immigration from the East comes and does not go, but remains to make a new history in the world.

CHAPTER XIX

THE TYRANTS OF PARAGUAY

AFTER the expulsion of the Spanish the first tyrant of Paraguay was Dr. Francia. He was born in Asuncion, 1761. By profession he was a lawyer. He was made consul in 1811, Dictator for three years in 1814, and Dictator for life in 1817. He recognized no law but that of his own will. He arrested and executed innocent men without any trial. He was to the last degree cruel and unpatriotic. He died in his native city in 1840.

Thomas Carlyle has a word of charity for him. In his essay on Dr. Francia, he says: "Francia's treatment of Artigas, his old enemy, the bandit and firebrand, reduced now to beg shelter of him, was good, humane, even dignified. Francia refused to see or treat with such a person, as he had ever done; but readily granted him a place of residence in the interior, and 'thirty piasters a month till he died.' The bandit cultivated fields, did charitable deeds, and passed a life of penitence for his few remaining years. His bandit followers, such of them as took to plundering again, says M. Rengger, were instantly seized and shot.'

"On the other hand, that anecdote of Francia's dying father requires to be confirmed. It seems the old man, who, as we saw, had long since quarreled with his son, was dying, and wished to be reconciled. Francia 'was busy; what use was it? could not come.' A second still more pressing message arrives: 'The old man dare not die unless he see his son; fears he shall never enter heaven if they be not reconciled.' 'Then let him enter,' said Francia; 'I will not come!' If this anecdote be true, it is certainly of all that are in circulation about Dr. Francia by far the worst. If Francia, in that death-hour, could not forgive his poor old father whatsoever he had done, or could in the murkiest, sultriest imagination be conceived to have done against him, then let no man forgive Dr. Francia! But the accuracy of public rumor in regard to a dictator who has executed forty persons is also a thing that can be guessed at. To whom was it, by name and surname, that Francia delivered this extraordinary response? Did the man make, or can he now be got to make, affidavit of it to credible articulate-speaking persons resident on this earth? If so, let him do it, for the sake of the psychological sciences.

"One last fact more. Our lonesome Dictator, living among Gauchos, had the greatest pleasure, it would seem, in rational conversation with Robertson, with Rengger, with any kind of intelligent human creature, when such could be fallen in with, which was rarely. He would question you with eagerness about the ways of men in foreign places, the properties of things unknown to him. All human interest and insight was interesting to him. Only persons of no understanding being near him for the most part, he had to content himself with silence, a meditative cigar, and cup of mate. Oh, Francia, though thou hadst to execute forty persons, I am not without some pity for thee!"

The principal tyrant of Paraguay was Francisco Solano Lopez, or Lopez the Younger. He was born July 24,

1826, or, according to another authority, July 26, 1827. His early life was passed in the Paraguayan military service, in the times of the tyrant Dr. Francia, and in that he learned little but the arts of a spy.

Paraguay declared her independence of Spain in 1810. In 1814 Dr. Francia was proclaimed Dictator for three years, and afterward for life. He held the office until his death in 1840, which was followed by anarchy. In 1842 the Congress elected two nephews of Dr. Francia, Don Alonso Lopez and Don Carlos Antonio Lopez, consuls of the republic. In 1844 a new constitution was proclaimed, and Don Carlos Lopez, called Lopez the Elder, was made President with dictatorial power for a term of seven years, which office was continued. He died in 1862, when he was succeeded as Dictator by his son Don Francisco Solano Lopez, then thirty-six years of age.

This man, the South American Nero, may be regarded as the darkest character in all American history. To him may be directly or indirectly assigned the deaths of hundreds of thousands of human beings. He caused his own brother to be murdered, and his mother and sisters to be tortured. He had a passion for blood that was never satiated. Scarcely a day passed in his last years that the torture of innocent people was not made to feed his passions. He was governed by the lowest and basest of animal passions, without any regard for justice or mercy, yet he claimed to govern by the appointment of God. If he imagined that any man looked unfavorably upon his monstrous crimes he brought him to torture and death, without judge or jury. "He was not a man; he was a monster," said one of his own blood after his miserable death.

Like all tyrants, he was a coward, and surrounded himself by spies. Lopez had nearly all the vices, and was a slave to them all. He practised them openly. To rebuke him for these was death. He had no fear of the laws of God, yet he believed that his office was ordained of God. He did not fear priests. He compelled priests not only to confess to him as the " Lord's anointed," but to reveal to him the secrets of the confessional. He was as vainglorious as he was depraved.

The Hon. Charles A. Washburn, commissioner and minister resident of the United States at Asuncion from 1861 to 1868, thus pictures this tyrant:

"In person he was short and stout. His height was about five feet four, and, though always inclining to corpulency, his figure in his younger days was very good. He dressed with great care and precision, and endeavored to give himself a smart and natty appearance. His hands and feet were very small, indicating his Indian origin. His complexion was dark, and gave evidence of a strong taint of Guarany blood. He was proud of his Indian descent, and frequently used to boast of it. As he could not pretend to be of pure Spanish blood, he would rather ascribe his swarthy color to a mixture with the Indian than the negro race. Hence he was as prone to talk of his Indian ancestry as ever were the descendants of Pocahontas. He also had many of the tastes peculiar to the savage. Before going to Europe he dressed grotesquely, but his costume was always expensive and elaborately finished. He wore enormous silver spurs, such as would have been the envy of a Gaucho, and the trappings of his horse were so completely covered with silver as almost to form a coat of mail. After his return from abroad he adopted a more civilized costume, but always indulged in a gorgeous display of gold lace and bright buttons. He conversed with fluency and had a good command of language, and when in good humor his manners were courteous and agreeable. His eyes, when he was pleased, had a mild and amiable expression; but when he was enraged the pupil seemed to dilate till it included the whole iris, and the eye did not appear to be that of a human being, but rather of a wild beast goaded to madness. He had, however, a gross animal look that was repulsive when his face was in repose. His forehead was narrow and his head small, with the rear organs largely developed. He was an inveterate smoker of the strongest kind of Paraguayan cigars. His face was rather flat, and his nose and hair indicated more of the negro than of the Indian. His cheeks had a fulness that extended to the jowl, giving him a sort of bulldog expression. In his later years he grew enormously fat, so much so that few would believe that a photograph of his figure was not a caricature. He was very irregular in his hours of eating, but when he did eat, the quantity consumed was enormous. He was a gormand, but not an epicure. His drinking was in keeping with his eating. He always kept a large stock of foreign wines, liquors and ale, but he had little discrimination in the use of them. . . . Though he habitually drank largely, yet he often exceeded his own free limits, and on such occasions he was liable to break out in the most furious abuse of all who were about him. He would then indulge in the most revolting obscenity, and would sometimes give orders for the most barbarous acts. When he had recovered from such debauches he would stay the execution of his orders, if they had not already been enforced. . . . It would generally be too late, the victims having already been executed.

"Of the three most noted tyrants of South America, Francia, Rosas, and the second Lopez, all have been distinguished for one quality, that is, personal cowardice. Francia was in such perpetual fear of his life that he kept himself constantly surrounded by a guard, and imagined that an assassin lurked behind every bush or wall or building he passed. Rosas was a notorious coward. Many instances in which he showed the most craven fear are well known to the older residents of the Plata. But the cowardly nature of Lopez was so apparent, he scarcely took pains to conceal it. He never exposed himself to the least danger when he could possibly avoid it. He usually had his headquarters so far in the rear that a shot from the enemy could never reach him. . . . Nevertheless, such a thing was possible, and he therefore had another house built close adjoining the one in which he lived, surrounded on all sides with walls of earth at least twenty feet thick, and with a roof of the same material, so thick that no shot or shell that might light upon it could ever penetrate deep enough to do any damage. While all was still along the enemy's lines Lopez would bravely remain in the adjoining house; but so surely as any firing was heard in the direction of the enemy's nearest batteries, he would instantly saunter out in feigned carelessness, trying hard to disguise his fear, and slink into his hole, and not show his face again outside until the firing had ceased. . . . At the very time he was thus hid away from danger he had his correspondents for the 'Semanario' around him, writing the most extravagant articles in praise of his valor, his sacrifices, and his generalship. The people of Paraguay could never pay the debt they owed him, who, while they were living in security and abundance, was daily leading his legions to battle."

Colonel George Thompson, in his history of this dark period, draws a like picture. He says: "One evening I was waiting to see Lopez, as were also several officers, and a sergeant of the guard entered into conversation with me. After a short time there was a great stir, officers going in and out of Lopez's room, the guard relieved, and the other officers who were waiting all arrested. One of Lopez's aides-de-camp came and said to me : ' His Excellency sends word to you to write down all the conversation you have had with the sergeant of the guard, and bring it to-morrow morning.' I went away, not expecting to be able to remember a twentieth part of the silly talk of the sergeant; but as things looked serious, I tried, and probably remembered it all. It filled a whole sheet of paper, and was all of it somewhat in this style: 'The sergeant asked me if Queen Victoria always wore her crown when she went out to walk. The sergeant asked me if I should wear the Paraguayan uniform when I went to England.' It was sealed and taken next morning to Lopez, about 7 A. M. He was not up yet, but the sergeant was already shot, and all the soldiers of the guard had received one hundred lashes each."

In the troubles of Uruguay, Brazil had intervened. Lopez declared war against her. This involved him in war with the Argentine Republic. On May 1, 1865, Brazil, the Argentine Republic and Uruguay (Banda Oriental) formed an alliance against him, which led to one of the most desolating wars ever known in South America, and which in the end scarcely left him a thousand men.

As the war between the allies and Paraguay went on in merciless savagery, Lopez became involved in troubles with foreign powers. Asuncion fell.

In 1868 the allied army, well prepared for the overthrow of Lopez, numbered thirty-two thousand men. The Brazilians took up a position near Villeta, north of Angostura, on the pass of the river Paraguay made famous by the exploits of Sebastian Cabot in 1526, nearly three hundred and fifty years before. Lopez had planted his guns so as to command the river.

The Brazilians marched into the rear of the Paraguayan army by the way of Chaco. They outnumbered the Paraguayans three to one. If Lopez should be defeated here, it would be the end of his power. The battlefield is known in history as the Pikysgry. Lopez made his headquarters on a hill overlooking the country for leagues around, some four miles from Angostura. The Brazilians from the first saw that they had Lopez in their power. The latter could trust only to the valor of his men for victory. The battle began with a furious attack on the Paraguayans. Lopez took a position on horseback behind the walls of his adobe house, ready to run at a moment's notice. It is said to have been the first time that he had been under fire since the war began. He was filled with terror from the first rattle of the musketry. At first the Paraguayans fought with desperate valor. After a four days' battle both armies were greatly reduced, and the Paraguayans almost utterly destroyed. Lopez saw that his men could not long sustain the bombardment. He prepared for flight with a body-guard. While his officers, after a week's valor, were leading their few remaining troops against the victorious allies, Lopez suddenly disappeared. There were not left of his army a thousand men. Lopez now began the flight of death. He was shot like a dog in a muddy stream, as he was struggling to recover himself from a lance thrust from his victorious pursuers. His last words are reputed to have been: "I die for my country."

The battle of Pikysgry brought to an end the life of Lopez and tyranny in Paraguay.

CHAPTER XX

EDUCATION IN ARGENTINA AND THE OTHER REPUBLICS—SARMIENTO

THE history of the progress of Argentina along educational lines is that of Sarmiento, who once said: "The primary school is the foundation of national character."

This man read the works of Horace Mann, and visited the great apostle of education in America. The friendship between him and Mr. and Mrs. Mann and Miss Elizabeth Palmer Peabody had a great influence on his own character, and through him, as the great educational President, upon Argentina. Senator Sumner was Sarmiento's friend during his diplomatic life. His biography has been written by Mrs. Mary Mann, who has also translated from the Spanish his "Civilization and Barbarism," under the title of "Life in the Argentine."

He founded in Argentina the North American Normal School, a sign which was long seen in some of the principal cities, and the work of which prepared the way for universal education not only in Buenos Ayres but in the lands of the Andes. On one of the reliefs of his tomb in the *recoleta* of Buenos Ayres he is represented as a schoolmaster, with the children of the republic around him.

His history reads like a romance, especially as interpreted by the sympathetic pen of Mary Mann. The influences of Mrs. Mann and of her sister, Miss Peabody, live in Argentina, and that of the latter has found new expression in the growth of the kindergarten.

Don Domingo F. Sarmiento was born in 1811. His family was a worthy one, but had suffered from war. He was descended on one side from a Saracen chief. His education was of the best, and his early accomplishments were many.

He describes his education in his address at the laying of the corner-stone of the Sarmiento School in San Juan, in 1864. I quote from Mrs. Mann's translation. "The inspiration to consecrate myself to the education of the people came to me here in my youth. My labor of thirty years, that of serving the countries where I resided with schools, turns now to its point of departure, to the very simple idea of the importance of primary-school education over all other education, to insure the happiness of nations. If I had been born in Buenos Ayres or Cordova, or in Santiago de Chili, the primary education of this part of the country would not have arrived at this point, when all are striving for that end. I should have been preoccupied with the brilliant university, and should have aspired to its honors. But I was born and educated amid the people of a province where there was no other education than that of the public school; and the *escuela de la patria* was one of the first order, without a rival in any private one, conducted by a man so respected by the people and the government that at that time the schoolmaster was looked upon as one of the first magistrates of the province. Observe, then, by what singular circumstances the school, as an institution, was destined to acquire in my mind that supreme importance which I have never ceased to give it; and how, at the close of my travels, I found in the United States that the school occupied the same place as in San Juan, and brought forth like results. The truth is that the first ideas in the child's mind keep the same relative position always, and, however slightly they meet with confirmation, grow and develop, and determine the career in life. If I should express all my thoughts I should say that the school of *la patria*, in San Juan, associated in my mind with the recollections of the only form of education with which I was acquainted, went forth with me from this province, and accompanied me in all my wanderings. In Chili it took the form of normal schools; in Europe I connected it with the study of legislation; in the United States with the spectacle of its wonderful results, of its temple school-houses, and of the prominent place it holds among the institutions of that country. In Buenos Ayres I reproduced it as a seed sown in good ground, and I return to do the same to-day in San Juan, by reëstablishing the school of *la patria*, completed as an educational institution, and also as a democratic one, and I bring to it all the acquisitions made in my long and various travels. No longer confined to three halls that contained in all but three hundred pupils, we have here an edifice that will enable us to throw off the swaddling-clothes of infancy. To-day we lay the stone which consecrates to education these beginnings of an unfinished temple. And that you may see how advanced ideas have grown, I will repeat to you what I have replied to those who have wished this edifice kept to its first destination, and who yet abandoned it to sterility and destruction.

"At the corner of the next block, thirty steps from here, thirty years ago, I was a merchant's clerk, and here pursued my solitary studies. Even at that time I saw that a spacious school-house might be erected within these walls, and, with your assistance, I now realize my thought after the delay of so many years."

Of the influence of certain books on his life he says: "From that time I read every book that fell into my hands, without arrangement, with no other guide than the chance which brought them to me, or the knowledge I had acquired of their existence in the scanty libraries of San Juan. The first was the 'Life of Cicero' by Middleton, with very fine plates, and in that book I lived a long time with the Romans. If I had then had half the means of doing it, I should have studied law to make myself an advocate and to defend causes like that distinguished orator, who was the object of my passionate love. The second was the 'Life of Franklin,' and no book has ever done me more good. The 'Life of Franklin' was to me what 'Plutarch's Lives' was to Rousseau, Henry IV., Mme. Roland, and so many others. I felt myself to be Franklin; and why not? I was very poor, like him; I studied, like him; and following in his footsteps, I might one day come, like him, to be a *doctor ad honorem*, and to make for myself a place in letters and American politics. The 'Life of Franklin' should be in every primary school. His example is so inspiring, the career he ran so glorious, that there would not be a boy at all well inclined who would not try to be a little Franklin, through that noble tendency of the human mind to imitate models of perfection that commend themselves to it."

His family was obliged to flee to Chili during the revolutions in San Juan. He there became a teacher, and also followed other occupations. He continued his studies. His thirst for knowledge was insatiable. It is said that for sixty days he translated a volume a day of the works of Sir Walter Scott. While this is without doubt an exaggeration, the statement will convey some idea of his industry in literary work.

In 1836 he returned to San Juan destitute, as one coming back from exile. He sought the society of educators, and founded there a college for young ladies. Its life lasted only two years, but furnished a model for the future. Here he had a library of the most scholarly works, which he carefully studied. He mastered the literature of the world.

His methods of a long self-education he thus describes: "It was in 1837 that I learned Italian, in company with young Rawson, whose talents had then begun to show themselves strikingly.

"Several years afterward, when editing the 'Mecorio' in Santiago de Chili, I familiarized myself with Portuguese, which is very easy. In Paris, still later, I shut myself up fifteen days with a German grammar and dictionary, and translated six pages to the satisfaction of an intelligent man who gave me lessons. That supreme effort left me an incomplete scholar, although I thought I had caught the structure of that rebellious idiom.

"I taught French to many persons for the sake of spreading good reading among them; and to sundry of my friends I taught it without giving them lessons. To put them in the path which I had trodden, I said: 'You must not fail to study—I am coming.' And when I saw their self-love fairly piqued, I gave them a few lessons upon the way to study for themselves."

He again emigrated to Chili with the intention of founding a college there. The idea of public education made his feet restless. He had but one vision. It was like that of Horace Mann. It dominated his life.

The states of South America became jealous of their

heroes and national glory. Chili had caused to be erased from her historic records the noble name of the unconquerable Argentine, San Martin. The chivalrous soul of Sarmiento was fired by the injustice. He wrote anew the true history of this man's deeds. He carried public opinion with him. The equestrian statue of San Martin now faces the Andes from the beautiful boulevard of Santiago. Sarmiento now became an editor, and thus sought to educate public opinion. He endeavored to organize primary instruction in Chili. He wrote the first spelling-book with accents, and founded the " Monitor for Schools." In 1842 he founded the first normal school in South America, and for a time brought to it his own varied learning. In 1843 he founded the first paper that was printed in Santiago de Chili. It was called " El Progreso " (" The Progress ").

He was persecuted in Chili by some who were jealous of him. Envy called him a " foreigner." Slander made his life miserable. His person was in danger, but he lived in his purpose, and his purpose lived in him. His ambition was to be the apostle of education.

He went to Europe. He there met Thiers, Guizot, Humboldt and Cobden. In the latter he found a congenial spirit. In England he met with the great educational report of Horace Mann. Here, too, he found a twin soul, and from his thought knew his brother worker in the interests of mankind. He returned to South America with a stronger enthusiasm for education. He succeeded in obtaining for educational purposes in Buenos Ayres $127,000, and erected a model school building in that city, which exerted a powerful influence on the thought of the whole country. In 1860 he had the satisfaction of seeing 17,279 children in Buenos Ayres in the public schools. " Give me the department of schools," he said; "this is all the future of the republic." In 1858 he was elected a senator from Buenos Ayres, and secured an appropriation of lands worth $1,000,000 for public education.

He became a great leader of the liberal party, and minister of state. He was assigned by the national government to the office of minister to the United States. Here he met the great educators of North America. On his return he was elected President of the Argentine Republic. He led the country into that period that will be remembered as the golden age of its history. He made education the glory of Argentina, and did a similar work in Chili and Peru.

He died at Asuncion, Paraguay, September 11, 1888. His life was one of beneficence. Under his influence the republic made use of her great opportunity. The children of the country will ever honor his name. The progress of education in South America has largely followed the views of Sarmiento, who especially valued the primary and the normal school.

The population of the South American republics is now increasing so rapidly that statistics are altered yearly, but the following facts from recent official reports will give the reader a view of the educational field outside of the Argentine Republic:

BOLIVIA, 1893.—Area, 784,544 square miles; divided into 9 departments, the littoral being occupied by Chili;' population, 2,333,350, of which 1,000,000 are Indians of pure blood, and 600,000 are creoles; schools, 493, and 4 universities.

BRAZIL, 1893.—Area, 3,251,829 English square miles; divided into 20 states; population uncertain, but exceeding 14,000,000; immigration in 1891, 216,659; schools, public, private and normal, 7500, with 300,000 pupils;

especial attention given to primary and normal-school education.

CHILI, 1893.—Area, 290,828 square miles, divided into 23 provinces; population, 2,817,552 (now 3,267,441); 1201 free public schools, with 101,954 pupils; national library, 70,000 volumes.

COLOMBIA.—Area, 504,773 English square miles; population, 4,000,000, including 220,000 Indians; schools, 16 normal, 1734 primary; primary education free.

ECUADOR.—Area, 248,350 square miles; divided into 17 provinces; population, 1,272,065; schools, 856, with 1137 teachers; 17 journals are published in the republic.

PARAGUAY.—Area, 88,807 square miles; population, 600,000; primary schools compulsory; the Normal College has 15 professors.

PERU.—Area uncertain, estimated at 483,147 square miles; population, 2,621,844; schools, 1177 primary; library of University of Lima, 20,000 volumes.

URUGUAY.—Area, 72,172 square miles; population, 706,524; schools, 470 primary; primary education compulsory between the ages of six and fourteen; the normal school has 19 professors.

VENEZUELA.—Area, 599,538 square miles; population, 2,323,527; schools, 1415; primary instruction obligatory.

CHAPTER XXI

DOM PEDRO II. AND THE PROGRESS OF BRAZIL—
THE HISTORY OF THE AMAZON

THE history of the progress of Brazil is inwoven with that of the beneficent Emperor, Dom Pedro II. He was crowned July 18, 1841, at the age of fourteen and a half years. The sixtieth anniversary of his birthday, celebrated on December 2, 1885, was made the occasion of the liberation of one hundred and thirty-three slaves by a private subscription. During the ceremony of conferring liberty on these slaves, the emperor said: "I hope that God will give me life to bestow liberty upon the last slave in Brazil." His hope was fulfilled. After a work so beneficent he was compelled to abdicate and to leave the country.

"The emperor," says Andrews ("Brazil: Its Conditions and Prospects"), "is six feet tall. He has an intellectual head, eyes of grayish blue, beard full and gray. He is erect and has a manly bearing. Being now upward of sixty years of age, he is not, of course, so sentimental a man as when, at thirty years of age, he used to talk to American travelers about our poets."

The last touch of this picture draws us toward him. Dom Pedro II. loved the poems of the Quaker poet Whittier. At a reception in Boston, tendered to him by the Radical Club, he met the poet. Dom Pedro II. was himself a poet. He thus expresses his opinion of the position to which he had been called and of the duties it entailed. This opinion found practical expression in every act of his long and illustrious reign.

> If I am pious, clement, just,
>   I 'm only what I ought to be:
> The scepter is a mighty trust,
>   A great responsibility.
>
> And he who rules with faithful hand,
>   With depth of thought and breadth of range,
> The sacred laws should understand,
>   But must not at his pleasure change.
>
> The chair of justice is the throne:
>   Who takes it bows to higher laws;
> The public good, and not his own,
>   Demands his care in every cause.
>
> *Translation of D. Bates.*

The political affairs in Brazil from the beginning of the republican movement in South America had had a liberal tendency. Dom Pedro II. was only five years of age when, by his father's abdication, he succeeded to the throne. The regents during his minority were chosen for him in accordance with the public will. He was declared of age before he was fifteen, and the heart of the boy emperor, from the first days of his reign, went out to the people who had desired to see him thus early upon the throne. In 1843 he married the Princess Theresa Christina Maria of Naples. Two princes, who died young, and two princesses were the result of this union.

He offered aid to General Urquiza in the war against Rosas, and thus secured the free navigation of the Rio de la Plata.

In 1850 the slave-trade was suppressed in Brazil. This was the first step toward the emancipation of slaves, an act which gave Dom Pedro II. a place among the greatest benefactors of humanity. In 1800 Brazil possessed a population of 3,200,000, nearly one half of which was negro slaves. A law for the gradual abolition of slavery was passed in 1871. This was followed by the abolition of slavery in 1888.

In 1865 Dom Pedro declared war against the tyrant Lopez of Paraguay, who had refused the free navigation of the Paraguay River, one of the sources of supply of the great province of Matto-Grosso in Brazil. The war ended in a complete victory for Brazil. It cost Brazil $315,000,000.

Years of peaceful progress in Brazil followed the Paraguayan war. The emperor gave himself to the study of the welfare of his people. He shared his great revenues with the poor. The freedom of the press was guaranteed; education was encouraged, and institutions of beneficence founded.

Emancipation was followed by a great European immigration to Brazil. In the single year 1888, 132,000 immigrants arrived.

On an island in the harbor of Rio de Janeiro, now called Villegaignon, but named Coligny by the first settlers, the French Huguenots, in 1555, planted one of the first Protestant settlements in the New World. The colony was reinforced from Geneva by a missionary colony. Thus the first Protestant missionary work in America was begun more than a half-century before the coming of the Pilgrim Fathers to New Plymouth, or three hundred and fifty years ago.

In 1818 two thousand Swiss colonists founded Novo Fribourgo, one hundred and fifty miles north of Rio de

Janeiro. The place is very beautiful and healthful, and is a favorite summer resort of the inhabitants of Rio de Janeiro.

German immigrants founded the colony of São Leopoldo on the Rio Grande do Sul in 1824. The colony grew to 40,000 inhabitants. There are to-day some 250,000 inhabitants of German origin in Brazil. They are prosperous, and are constantly growing in numbers, resources and wealth. São Leopoldo was the mother of German colonies. Out of this colony forty-three others sprang.

The German colony of Santa Cruz was founded in 1849, and has now a population of more than 5000. These Germans cultivate corn, rice, tobacco, sugar-cane, flax and the vine.

The colony of Blumenau was founded in 1860, by Dr. Herman Blumenau, and has a population of 11,000 or more.

The colony of Santa Leopoldina, on the river Santa Maria, cultivates coffee and sugar-cane. Its export of the former numbers millions of pounds. There are several coffee-producing colonies in the different states.

At times the ocean passage of immigrants has been paid by the Brazilian government. Under the provision of the law of 1867, newly arrived immigrants, while awaiting transportation, were lodged and fed at the expense of the government. On taking possession of the government land they were furnished with food for ten days. They were given eleven dollars in money, ten acres of land and a temporary house. The immigrant was debited with such advances, but was allowed a long time in which to pay the loan.

On November 15, 1889, after a bloodless revolution, Brazil became a republic. The republican flag took the place of the imperial banner. It represented twenty-one states—the United States of Brazil. The emperor sailed for Portugal, bringing to a close his beneficent and illustrious reign.

The history of the navigation of the Amazon is full of dramatic incidents. No river promises to contribute more to the world's development. It is three thousand miles long. Its branches would add to its main current another three thousand miles. It rises in the Andean Alps, fourteen thousand feet above the sea, and dashes down through the crystal Cordilleras to the plains.

The first voyager on the Amazon was Francisco de Orellana, a Spanish adventurer. His story, which filled Europe with wonder, is as follows: Gonzalo Pizarro, the half-brother of the conqueror of Peru, received the appointment of governor of Quito. He had heard wonderful tales of the land of cinnamon, and of a mighty river that leaped down the Andes and went rushing to the sea. He wished to visit the land of spices and to discover this river. For this purpose he mustered three hundred and fifty Spaniards and four thousand Indians. He gathered for the expedition a great quantity of provisions.

In the year 1540 he set out on this expedition to the cinnamon-groves. He marched through the old land of the Incas as in a triumphal procession. When he came to the cold, bare, lofty ranges of the Andes, among new tribes of barbarous people, his men began to suffer. Besides the cold of the Cordilleras, he met with an earthquake which rent the earth asunder, poured forth sulphurous vapors, and swallowed up a village. Five hundred houses were destroyed. On descending the eastern slopes of the Andes, the cold changed to heat, and heavy thunder-clouds hung over the passes. After months of travel they reached the land of cinnamon. They came to the river Napo, one of the tributaries of the Amazon, a river that, in this region, rolls foaming and tumbling down toward the plains. It is said that the roar of this river may be heard for leagues. It flows through a pathless wilderness, gigantic forests inhabited by the alligator, the boa, and an unknown people almost as wild as the beasts.

In this expedition was one Francisco de Orellana, an ambitious cavalier. Gonzalo Pizarro caused a boat to be built. He intrusted to this man an expedition in search of food, for his men were dying for the want of supplies. The last of their horses had been eaten, and the gloomy forests offered no adequate sustenance for so many men.

Orellana had heard that the Napo emptied into a greater river, and, with high hopes, he started with his boats and a crew of fifty men. He sailed down to the plains, over the foaming currents, and found a mighty stream. Orellana desired to explore this majestic river. His duty was to return to the famished men he had left, but his ambition rose above his sense of duty. Whither did this grand river flow? To the ocean? If so, to follow it to the ocean would make him famous. He continued his course on the broad river, and he and his companions were borne through lands of wonder to the ocean. He reached the isle of Cahagua, and there found passage to Spain. He thrilled the Spanish court with his story, and obtained royal permission to occupy the lands that he had discovered.

In his reports of this perfidious expedition he claimed to have found a nation of Amazons, women warriors like those fabled to have lived in Scythia. He did not live to fulfil his dream of repeating the deeds of a Pizarro. His marvelous story of the Amazons gave the name to the river.

The Amazon was first described in modern travel by

M. de la Condamine, a French traveler, who embarked upon it in 1743. It was explored in 1799 by Humboldt, and in 1867 by Professor Agassiz.

In 1866 the Peruvian government organized an expedition to ascertain if it would be possible to establish communication between Lima and the town of Magro, at the foot of the Andes in Upper Peru. After many difficulties it found the desired waterway to the tributary of the Amazon. From Magro to Lima is a distance of four hundred or more miles. It is proposed to make over this route a new waterway to the Amazon, and so from Peru to Para, from the Pacific to the Atlantic.

The india-rubber trade began to fill the Amazon with river craft. The great ocean steamers followed, and to-day a person may travel by steamer from New York to Para, from Para to Marañon, and thence to Peru by a continuous waterway.

The navigation of the Amazon has of late been developed in a wonderful manner. The report of the Bureau of American Republics (Brazil) says of this development: "The possibilities of the navigation of the Amazon and its affluents have only begun to be developed; and yet the following 'magnificent distances' are navigated already by steamers: from Belem (Para) to Manaos, 1100 miles; Manaos to Iquitos, Peru, by river Solimoens, 1350 miles; Manaos to Santa Isabella, by river Negro, 470 miles; Manaos to Hyutanahan, by river Purus, 1080 miles; Manaos to São Antonio, by river Madeira, 470 miles; Belem to Bayao, by river Tocantins, 156 miles; Leopoldina to Santa Maria, 570 miles—making a total of 5196 miles of steam-navigation on the Amazon and its southern affluents; and this total does not include the navigation of the branches of the above-named rivers, which would increase the amount by some 3000 miles more."

Rubber, coffee, sugar, cocoa and mandioca (tapioca) here find one of the finest soils in the world.

The coffee-plant was brought from Africa to Brazil. In 1800 the empire exported 13 bags of coffee; to-day the republic exports 6,000,000 bags of 132 pounds each.

The port cities are growing populous and rich with increasing commerce. Rio has a population of more than 400,000, Bahia of nearly 200,000, and Pernambuco of 150,000 or more.

Para, the port city of the Amazon, called Belem in Brazil, has a harbor in which are found ships from all parts of the commercial world. Through this port pass the growing imports and exports of the broad Amazon valley. From January to July, in 1888, there were exported from Para rubber to the value of $6,462,000, and cocoa to the value of $670,000. The city of Para is one of the most rapidly growing commercial centers of South America.

Rio, with its beautiful harbor, is the port from which coffee finds its way to many lands, but most largely to the United States. In 1888, in eleven months, 3,330,-185 bags were exported. The state of São Paulo, which connects with Rio, is the great coffee region of Brazil, and is the home of the planters whose enterprise has caused them to be called the "Brazilian Yankees."

The Golconda of South America is the diamond region of Brazil, known as the Serro do Frio, or the "Mountains of Cold." The diamond district is small in extent. It was once so jealously guarded that no one was allowed to enter it without special permission. Travelers thither were escorted by soldiers. They were not allowed to remain for any considerable time. The town where the officers and explorers resided was called Tejuco. The mines were discovered by accident in the early part of the last century. Their product then belonged to the crown.

The discovery of these mines is associated with a very curious story. The lofty, cold range of Serro do Frio was explored for gold. In searching for the precious metal some singular stones, supposed to be pebbles, were found. Their luminous qualities and geometrical forms excited the curiosity of the negro laborers, who showed them to their masters. The laborers collected these shining pebbles as curiosities. Card-playing was a favorite amusement in these cold, lonesome mountain regions, and it became a custom to use these luminous pebbles as counters in the game. One day an officer who had been in India arrived in this region. He saw shining pebbles, and was led to examine them on account of their geometrical forms. He had a suspicion that they might have value. He compared the weight of these pebbles with that of other pebbles, and found a great difference. The result led him to believe that they were gems. He sent some of them to Lisbon to be examined. The Dutch consul there saw them. "They are diamonds," he said. The Dutch consul forwarded some of them to Holland, where they were pronounced to be diamonds equal in value to those of Golconda.

A more extraordinary story is associated with the Braganza diamond of Brazil, the largest diamond in the world, once the glory of the jewels of Portugal. "It was found," says Mawe, "in 1791. Three men convicted of capital offenses, named Antonio de Sousa, José Felix Gomez, and Tomas de Sousa, were sent into exile, into the wilderness of Morias, among cannibals and wild beasts. They searched for treasures. They were forbidden to enter any city or to hold communication with the world. While washing for gold in the Abaite River, in a dry season, this diamond gleamed upon them. There was a law against diamond-washing. The three exiles took the wonderful gem to a priest. He had an honest, trusting soul, and he ventured to lead them to Villa Rica, where the governor of Minas then lived. Notwithstanding the law, he presented the diamond to the governor, and asked him to test its worth. This was quickly done, and the priest was commended. ' I want you to pardon these men,' said the priest. The pardon was granted. The King of Portugal confirmed the pardon granted by the governor."

The discovery of the value of india-rubber followed the diamond excitement, which latter lasted from 1728 to the close of the last century. The india-rubber groves of the Amazon became the source of a commerce more rich than the diamond-fields. For a century the uses of rubber have multiplied, and the rubber-tree has come to be one of the most beneficent products of the world.

Brazil is a prolific land. Her territory could sustain an immense population. Her natural products are inexhaustibly rich. She has diamond-fields indeed, but her soil and her forests are the sources of her prosperity. The mighty arms of the Amazon will forever gather her wealth to feed the world.

Brazil faces the future with such abundant and undeveloped resources that her progress in the twentieth century is likely to be phenomenal. We cannot wonder that Dom Pedro II. left the beautiful land with regret, and that the empress, when compelled to live in other lands, languished and died.

CHAPTER XXII

THE CONGRESS OF THE REPUBLICS AT LIMA, 1847—THE PROGRESS OF THE WEST COAST—BALMACEDA—GUIANA—THE PAN-AMERICAN CONGRESS, 1889-90

THE Panama Congress, although a partial failure, suggested the destiny of the Pan-American republics. The spirit of that congress was unity, peace and progress. "*Adelante!*" (" Onward!") became the order of the march of the South American states. The genius of Bolivar caused the new republics of the Sun to see their future possibilities and opportunities. The lands of the palm, of the Cordilleras and the Southern Cross could become new empires of the world. The peoples of the outworn tyrannies of the East, the earliest nations of the world, would come to them.

Five years after the Panama Congress Mexico sent out an invitation to the Southern republics to meet in a new congress at Tacubaya, Panama or Lima. The plan failed. In 1838 Mexico renewed the invitation. The favorite scheme of Bolivar had taken hold of the hearts of the new republics. The Liberator, though dead, lived in this spirit that he had inspired. Mexico made this second appeal with these words, than which nothing could be more noble : " We desire the union and alliance of the new states for the purposes of defense against foreign invasion, and the acceptance of friendly mediation of the neutral states for the settlement of all disagreements and disputes, of whatever nature, which might happen to arise between sister republics." The plan again did not take form, though the spirit of it lived and grew.

In 1840 New Granada joined with Mexico in inviting the South American republics to a conference, and suggested the historic Tacubaya as the place of the meeting. The suggestion did not meet with a favorable response.

In 1847 the republics of Bolivia, Chili, Ecuador, New Granada and Peru decided to hold a congress at Lima. They invited the other republics to join them. The invitation was also extended to the United States. The congress met at Lima, on December 11, 1847. It held nineteen meetings. The result was a treaty of confederation. The United States was then at war with Mexico, so these republics did not take part in the conference. At this congress there was brought forward a secret plan of Spain to form Cuba, Porto Rico and Spanish Santo Domingo into a monarchy for the purpose of reconquering New Granada and the ancient possessions of the Peninsula on the Spanish Main.

The expedition of General Walker in Nicaragua caused a new alarm, and another continental congress assembled, this time at the city of Santiago, on September 15, 1856. Here again the great plans of Bolivar for the purpose of continental unity and peace were discussed.

In 1864 the government of Peru issued an invitation to all of the Spanish republics to meet in congress at Lima. This congress met there on November 14, 1864. It was opened by the celebration of the birth of Simon Bolivar.

In 1881 Colombia issued a call for a congress to be held at Panama. This was to bring together the representatives of all the republics of the western world. The United States was invited to be represented. The purpose of this congress was to unite the republics of America against foreign dictation and to promote among them fraternity, progress and peace. The Argentine Republic, in accepting the invitation, said: "Peace is certainly most necessary for Spanish America. Europe no longer entertains thoughts of conquests or recoveries. These were abandoned in view of our unconquerable attitude." The proposed congress was never held, owing to the disturbed relations into which the republics were unexpectedly thrown.

But the soul of the movement lived, and another congress was convoked, to meet at the city of Washington, in 1882. The call for this congress came from our own land. Mr. Blaine, from the Department of State, issued a manifesto in which are the following notable words: "For some years a growing disposition has been manifested by certain states in Central and South America to refer disputes affecting grave questions of international relationship and boundaries to arbitration rather than the sword. It has been on several occasions a source of profound satisfaction to the government of the United States to see that this country is in a measure looked up to by all the American powers as their friend and mediator. The existence of this growing tendency convinces the President that the time is ripe for a proposal that shall enlist the good will and active coöperation of all the states of the western hemisphere, both north and south, in the interests of humanity, for the common weal of the nations." Internal dissensions in South America caused this proposed congress to be postponed till 1890.

Thus the principles of Bolivar grew. The Panama

Congress, one of the first ever held in the interests of humanity, did not fail. It was to find expression in the International American Conference of 1889-90.

Before considering the proceedings of this congress I shall describe the growth of independence among the South American republics.

The word "Chili," spelled also "Chile," is probably derived from the Quichua *chiri*, cold. The plains and gardens of the flowery empire lie under the snow. Aconcagua rises into the silence of eternal wonder, 22,427 feet high. The historic mountain of Maypo is 17,664 feet high. The Uspallata Pass, from Argentina to Chili, is 13,125 feet above the sea-level. Chili is a land of fruit, of pastures and waving palms, but one looks from the vegetation to mountain-crowns of snow. These mountains begin in the wild Patagonian seas and sink at Darien, to rise again in the Central American Andes.

The Inca Yupanqui led his army across the desert of Atacama to conquer a part of Chili. The Peruvian dominion of Chili ceased with the death of Atahualpa, 1533. In the latter days of the two republics Chili has come to dominate over the rich deserts of Peru.

After the war of liberation of Chili under San Martin, Chili became the seat of the naval operations on the west coast, under the lead of Lord Cochrane. The national government began in 1817, under the dictatorship of General O'Higgins, who held the office until 1823. He was succeeded by General Freire. The government by dictators lasted until 1828, when, under the administration of General Pinto, a constitution was promulgated. On May 25, 1833, the present constitution was promulgated. Under it a succession of presidents has governed. These presidents have for the most part been able men, with noble aspirations for the progress of the country. The Araucanian race to-day is not as large as the European and North American colonists.

Chili has a present area of 300,000 square miles. The population, after the estimate of 1889, is 3,413,576. The foreign population is something more than 80,000, of whom about 35,000 are Peruvians. The Germans number about 7000, and the English upward of 5000. The foreign colonization south of Concepcion is almost wholly German.

By the constitution of 1833, the sovereign power is declared to lie in the people. The legislative power is administered by a national Congress consisting of a Chamber of Deputies and a Senate. The Chamber of Deputies is composed of one hundred or more members. They hold office for three years. The President is the executive, and the supreme head of the nation. He is elected for five years, after which he may not be reelected until the expiration of another five years.

The present constitution of Chili, framed under the influence of Portales in 1833, may be considered to be the beginning of the new progress. The railway system has aided this progress, as the building of roads had done in no other land. Religious toleration followed, and education came in through this open door. The population increased as the world began to see the opulent valleys of the mountains whose eternal whiteness crowns the western world. Artisans and agriculturists, the true army of the future, came. In 1843 Chili had 1,083,801 inhabitants; in 1854, 1,819,222; in 1865, 2,075,971. Then the mining industry began, and the unemployed world flocked toward the long shining strip of land on the calm Pacific. Valparaiso became a city of 75,000, Santiago of 175,000 inhabitants. At the beginning of the year 1879, Chili had more than 1000 miles of railroads, and 15,370 miles of

CHILLAN VOLCANO, IN THE ANDES IN CHILI. HEIGHT 9446 FEET.

carriage-roads. Her rainless territory, the nitrate region, became a great source of wealth. This district, now the principal source of supply of artificial plant-food, has a littoral line of some 400 miles. The money value of this region cannot be computed. The world gets its supply of nitrate and iodines there.

In 1884 Albert G. Browne, Jr., opened an address before the American Geographical Society with the following words: "I will apply the evening you have invited me to occupy to some considerations of the growing power of the republic of Chili, on the Pacific. There are sound reasons why the United States should be the foremost of American powers whose territory borders on the Pacific, and the fact that we are suffering ourselves to be surpassed there in political influence, in commerce and naval strength, by a country whose population is less than a twentieth of ours merits more notice than is accorded to it by Congress or the public."

The silver ores in the province of Atacama were discovered by a shepherd as late as 1832. The wonderful events on the desert of Tarapacá are of later date. Valparaiso was until a half-century ago little more than a calling-place for ships going around the Horn.

The formation of Alta Peru, the Switzerland of America, into the republic of Bolivia was a menace to the power of Chili. The latter republic attempted to prevent the union of the republics.

José Manuel Balmaceda was born in Santiago in 1842. He came of an ancient and honorable Castilian family. He was educated for the priesthood. He had an ardent nature, and quick sympathies with whatever tended to the advancement of mankind. He joined the Reform Club, and became a leader of progressive Chilians. He sought to liberalize the Chilian constitution. He was elected to Congress at the early age of twenty-eight. He became the natural leader of the Liberal party, and young Chili saw in him a rising star. He instituted reforms. He favored universal education. He rose to be a senator, a minister of the interior, and a foreign minister. In 1886 he was elected President of Chili by an overwhelming majority. He was inaugurated amid the plaudits of the people. At that period he seemed to be their idol. Under his influence Chili advanced; public education was stimulated; improvements multiplied. Those were prosperous days. The Conservative party in Chili was from the first opposed to his progressive ideas and enterprises. Its opposition grew. The old capitalists thought their investments were in danger. The Conservatives became a controlling power again. The heart of Balmaceda was in the progress of his reforms, and he at first sought to retain power by indirection. He caused himself to be made Dictator. His ungoverned will was his ruin. The Conservatives organized a powerful movement against his usurped authority, and defeated him in a battle near Valparaiso. After the battle Balmaceda vanished. It was suspected that he had found refuge on an American ship. He was discovered in the Argentine consulate. Rather than be captured, he ended his short life by a pistol-shot on December 19, 1891.

Peru, the land of the ideal government of the Incas, that gave to the world the cinchona, the potato, and a wealth of new varieties of flowers, that enriched Spain with gold, and the worn-out lands of many countries with plant-food, has been subject to many misfortunes in the last half of the century; but she has made progress in education and the enterprises of industrial art.

·The presidents and chiefs of Peru from 1829 to 1844 were as follows: Agustin Gamarra (from 1829 to 1833);

Luis José Orbegoso (1833-35); Felipe Santiago de Salaverry (1835-36); Andres Santa Cruz (1836-39); Agustin Gamarra (1839-41); Manuel Mendenez (1841-44). In 1845 General Ramon Cortilla was elected President of Peru, and there followed a long period of peace and prosperity.

We have spoken of the flag of the Army of the Andes, the banner of the Sun. The flags of the patriotic movements were usually adopted before the declarations of independence. They sprang into life spontaneously.

The flag of Chili had an American origin. In 1812 the first printing-press was established in Chili, and on February 13 appeared the first newspaper there, called " La Aurora de Chili," edited by a priest. With the printing-press from the United States came Mr. Poinsett, a patriotic consular agent, whose heart beat in sympathy with the new ideas of the country. This man celebrated the Independence Day of his own country, at the consulate on July 4, 1812. He unfurled the Stars and Stripes. With it he launched in the air a new flag of three colors with one star in its corner. The one star stood for Chili. The three colors became the cockade of the patriots. On September 30 the tricolor and one star was adopted as the national ensign. When the Republic of Colombia was decreed in the eventful year of 1819, the tricolored flag raised by Miranda in 1806 became the national emblem. This was the flag of yellow, blue and red, the national ensign that Venezuela had borne from the days of Miranda, in her struggles for liberty. The flag of the Sun that San Martin had borne over the Andes, with colors of white and scarlet, was made on October 24, 1820, the escutcheon of the republic of Peru. The figure was that of the sun rising over the mountains, on a tranquil sea.

The republics of South America began their independent existences as follows: The first declaration of independence in South America was made by the Congress that convened in Caracas on March 2, 1811, one of the deputies to which was Miranda. This man urged an immediate declaration of the independence of Venezuela, and carried the measure of July 5. On the same day the flag of yellow, red and blue was adopted as the national ensign. The province of Cartagena followed, declaring herself an independent state on November 11, 1811. Argentina made her declaration of independence at the Congress at Tucuman on July 9, 1816, under the influence of San Martin. The general of the Army of the Andes believed in the independence of the country from Spain, and in the rule of the representatives of the people; but at one period of his life he seems to have looked favorably upon the English form of government, a constitutional monarchy. He was a conservative man. He weighed everything, and desired to found things that would last. His conservatism brought him under the criticism of those of more advanced and radical views. He was, however, more concerned with the gaining of the independence of the country than deciding upon forms of government.

Bolivar gradually came to believe in the unity of the republics of South America under the rulers elected by the people. He at one time held the views afterward advocated in some measure by the Pan-American Congress, or International American Conference, of 1890. The Chilian people had voted for independence on November 17, 1817. On January 20, 1818, the independence was proclaimed at Talca, and afterward at Santiago by a solemn assembly in the great square. Among the first who swore on the latter occasion to support the independence were San Martin and the bishop of Santiago. The independence of Peru was proclaimed with an inspiring ceremony, in the great square at Lima, on July 28, 1821. San Martin, who had been present at the birth of two republics, here displayed the new flag of Peru amid the thunders of cannon and the vivas of the people. The triumphal procession of liberty passed through the streets of rainless Lima amid showers of flowers. We have already spoken of the declaration of independence of Brazil. Several provinces declared themselves independent, as Panama and Maracaybo, but later reunited with the republics of which they naturally formed a part. The year 1830 found South America practically free and independent, but in the unsettled state that for a time generally follows a radical change of government. The independent republic of Venezuela, New Granada, and a part of the country now known as Ecuador was proclaimed on May 9, 1821. The constitution of Bolivia was formed in 1826, and in 1830 Simon Bolivar retired from active life, being voted the " first and best citizen of Colombia," and allotted a pension of three hundred thousand dollars a year. From that date the republics of the South were, as a rule, left to work out their own political destiny.

South America was now a land of republics, except a territory between the Amazon and the Orinoco, called Guiana. This remained a foreign possession, subject to England, France and Holland, and was divided into three parts, English Guiana, French Guiana, Dutch Guiana.

British Guiana abounds in forests of gigantic trees; in beautiful flowers, among them the *Victoria regia;* and in wonderful orchids. It produces sugar, coffee, cotton, cocoa, vanilla, cinnamon and tobacco. It is the home of the jaguar, puma, tapir and peccary. The boundary of the territory west of the Essequibo River, between British and Dutch Guiana, became a matter of dispute after the discovery of gold within the mid-river region. A commission was appointed to settle the question. The population of British Guiana in 1891 was over 288,000.

Dutch Guiana (Surinam) lies between British and French Guiana, and has like productions. Its area is 46,060 square miles. Its population in 1890 was 56,873.

French Guiana is the smallest of the three divisions. It is a fertile country, abundantly watered, a land of coffee, cane, cocoa, indigo and spices. It had a population in 1891 of 25,796. Cayenne is the seat of government.

The action of the Congress of the United States which preceded the decision to call the International American Conference of 1889-90 was briefly as follows: On January 21, 1880, the Hon. David Davis of Illinois, at the request of Hinton Rowan Helper, the publicist, introduced into Congress a bill for the encouragement of closer commercial relations between the United States and the republics of Mexico, Central America, the empire of Brazil, and the several republics of South America. The bill called for a conference in regard to the building of an international railway "running from the northern to the southern termini of the eastern slope of the great mountain-chain, which would open that vast interior region to our manufactures and commerce."

On April 24, 1882, Senator Morgan of Alabama introduced a bill into the Senate, a sentence of which reads thus: "That the President of the United States be, and he hereby is, requested to invite all the governments of the said [Latin-American] republics and the empire of Brazil to send delegates to meet in the city of Washington." Adverse action followed.

In 1884 the Senate took favorable action on a similar bill, which was followed by like action of the House of Representatives. This latter bill was accompanied by a report which clearly set forth the great opportunity of the United States in South America.

As a result of this legislation a South American commission was authorized. On January 26, 1886, a joint resolution was introduced into the House of Representatives to promote arbitration among the republics of America.

The International American Conference assembled at Washington, October 2, 1889. The government of the United States had appropriated seventy-five thousand dollars for the expenses of this conference. The proceedings were published, at public expense, in the English, Spanish and Portuguese languages. Later an additional appropriation of fifty thousand dollars was made. Eighteen invitations were extended to as many different states. While here the visiting delegates made a tour to the commercial and manufacturing cities of the country. A special train conveyed the party through the leading states, a distance of nearly six thousand miles. The party returned to Washington on November 13, after an absence of forty-two days.

The business of the conference began on November 18. The Hon. James G. Blaine was elected president. After organization the congress adjourned until January 2, 1890.

At this congress reciprocity and the commercial relations of the Latin-American republics were discussed. Señor Quintana said: "The real constitution of the famous Council of the Amphictyons, from which the constitution of the United States was taken, was nothing more than a great council of arbitrators between the towns of Greece." Said Señor Zelaya: "Civilization, humanity and Christianity cry out for this remedy of arbitration for all conflicts in the future which may arise between American nations."

The three principal topics that engaged the attention of this assembly were the international railroad, the Nicaragua Canal, and arbitration.

In a letter to the President, May 12, 1890, Mr. Blaine submitted a plan "for a preliminary survey for a railway line to connect the commercial cities of the American hemisphere." He wrote: "Under the generous and progressive policy of President Diaz the railways of Mexico have been extended southward as well as northward, and toward the two oceans. The development of the Argentine system has been equally rapid. In the other republics similar enterprise has been shown. Each has its local lines of railway, and to connect them all and furnish the people of the southern continent the means of convenient and comfortable intercourse with their neighbors north of the isthmus is an undertaking worthy of the encouragement and coöperation of this government. In no other way could the government and the people of the United States contribute so much to the development and prosperity of our sister republics, and at the same time to the expansion of our commerce."

President Harrison, in submitting the report, May 19, 1890, said: "But it should not be forgotten that it is possible to travel by land from Washington to the southernmost capital of South America, and that the opening of railroad communication with these friendly states will give to them and to us facilities for intercourse and the exchanges of trade that are of special value. The work contemplated is vast, but entirely practicable."

The moral influence and result of the congress centered in arbitration. In 1890, after long discussion, the delegates adopted a declaration which was a prophecy of the future. The declaration began as follows:

"The delegates from North, Central and South America, in conference assembled, believing that war is the most cruel, the most fruitless and the most dangerous expedient for the settlement of international difficulties;

"Do solemnly recommend to all the governments by which they are accredited that they conclude a uniform treaty of arbitration in the articles following:

"ARTICLE I. The republics of North, Central and South America hereby adopt *arbitration* as a principle of American international law for the settlement of the differences, disputes or controversies that may arise between two or more of them."

The other articles recommend the establishment of a high court of nations to which all controversies shall be submitted for final decision.

The International American Conference is the prophetic vision of the twentieth century. All that it saw is likely to become a part of the history of the next generation.

CHAPTER XXIII

THE CHILI-PERUVIAN WAR—THE AFFAIR OF THE "ESMERALDA," AND THE HEROISM OF ARTURO PRATT—THE BATTLES OF TARAPACÁ AND MIRAFLORES.

NORTHERN Chili is a long avenue of coast-land between a high chain of the Andes and the Pacific Ocean. It originally formed a part of the empire of the Incas.

Fifty-four years elapsed between the battle of Ayacucho and the Chili-Peruvian War. The cause of the latter was a dispute as to the boundary of this narrow strip of arid land between the Andes and the sea. The land is a white, rainless desert, known as the desert of Tarapacá. South of it is the desert of Atacama. At the time of the independence of Peru nothing on earth could have been deemed of less value than these two deserts. It is said that there were Inca villages on Tarapacá, and that to lose one's way in finding them was death, for the winds obliterated every track in the white, blinding sands, and there was no tree or object of any kind to guide the traveler. In the course of time it was discovered that these deserts, so barren and seemingly valueless, abounded in wealth. There were rich silver-mines in Atacama—in fact, among the richest in the world. Tarapacá was found to abound in plant-food more valuable than the fertilizing products of the guano islands. It was a great chemical laboratory

A PARTY OF INDIANS CONDUCTING A BAGGAGE-TRAIN OF LLAMAS, CHILI.

of nitrate of soda. The impoverished lands of Europe needed the riches of this forbidding desert. Colonel North, of English fame, saw his great opportunity there.

If this almost boundless wealth had not been brought to light, there probably would have been no Chili-Peruvian war. The boundary would not have been a matter of moment. When the riches of the desert of Tarapacá became known, Chilian enterprise began to find a field there. Chilian laborers immigrated there, and planted industries there on soil claimed by Bolivia, which had been Peru. When the South American republics became independent of Spain, their boundaries followed those of the viceroyalties. On this principle, Peru, or Bolivian Peru, claimed the province of Tarapacá, which had been occupied by immigrating Chilians. The province extended from the southern limit of Peru to the northern limit of Chili. The Peruvian land was that of the province of Tarapacá. Hence Peru and Bolivia both claimed the deserts of Tarapacá and Atacama, the resources of which the enterprising Chilians developed. The territory was Bolivian Atacama, and Peruvian Tarapacá, of Chilian occupation.

In 1870 the rich silver-mines of Caracoles were discovered. The Bolivian government, in consideration of ten thousand dollars, granted a concession to a company to work the nitrate deposits and to open a road to the silver-mines. The company built a railroad and employed largely Chilian labor. Under this arrangement the deserts came under Chilian influence. Bolivia claimed the right to tax such enterprises, which Chili denied.

A defensive treaty was formed between Peru and Bolivia to protect their hereditary boundaries, which Chili had sought to overthrow. Chili regarded this treaty as detrimental to her interests, and a cause of war. She declared war upon Peru on April 5, 1879.

Chili had been preparing for war on the land and the sea. She had a strong navy. The Chilian army was well drilled and equipped. Its artillery was especially effective. It was armed with Krupp and Gatling guns. The Peruvian navy consisted chiefly of four ships.

The war began February 14, 1879, when the Chilians seized the Bolivian port of Antofagasta. They next occupied the station of the rich silver-mines of Caracoles. General Daza, President of Bolivia, declared war on Chili March 1, 1879. General Brado, President of Peru, took command of the Peruvian army. It was a war for the riches of the deserts.

A Peruvian squadron, consisting of two ships, the *Huascar*, commanded by Captain Grau, the *Independencia*, by Captain Moore, and some transports, sailed south. At the same time the Chilian admiral Williams made a reconnaissance to the north. A very heroic and dramatic event grew out of this situation, one that has been celebrated in song. It is known as the "affair of the *Esmeralda*." The blockade of Iquique by the Chilians was sustained by two vessels, the *Esmeralda* and the *Covadonga*. Commander Grau landed the President of Peru at Arica, and then proceeded to Iquique with the *Huascar* and *Independencia*. He sighted the Chilian blockading corvette *Esmeralda*, commanded by Captain Arthur Pratt (Arturo Pratt), and the gunboat *Covadonga*, commanded by Captain Condell. Grau at once attacked the *Esmeralda*. Captain Pratt saw the danger of the small corvette, and attempted to draw the war-ship *Huascar* into shoal water. At the critical moment, one of the boilers of the corvette became disabled, reducing the speed of the craft. Pratt put the crew to the guns of his little craft, and commenced action against the man-of-war. It required heroism to do this, but honor demanded it should be done. The little *Es-*

meralda poured a broadside into the *Huascar*, and for two hours a cannonade was kept up between the two vessels. Captain Grau now made use of the ram. He struck the *Esmeralda* at her port side. The two vessels came in contact. As they did so, Captain Pratt, sword in hand, leaped on board the *Huascar*, calling to his officers and men, "Follow me!" The two vessels suddenly became disengaged, and only one man was able to follow the captain's command. Pratt rushed along the deck of the *Huascar* as though he himself had captured the ship. Captain Grau must have admired his heroism. "Surrender, captain," he cried; "we wish to save the life of a hero!" Pratt began to wage war on the deck, and was killed sword in hand. Captain Grau again used the ram against the *Esmeralda*, when the men of that ship once more tried to obey the command of their fallen commander by leaping on board of the *Huascar*. The effort was in vain. The *Esmeralda* went down. Out of a crew of two hundred men only fifty were saved.

In the course of the war the Peruvian navy was destroyed, and Admiral Grau died in defending the *Huascar*.

The war on the land now centered at Tarapacá. The province of Tarapacá contains nitrate of soda sufficient to fertilize the gardens and fields of Europe for centuries to come. The refining-works of this immense industry are called *oficinas*. In these are employed thousands of men from nearly all lands. The ports of the deserts are full of vessels, and look like towns on the sea.

The invading Chilian army numbered some ten thousand men, and was disembarked at Pisagua, which was bravely defended. A battle was fought at San Francisco, and the Peruvians retreated to the town of Tarapacá. The Chilian general planned to surprise and destroy the Peruvian army there. On the morning of the 27th of November the Peruvian troops were resting under willow-trees in the gorge that opens from the stupendous peaks of the Andes, as high as Mont Blanc. The crest of the ravine, in whose heart a mountain stream was lost, seemed to wall the purple sky. A muleteer galloped up to the encampment and announced: "The enemy is on the height!" A sub-lieutenant, a mere lad, came running into the camp in great excitement, saying: "The enemy is surrounding us!" An officer patted him on the back doubtfully, but looking up beheld columns of men marching high above him, as on the sky-line. The Peruvian commander ordered his troops to march up the sides of the ravine, which were precipitous. The march was like scaling a wall. The Chilians had gathered above them in force, and had planted on the heights their Krupp guns. The Peruvians reached the crest. Their force consisted in part of Inca Indians. They charged. One by one their leaders fell; but the mountaineers captured the Krupp guns, and compelled the invaders to fall back. The best blood of Peru flowed like water. The Chilians were defeated, and retreated. In the battle twelve hundred and twenty men fell.

But though the Peruvians gained the victory at Tarapacá, the advantage of the war was still with the powerful army of the Chilians. The Peruvians retreated to Arica. Nicolas de Pierola became the supreme chief of Peru. General Campero was President of Bolivia, Arica and Callao were blockaded by the Chilians, and the year 1880 brought defeat to Peru and Bolivia. The Chilians had destroyed the Peruvian fleet, and had secured the nitrate province. The allied army was intrenched at Tacna, a town on the Pacific side of the Andes, in a fertile plain among the hills. It had a population of about twenty-four thousand. The allied army consisted of fourteen thousand. A bloody battle was fought at Tacna. The allies were defeated. Arica fell before the conquering Chilians. The way was now open to the Chilians for the conquest of Peru.

In October, 1880, the United States offered her services as mediator. The offer was declined. The conquerors now set their faces toward Lima. They landed south of Lima. A battle was fought at Chorrillos, a beautiful town near Lima, and a favorite pleasure-resort. In this battle more than two thousand Chilians were killed and wounded. The Peruvians defended their capital bravely. They made, as it were, a human wall against the invaders. Four thousand lay dead on the field.

There is a beautiful resort near Lima, with which it is now connected by railway, called Miraflores. It is overlooked by the Andes, and it overlooks the sea. The land is full of orchards and flowers. Inca ruins are there. Villas of the nobility make the spot an earthly paradise. San Martin loved the place, as have statesmen, scientists, poets for centuries. An armistice was sought by the foreign ministers, who had taken refuge at Miraflores. The conference was ended by a cannonade.

At Miraflores the Peruvians made their last stand. They were defeated after a great slaughter, losing six thousand in killed and three thousand in wounded. Lima fell and was sacked, and the Chilians were enabled to dictate their own boundaries of the desert of Tarapacá.

CHAPTER XXIV

HISTORY OF LIBERTY IN CUBA—THE CUBAN HEROES—
THE DESTRUCTION OF THE "MAINE"

COLUMBUS discovered the island of Cuba on the morning of October 28, 1492. He declared the land to be the most beautiful that eyes had ever beheld. He named it Juana, from the son of the royal family. Poets later called it the "Isle of June." There was a tall ceiba- or cottonwood-tree near the place where he landed. Here he caused a wooden cross to be raised, and mass to be celebrated. A temple stands on the place now as a memorial of the event. Columbus believed that Cuba was a continent, a part of the enchanted land of far Cathay, whose wonders and glories had been described by Marco Polo. He sailed along the coast, in view of the majestic forests and mountains. He visited again those beautiful shores on his fourth voyage to America. On his death his body was buried in the cathedral near the place where he had first heard mass under the cottonwood-tree. His tomb may be seen in the simple but ancient walls.

The island was conquered by Velasquez in 1511. The conqueror divided the land and the natives among his followers. He founded many towns, among them Havana and Santiago de Cuba, the two mentioned about the year 1515.

The simple inhabitants began to disappear. Hernando Cortez became a governor of Cuba in 1537, under Velasquez. He sent the suffering Indians to the copper-mines. The Indians were killed by the forced service. From this island he went forth to the conquest of Mexico.

Negro slaves were introduced to take the places of the perishing Indians. Great plantations were cultivated, and the island was made to yield rich revenues to the Spanish crown. The trade of the sea was held in slavery, and as a consequence filibusters filled the coasts.

On June 6, 1762, at the period when Charles III. of Spain was at war with Great Britain, there appeared off Havana an English squadron of thirty-two ships and frigates, with two hundred or more transport-vessels. The armament was the largest that had ever appeared in America. It was commanded by the Duke of Albemarle. The English landed a force of twelve thousand men. The Spanish garrison consisted of only twenty-seven hundred men, but received the aid of volunteers. The invading army occupied the heights near Morro Castle and the city, and opened fire upon both of the latter places, but was itself exposed to a fire from the Spanish on the Cabanas. The Spaniards blocked the entrance to the harbor by sinking two vessels in the channel. This was done to protect the Spanish vessels inside of the harbor. The precautionary defense proved a snare, for it shut the Spanish in while it shut the English out. This gave the English the advantage of concentrating their force on a land attack. The little garrison defended itself long and bravely. It finally surrendered, and was permitted to march out with the honors of war. The English held the fortifications until the peace of Paris in 1763. The "Pearl of the Antilles" was then restored to Spain, and for many years the date of the restitution was observed as a festival.

From this period the island grew in wealth, and its viceregal court in splendor. Slavery increased. The plantations were among the richest harvest-fields of the world.

The creoles began to hear of the struggles for liberty in the provinces of the Andes, but liberty slumbered in Cuba. In 1823 a society, "Soles de Bolivar," made a movement for the freedom of the island. In 1829 the secret society of the Black Eagle made a similar attempt. It was unsuccessful.

In 1844 the condition of the slaves had become intolerable. They planned an insurrection for freedom. They struck and were stricken down.

The expedition of Narcio Lopez, a Spaniard, who sailed from the Southern ports of the United States with a few hundred men, has already been briefly pictured. Lopez was the Miranda of Cuban freedom. His expedition was one of those failures that lead to success, that present ideals that do not fade. His heroic and tragic death was never forgotten.

In 1868 there was a rising of patriots against the tyranny of Spain, led by men of intelligence, character and purest patriotism. These heroes threw to the breeze the banner of liberty. Puerto Principe, another patriotic city of a patriotic province, rose in arms. The rebels were poorly armed, but were inspired by the righteousness of their cause. Fifty thousand Spanish troops and seventy thousand volunteers confronted them. The mountains and marshes were their defenses. They continued the struggle until diplomacy did what force of arms could not do, namely, secured the liberation of the slaves.

Again liberty slumbered, but not as before; it dreamed now. The hope of independence was left. It lived and grew. Spain had promised the patriots justice, but had pursued her old policy. Spanish officers, bent only on making fortunes, filled the places of government. Three fourths of the office-holders were Spaniards. They gorged themselves with the products of others' toil. The system of taxation became unbearable. Human rights were ignored, and the blood of cruelty flowed as of old.

In the winter of 1895 local outbreaks indicated the beginning of another war for liberty. Maximo Gomez, a patriot leader, and the two Maceos were again in the saddle. Marshal Campos attempted to subdue the patriots, but in vain. He was succeeded by Weyler, another Boves. Weyler began a campaign of the trocha. He built a line of fortifications across the island. He compelled the non-combatants, the reconcentrados, as they have come to be called, to be gathered together in fortified cities, and a line to be drawn around them, to pass beyond which was death. Here they were left to starve. Two hundred thousand people, and, according to some writers, a larger number, were, under this policy of concentration, starved to death. The land was covered with heaps of dead bodies.

Excessive cruelty defeats itself. The call of the Cubans to humanity, for help, fell at first upon unbelieving ears, then upon startled ears. Finally it touched the heart. Spain seems to have seen the coming judgment. She withdrew Weyler from Cuba. General Blanco took up the cause of the Peninsula with a more humane heart. It was too late for military success. Of over two hundred thousand soldiers sent by Spain to Cuba more than one half died or returned disabled.

Spain, now seeing the necessity for a change of policy toward the wronged island of Columbus, proposed to the Cubans autonomy, or local self-government. Such a government was formed, but without power.

In the former struggle for liberty a republic had been

formed, with Señor Céspedes as President. A new Cuban republic was proclaimed by the patriots of 1895.

The rise and progress of the new republic may best be pictured by narratives of the lives of its leading heroes.

Maximo Gomez, the general-in-chief of the insurgent forces, was born in 1823. He entered the last struggle for Cuban independence when past seventy years of age. "He is a grim, resolute, honest, conscientious, quizzical old veteran," wrote Consul-General Lee in 1898, "now seventy-five years old, who has thoroughly understood the tactics necessary to employ in order to waste the resources of his enemy." He served as a lieutenant in the Spanish cavalry in the revolution of Santo Domingo. The cause of the patriots of Santo Domingo seems to have set him to thinking. He became a republican, and joined the Cubans in their long struggle for liberty. He was one of the heroes of the ten years' war.

His policy in the final Cuban war was to prevent Cuba from affording resources for the Spanish army. He forbade the planters to grind cane, in order to deprive the Spaniards of their revenue. The cane-fields went up in smoke wherever he marched. He believed in sacrificing everything to the cause of liberty, and was fond of relating that the semi-civilized Indians threw their gold into the rivers on the approach of the Spaniards.

He had some sterling qualities. He never allowed the wounded to be deserted. "The wounded are sacred," he said. To him liberty was more than life. Flint relates that Gomez once met a farmer in the fields, and asked him why he was at work. Gomez probably received the answer that the farmer worked to support his family. "To support your family!" Gomez responded. "It were better if you fed them on the roots of the forest or left them to starve, as my men have left their wives and children and parents to starve for the sake of the fatherland. Do you know that you make the land richer for Spain?"

Such was the spirit of Gomez. His faith in the future was perfect; his views were unyielding. Flint reports one of Gomez's officers as saying: "The life of one entire generation is not too great a sacrifice to the prosperity of countless generations to come." Such was Gomez's opinion. War has seldom found so old a hero who was so young in heart, and so full of thought for the welfare of man and of the future that he would never see.

Masso, President of the Cuban republic, was a man of uncompromising integrity and of sublime faith in the success of the patriot cause. In the September elections of 1897 Domingo Mendez Capote had been chosen President. The military chiefs questioned whether or not Capote had the strength of character to resist overtures of peace from Spain in case of great disasters. In the ten years' war the patriots had lost by diplomacy and the acceptance of false promises what they had a right to demand as the results of their valor. They wished to avert a similar fate now. Hence they needed a man of iron. Such a man was Masso. A new election was ordered, and Masso, then about sixty-two years of age, was elected President.

"Let no one enter our camps with any offer of terms of peace from Spain," was the voice of insurgent chiefs. "Independence or death is our unalterable purpose!" Masso was a man of this mold. He was among the first of the Cuban commanders in the ten years' war, and he remained in the field to the last. When the agreement of peace was made he distrusted the Spanish pledges of reform. For this reason he was imprisoned in Morro Castle and deported to Spain. In 1880 he returned to his ruined estates, and became successful as a sugar-planter. In 1895, on his own estates, near Manzanillo, he proclaimed the independence of Cuba. He took command of the patriot volunteers there until the arrival of Maximo Gomez and José Marti, who organized the war of liberation. Though firm in his conviction of right, Masso was just and liberal. In a proclamation issued February 24, 1895, entitled "To the Spaniards," he said: "While you remain friendly to us we will consider you and treat you as Cubans, and shall respect your lives, your families and property. What we want is independence for all, a country and liberty!"

It was Marti who organized the new revolution, which may be said to have begun on February 24, 1895. Marti was born of Spanish parents. Liberty was his native air. Early in life he became the friend of political prisoners. He knew the spirit of the old monarchy well, its politicians and bureaucrats who aimed only at robbery. He was exiled from Cuba to Spain. He escaped from Spain to the United States in 1879, about the time that General Calixto Garcia, a Cuban patriot, arrived in New York. The two planned an expedition to Cuba in aid of the cause of independence. Their purpose was delayed, but each became a leader in the movement of 1895.

Near the end of 1896, at the head of a charge *al machete*, there fell a mulatto general, Antonio Maceo. On his body were twenty-three wounds, received in many engagements. He had been one of the heroes of the ten years' war. This man belonged to a family of heroes of the patriotic province Santiago de Cuba, a province of the Southern seas.

The family tradition of the Maceos of Sanitago is a very noble one. The elder Maceo had ten sons. He saw the oppression of the creoles and his own race. He dedicated these ten sons to the cause of liberty. Five of these sons fell in the ten years' war. Of these ten sons two became famous, and did deeds that merit a place among heroes. They broke through the trocha, and made an open way from Santiago to Pinar del Rio. They were José Maceo and Antonio Maceo, both of whom came to tragic ends under the most heroic and thrilling circumstances. The death of Antonio Maceo, the greatest of this family of born patriots, is worthy of commemoration in art and song. In the beginning of the winter of 1896 he resolved to lead his cavalry into the province of Havana, to threaten the port city, and to give the Spaniards a surprise at their own doors.

He prepared for this daring and hazardous exploit with consummate generalship. He organized the patriot army of the mountains of Pinar del Rio, and put it under General Rius Rivera, with whom he had fought in the ten years' war. He made strong the prefectures of the interior by provisions which would last for months. Arms and ammunition had been landed, and the Cuban army was in a condition for aggressive work. On December 4, 1896, General Antonio Maceo crossed the trocha, and entered the province of Havana with about fifty raiders, among them his chief of staff and other most ardent and brave officers. Weyler was searching for him in the mountains of Pinar del Rio. Antonio's purpose was to destroy the suburbs of Havana, and then to join General Maximo Gomez, who was marching from the west, and to arrange with him a plan for the winter campaign. It was a dashing raid on December 5, 1896. The raiders crossed the trocha, and a few days later they were joined by a force of some three or four hundred men. They were opposed by a Spanish force under Major Cirujeda, an officer notorious for his cruelty. Maceo arranged his force to strike the enemy, and said: "This goes well. *Al machete!*" He obeyed his own order, and led the way on his fiery war-horse. The patriots were met by a discharge of Spanish rifles. A bullet pierced the head of Maceo; another entered his body. He reeled back and fell dead among his faithful officers, who were falling around him. The greatest of the heroes of the Maceo family was no more. On seeing their leader fall, the Cubans retreated, and the body of the dead Maceo fell into the hands of the Spaniards. The latter robbed it, and, tying it to the tail of a horse, dragged it about. They finally left it on the field and returned to their camp. The command of the Cubans now devolved in part upon General Miro. This officer recovered the corpse of Maceo, and called his officers around him. "We must bury our leader in a secret place, and you must take an oath never to reveal the spot until the cause of Cuban liberty is won." This oath was taken, and the body of Antonio Maceo was hidden, for disinterment in future days. The body was covered with blood. General Miro dipped his handkerchief in the blood that had come from the open veins, and said: "Behold, I shall keep this for an ensign, to rally the people if their faith shall falter. He embodied patriotism and loyalty, and this blood will inspire the patriot to fight until the cause for which he fought is gained."

The death of José Maceo, the brother in blood and heart of Antonio Maceo, was almost as dramatic. On July 4, 1897, he and his staff and officers had celebrated the independence of the United States. On the next morning, setting out on a white horse, he led a cavalry charge. He was struck in the breast by a bullet, and was taken from his horse. He was borne in silence to the town of Tiarrba, where he died. His death proved an inspiration to the Cuban soldiers. They won a victory on that day over the

Spaniards, who lost eighty in killed and two hundred and sixty in wounded.

These heroes of the Cuban cavalry broke the trocha, which had been deemed invincible, and they held firmly the cause of Cuban independence in its dark and wavering days. They were like bridges over which an army passed to liberty.

What was the personal character of Antonio Maceo, who was an inspiration, a firebrand, a torch in these stern times? He was a Toussaint, and not a Dessalines. His heart was as full of mercy as those of his opponents were full of cruelty. His appeal to the people of the United States is a picture of his nobleness of soul. A part of it reads: "I would not like them to have to shed American blood for our liberty; we are capable alone—provided that within the laws of nations we can obtain all the elements which we need—to expel from Cuba the ruined power of Spain in America. What only troubles me are the victims which the Spaniards make of poor and innocent families, whom they assassinate daily. I wish that in this sense the Americans would interpose their good offices so that the Spanish wild beasts will cease the butchery of defenseless people. For the sake of humanity this intervention should be favored by all civilized countries and nations interested in the moral and material progress of mankind."

In the great battle of Bayamo (1895), in which General Campos was defeated with great loss, Antonio Maceo was the guiding spirit of the field. Campos hoped to shatter the army of Maceo and kill the revolution. In the engagement Campos was wounded, and his principal general, Santocildes, killed. At a shelter near Bayamo there were found thirteen Spanish officers dead. Campos himself escaped by the stratagem of being carried away with the wounded on a stretcher. He lost three hundred men. The character of Maceo was shown in the hour of his victory over the representative of Spain. He sent to the general the following letter:

"*To His Excellency the General Martinez Campos.*

"DEAR SIR: Anxious of giving careful and efficient attendance to the wounded Spanish soldiers that your troops left behind on the battle-field, I have ordered that they be lodged in the houses of the Cuban families that live nearest the battle-ground, until you send for them. With my assurance that the forces you may send to escort them back will not meet any hostile demonstration from my soldiers, I have the honor to be, sir,

"Yours respectfully,
(Signed) "ANTONIO MACEO."

As noble was his expostulation with General Weyler when the latter had begun to develop his merciless policy:

"What! must even the peaceful inhabitants (I say nothing of the wounded and prisoners of war) be sacrificed to the rage that gave the Duke of Alva his name and fame? Is it thus that Spain, through you, returns the clemency and kindness which we, the redeemers of this suffering people, have exercised in like circumstances? What a reproach for yourself and for Spain! The license to burn the huts, assassinations like those at Nueva Paz and the villa El Gato, committed by Spanish columns, in particular those of Colonels Molina and Vicuña, proclaim you guilty before all humankind; your name will be forever infamous, here and far from here, and remembered with disgust and horror!

"Out of humanity, yielding to the honorable and generous impulses which are identified with both the spirit and the tendency of the revolution, I shall never use reprisals that would be unworthy of the reputation and the power of the liberating army of Cuba. But I, nevertheless, foresee that such abominable conduct on your part and on that of your men will arouse at no distant time private vengeances to which they will fall victims, without my being able to prevent it, even though I should punish hundreds of innocent persons.

"For this last reason, since war should only touch combatants, and it is inhuman to make others suffer from its consequences, I invite you to retrace your steps, if you admit your guilt, or to repress these crimes with a heavy hand, if they were committed without your consent. At all events, take care that no drop of blood be shed outside of the battle-field. Be merciful to the many unfortunate peaceful citizens. In so doing you will imitate in honorable emulation our conduct and our proceedings.

"Yours,
"A. MACEO."

As noble is the following anecdote given by an American writer: "On one occasion twenty-six Spanish soldiers were captured in a small engagement near Sagua. They were placed in line in front of the headquarters of General Maceo, and when the chief stepped up in front of them they expected instant death. They had been told various stories of cruelty by their officers, and the limbs of every one, with the exception of a veteran surgeon, trembled with fear. 'Well, there is one of two things for you fellows to do,' said General Maceo; 'you can either stay here or go back to your own people. Now, which do you want to do?' They were struck dumb with astonishment, and several tried to kiss the hand of their preserver. They held a consultation among themselves. The surgeon and fifteen of the soldiers decided they would return to their own forces. The remaining eleven decided to join the forces of the rebels. General Maceo paroled the former, after writing a letter explaining to the Spanish commander the bravery of his men, and how they had been compelled to surrender. He then sent them back rejoicing, accompanied by an armed escort, carrying a flag of truce."

Such was the man who set at naught the trocha, and swept with his raiders from Santiago to the mountains of Pinar del Rio.

The following is a list of the leaders, colored and white, who faced the problem the solution of which was, at last, to make Cuba free:

President and political leader, José Marti, white; general-in-chief, Maximo Gomez, white.

First division, comprising the departments of Cuba, Guantanamo and Baracoa: major-general, Antonio Maceo, colored; brigadier-general, José Maceo, colored. General officers: Pedro Perez, white; Quintin Bandera, colored; Alfonso Goulet, colored; Felix Ruen, colored.

Second division, comprising the departments of Manzanillo, Bayamo and Cauto: major-general, Bartolomé Masso, white; brigadier-general, José Rabi, colored. General officers: Amador Guerra, white; Jesus Rabi, colored; Juan Vega, colored; Saturnino Lora, white.

Third division, comprising the departments of Holguin, Magari, Tunas and Guaimero: major-general (vacant); brigadier-general, Francisco Borrero, white. General officers: José Miro, white; Luis de Feria, white; Angel Guerra, white; N. Marrero, white.

The Hon. Richard Olney, at that time Secretary of State of the United States, wrote to President Cleveland on December 7, 1896, of this pivotal period of the Cuban contest: " Confined in the outset, as in the ten years' insurrection which began at Yara in October, 1868, to the eastern portion of the island, where the topography and absence of settled centers especially favored the desultory warfare apparently normal to this class of contests, the present insurrection very early took proportions beyond those of its predecessor, and therewith assumed an aggressive phase, invading the populous central and western districts. Passing the defensive lines, or trochas, traversing the island from north to south, formidable bodies of the revolutionary forces early in the year established themselves in the rich sugar-planting districts of Santa Clara, Cienfuegos and Matanzas, made hostile forays almost in sight of Havana itself, and advancing westward, effected a lodgment in the fertile tobacco-fields of Pinar del Rio, which has so far resisted all efforts of the Spanish forces to overcome.

"Although statistics of their military strength are attainable with difficulty, and are not always trustworthy when obtained, enough is certainly known to show that the revolutionists in the field greatly exceed in numbers any organization heretofore attempted; that with large accessions from the central and western districts of the island a better military discipline is added to increased strength; that instead of mainly drawing, as heretofore, upon the comparatively primitive population of eastern Cuba, the insurgent armies fairly represent the intelligent aspirations of a large proportion of the people of the whole island; and that they propose to wage this contest, on these better grounds of advantage, to the end, and to make the present struggle a supreme test of the capacity of the Cuban people to win for themselves and their children the heritage of self-government.

"A notable feature of the actual situation is the tactical skill displayed by its leaders. When the disparity of numbers and comparatively indefensible character of the central and western Vego country are considered, the passage of a considerable force into Pinar del Rio, followed by its successful maintenance there for many months, must be regarded as a military success of a pronounced character.

"So, too, the Spanish force in the field, in garrison on the island, or on its way thither from the mother-country, is largely beyond any military display yet called for by a Cuban rising, thus affording an independent measure of the strength of the insurrection.

"From every accessible indication it is clear that the present rebellion is on a far more formidable scale as to numbers, intelligence and representative features than any of the preceding revolts of this century; that the corresponding effort of Spain for its repression has been enormously augmented; and that, despite the constant influx of fresh armies and material of war from the metropolis, the rebellion, after nearly two years of successful resistance, appears to-day to be in a condition to prolong indefinitely the contest on its present lines."

On the evening of February 15, 1898, a terrible event occurred in the harbor of Havana. The shadows of nightfall had gathered upon the sea. The lights of the whole city glimmered in the mild air. Suddenly a red column of fire rose into the darkness and sank again. A rain of missiles fell upon the water. The boatmen near the column of fire had heard a dull, sullen roar in the sea, as though the bed of the water had been earthquake-riven. The column of fire had revealed the white ship from which it had seemed to proceed. It was a United States war-vessel, the *Maine*. Immediately the sea was filled with dying men. Two hundred and sixty-six officers and sailors perished. The ship had gone there, to a friendly port, for the protection of American citizens. She had doubtless been blown up by a secret mine exploded by conspiracy or accident.

The Spanish officials in the harbor who saw the column of flame rise into the darkness could hardly have felt the prophetic import of the event. The destruction of the proud battle-ship was to reveal to the American mind centuries of cruelty, injustice and wrong. It was to lead America, as with one voice, to demand that in the name of humanity and liberty the oppressions of Spain on the continent should forever cease. The judgment-day of three centuries was in it. Whose hand exploded the mine none know or ever will know, but the world saw in the explosion a resemblance to the deeds of the past. That column of flame, like a candle of destiny, made the past clear again, and aroused the human will to decide that in the future such things should not be. From that dark death of the martyrs of the *Maine* began an inquiry that gained the cause of all the Cuban patriots who fought for liberty. The *Maine* sank helplessly in the still waters; but the sunrise of freedom came in the morning. The hour of the fate of the *Maine* was that of the end of the Spanish empire in the western world.

CHAPTER XXV

PORTO RICO

"PORTO RICO," says an old writer, "is one of the coolest and healthiest parts of the West Indies." It is also one of the most populous islands of the Spanish Main. The larger part of the inhabitants are creoles. This new possession of the United States is likely to become one of the sea-gardens for the people of North America.

It is an island of beauty. One of the most interesting and suggestive of American legends is associated with the ruined palace of Ponce de Leon, which is still to be seen at San Juan. This poet-mariner and companion of Columbus had heard of Bimini, a fabled island in the new Spanish Main, which contained a fountain of magical influence, the waters of which would cause one to live in perpetual youth. He was growing old, and went in search of this fountain in the sunny waters. He found Florida. He was made governor of Porto Rico, and built a palace there.

The island is rectangular in shape. It is about a hundred miles long and fifty wide, traversed by a range of mountains, one peak of which rises 3670 feet above the sea. It is nature's own land of sugar, coffee, tobacco and tropical fruits. The cattle and sheep raised there are said to be superior. The island is comparatively free from noxious vermin.

The people of Porto Rico caught the spirit of Simon Bolivar, and, in 1820, made an attempt to throw off the Spanish yoke, and to follow the example of the South American patriots. The republican movement was crushed in 1823. Spanish supremacy was reëstablished more rigidly than before. Slavery was abolished in 1873, and also the mita.

In 1870 Porto Rico was made a province of Spain, and was allowed a representative government.

The climate has two seasons, the wet and the dry. The dry months are healthful, and are the time when the foreign visitor may live there without danger from malarious fevers. They begin with November and end in April. The mean heat in summer is about 80°; in winter about 70°.

The hills of palms abound with coffee-plantations, the valleys with sugar-farms and fruit-orchards, and the pastures are famous for succulent grasses.

The island has 470 miles of telegraph lines and 137 miles of railway. San Juan is the capital. Its harbor has an entrance 2000 feet wide, and is overlooked by a Morro or Moorish castle. The city is built on a coral reef. It is connected with the mainland by a picturesque bridge.

The population of the island in 1887 was 798,565. Of these 474,923 were white. The population of San Juan is 26,000; that of Ponce is about 15,000.

The Porto Ricans hailed with rejoicing the coming of the American flag of liberation. The island became a part of the republic of the United States on August 12, 1898, at the time of signing the famous protocol. By so doing the hopes of the patriots of 1820, with which they had been inspired by the victorious march of Bolivar, have been happily realized.

CHAPTER XXVI

THE SOUTH AMERICAN ORATORS—THE ORATIONS OF BOLIVAR—THE FAREWELL OF SAN MARTIN

BOLIVAR was the orator as well as the Liberator of South America. We give here some specimens of his grand oratory.

A general assembly of the Venezuelans, held at Margarita, had appointed Bolivar "Supreme Chief," with dictatorial powers. In the war which followed he was victorious. He conquered the Spaniards and secured the independence of Venezuela. Having accomplished that, he convened a congress, which assembled at Angostura, January, 1819. To that, composed of the direct representatives of the people, he resigned his powers as Dictator. In doing so he said:

"GENTLEMEN: I account myself one of the beings most favored by divine Providence in having the honor of reuniting the representatives of Venezuela in this august congress, the only source of legitimate authority, the deposit of the sovereign will, and the arbiter of the nation's fate.

"In delivering back to the representatives of the people the supreme power intrusted to me, I satisfy the desires of my own heart, and calm the fears of my fellow-citizens and of future generations, who hope everything from your wisdom, rectitude and prudence. In fulfilling this delightful duty, I free myself from the boundless authority which oppresses me, and also from the unlimited responsibility which weighs on my feeble hands.

" An imperative necessity, united to a strongly expressed desire on the part of the people, could alone have induced me to assume the dreadful and dangerous charge of *Dictator, Supreme Chief of the Republic.* Now, however, I desire to return the authority which, with so great risk, difficulty and toil, I have maintained amid as horrible calamities as ever afflicted a social body.

" In the epoch during which I presided over the republic, it was not merely a political storm that raged, in a sanguinary war, in a time of popular anarchy, but the tempest of the desert, a whirlwind of every disorganized element, the bursting of an infernal torrent, that overwhelmed the land of Venezuela. A man,—and such a man as I am!—what bounds, what resistance could he oppose to such furious devastation? Amid that sea of woes and afflictions I was nothing more than the miserable sport of the revolutionary hurricane, driven to and fro like the wild bird of the ocean. I could do neither good nor evil; an irresistible power above all human control directed the march of our fortunes; and for me to pretend to have been the prime mover of the events which have taken place would be unjust, and would be attaching to myself an importance I do not merit. Do you desire to know the sources from which those occurrences took their rise, and the origin of our present situation? Consult the annals of Spain, of America and of Venezuela; examine the laws of the Indies, the conduct of your ancient governors, the influence of religion and of foreign dominion; observe the first acts of the republican government, the ferocity of our enemies, and the national character. I again repeat that I cannot consider myself more than the mere instrument of the great causes which have acted on our country. My life, my conduct and all my actions, public and private, are, however, before the people, and, representatives, it is your duty to judge them. I submit to your impartial decision the manner in which I have executed my command, and nothing will I add to excuse. I have already said enough as an apology. Should I merit your approbation, I shall have acquired the sublime title of a *good citizen*, preferred by me to that of *Liberator*, bestowed on me by Venezuela; to that of *Pacificator*, given me by Cundinamarca; and to all others the universe could confer.

"Legislators! I deposit in your hands the supreme command of Venezuela, and it is now your high duty to consecrate yourselves to the felicity of the republic. In your hands rests the balance of our destiny and the means of our glory. You will confirm the decrees which establish our liberty.

"The supreme chief of the republic is, at this moment, nothing more than a simple citizen, and such he wishes to remain until his latest hour. He will, however, serve with the armies of Venezuela as long as an army treads her soil."

Bolivar surveyed the republics of the past, and pictured their rise and fall with masterly eloquence. He continued:

"Legislators! This is the proper time for repeating what the eloquent Volney says, in his dedication to the 'Ruins of Palmyra': 'To the growing people of the Spanish Indies, to the generous chiefs who conduct them to liberty! May the errors and misfortunes of the Old World teach wisdom and happiness to the New!' May they never lose themselves, but profit by the lessons of experience given in the schools of Greece, of Rome, of France, of England and of America, and be instructed by them in the difficult science of establishing and preserving nations with proper, just, legitimate, and, above all, useful laws, never forgetting that the excellency of a government does not consist in theory, form or mechanism, but in being fitted to the nature and character of the people for which it was instituted."

The speech ended with this grand peroration:

"Flying from present and approaching times, my imagination plunges into future ages, in which I observe, with admiration and amazement, the prosperity, the splendor and the animation which this vast region will have acquired. My ideas are wafted on, and I see my beloved nation in the center of the universe, expanding herself on her extensive coasts between those oceans which nature had separated, and which our country will have united with large and capacious canals. I see her the bond, the center and the emporium of the human race. I see her transmitting to earth's remotest bounds those treasures contained in her mountains of gold and silver. I see her distributing, by her salutiferous plants, health and life to the afflicted of the Old World. I see her imparting to the sages of other regions her inestimable secrets, ignorant until then how much her height of knowledge transcends her excessive wealth. Yes! I see her seated on the throne of freedom, wielding the scepter of justice, and crowned with glory, showing the Old World the majesty of the New.

"Legislators! Condescend to receive with indulgence the declaration of my political creed, the highest wishes of my heart, and the earnest petition which, in the name of the people, I have dared to address to you.

"Vouchsafe to grant to Venezuela a government purely popular, purely just and purely moral, which will enchain oppression, anarchy and crime; a government which will cause innocency, philanthropy and peace to reign; a government which, under the dominion of inexorable laws, will cause equality and liberty to triumph.

"Gentlemen! Commence your duties; I have finished mine.

"The Congress of the republic of Venezuela is installed. In it from this moment is centered the national sovereignty. We all owe to it obedience and fidelity. My sword, and those of my illustrious fellows in arms, will maintain its august authority. God save the Congress!"

The speech electrified the Congress. The Liberator followed it by presenting to the Congress the new constitution. "*Viva el Congreso de Venezuela!*" rang through the halls, which shout was echoed by the artillery. A President pro tem. was elected, Francisco A. Zea. Bolivar then rose and took the oath of allegiance to the written law of the people. He placed the President pro tem. in the seat that he as Dictator had just vacated, and said:

"Generals, chiefs and officers, my companions in arms, we are no more than simple citizens till the Sovereign Congress pleases to employ us in the class and rank which it may think proper. Relying on your submission, I am going to give, in my name and yours, the most evident proofs of our obedience, by surrendering to it the command with which I was charged."

On saying this he approached the President of the Congress, and presenting his general's baton, he continued: "I return to the republic the baton of general which she conferred on me. To serve her, in whatever rank or class to which the Congress destines me, is for me honorable; in it I will give the example of subordination and kind obedience, which should distinguish every soldier of the republic!"

The next day the Liberator was elected President of the republic.

One of the greatest of the orations of Bolivar was delivered in the south after the organization of the republic of Bolivia. It was addressed to the Congress of Bolivia.

"Legislators! In offering the project of a constitution for Bolivia, I feel overwhelmed with confusion and timidity, being convinced of my incapacity to make laws. When I consider that the wisdom of whole centuries is insufficient to compose a fundamental law which shall be perfect, and that the most enlightened legislator is perhaps the immediate cause of human unhappiness, and, if I may so express myself, the dupe of his divine ministry, what may not be said of a soldier born among slaves and buried in the deserts of his country, having seen nothing but captives in chains, and companions in arms to break them? . . .

"I have summoned all my powers of mind for the purpose of submitting to you my opinions respecting the best method of managing free men according to the principles adopted by civilized nations, although the lessons of experience exhibit only long periods of disaster checkered by some glimpses of good fortune. What guides can we follow in the shade of such dark examples?

"Legislators! Your duty calls on you to resist the shock of two monstrous enemies who mutually combat each other, and who will both attack you at one and the same time. . . . Tyranny and anarchy form an immense ocean of oppression, rolling round a small isle of liberty, perpetually beaten by the violence of the waves and by the hurricanes which incessantly threaten its submersion. Such is the sea on which you are about to launch, in a frail bark, with a pilot so inexperienced. . . .

"Legislators! From this day forward liberty will be indestructible in America. You see that the savage nature of this continent is of itself sufficient to repel the monarchical form of government. Deserts are favorable to independence. Here we have no grandees, either aristocratical or ecclesiastical. Our riches are but inconsiderable, and now they are reduced in a still greater degree. Though the church enjoys some influence, she is far from aspiring to dominion, being satisfied with her own preservation. Without such supports tyrants never remain permanent, and if some ambitious men should engage in raising empires for themselves, the fate of Dessalines, Christophe and Iturbide will warn them of what they have to expect. No power finds greater difficulty to maintain itself than that of a new Prince Bonaparte, who, having vanquished so many armies, could not succeed in overcoming this rule, which is stronger than empires. And if the great Napoleon was unable to maintain himself against the league of republicans and aristocrats, who may hope to found monarchies in America, in a soil warmed and illuminated by the bright flames of liberty, in a soil which consumes the materials used for erecting these legal platforms? No, legislators! Fear not any pretenders or aspirants to crowns. To them the diadem would be what the hair-suspended falchion was over the head of Dionysius. Those upstart princes, who are so blind as to raise thrones on the ruins of liberty, are erecting their own sepulchral monuments, which will announce to future generations that they preferred their infatuated ambition to liberty and glory. . . .

"Legislators! Slavery is the infringement of all laws. A law having a tendency to preserve slavery would be the grossest sacrilege. What right can be alleged in favor of its continuance? In whatever view this crime is considered, I am persuaded that there is not a single Bolivian in existence so depraved as to pretend that such a signal violation of the dignity of man can be legalized. Man to be possessed by his fellow-man; man to be made a property of! The image of the Deity to be put under the yoke! Let these usurpers of man show us their title-deeds. No one can break asunder the sacred dogma of equality; and is slavery to exist where equality reigns? Such contradictions would rather impugn our reason than our justice. We should then be deemed insane rather than usurpers.

"Legislators! I shall make mention of an article which in my conscience I ought to have omitted. No religious creed or profession should be prescribed in a political constitution, for, according to the best doctrines concerning fundamental laws, these are the guaranties of civil and political rights; and as religion touches none of those rights, she is in her nature not to be defined in the social order, and belongs to an intellectual morality. Religion governs man at home, in the cabinet, and in his own bosom, within himself; she alone has a right to examine his most secret conscience. The laws, on the contrary, consider and view the exterior of things; they govern only out of doors, and not within the houses of citizens. Applying these considerations, how can the state rule the consciences of its subjects, watch over the fulfilment of religion, and reward or punish, when the tribunals of all those matters are in heaven, and when God is the Judge? As all this belongs to divine jurisdiction, it strikes me at first sight as sacrilegious and profane to mix up our ordinances with the commandments of the Lord. It therefore belongs not to the legislator to prescribe religion; for the legislator must impose penalties on the infringements of the laws, to avoid their becoming merely expressions of counsel and advice. When there are neither temporal penalties, nor judges to inflict them, the law ceases to be law.

"Legislators! What generous and sublime thoughts must fill your souls when you see the new Bolivian nation already proclaimed! The accession of a new state to the society of those already existing forms a just subject of exultation for mankind, as it augments the great family of nations. What then must be the exultation of its founders, and my own, seeing myself placed on a level with the most celebrated sages of antiquity, with the founder of the Eternal City! This glory by right appertains to the institutors of nations, who, being their first benefactors, must have received immortal rewards; but mine, besides its immortality, possesses the merit of being gratuitous, not having been deserved. Where is the city, where is the republic which I have founded? Your munificence in dedicating a nation to me has surpassed all my services, and is infinitely superior to all the good which men can do to you.

"My despair increases when I contemplate the immensity of your reward; for even had I concentrated the talents, virtues, and the very genius of the greatest of heroes, I should be nevertheless unworthy of the name which you have chosen to give yourselves, my own name! Shall I talk of gratitude when that sentiment cannot otherwise than feebly express what I experience from your goodness, which, like the divine goodness, passes all limits? Yes; God alone had the power of naming this country Bolivia. . . . What means the word 'Bolivia'? A boundless love of liberty, at the receiving of which your enthusiasm saw nothing equal to its value. Your ecstasy, finding no demonstration adequate to the vehemence of your feelings, extinguished your own name, and gave mine to yourselves and all your posterity. This has no parallel in the history of the world. It is unexampled in the records of sublime magnanimity. So great an action will show to after times, which exist in the mind of the Eternal, that you aspired to the possession of your rights, which consist in the power of exercising your political virtues, in the acquisition of luminous talents, and in the enjoyment of being *men*. This noble deed, I repeat it, will prove that you are entitled to obtain the grand blessing of Heaven, the *sovereignty of the people*, the only legitimate authority of nations."

General Martin's proclamation on resigning his office recalls Lincoln's address at Gettysburg. Its very simplicity is eloquent; events are in every sentence. Nothing could be more dramatic than the words: "I hold in my possession the standard which Pizarro brought to enslave the empire of the Incas." The proclamation is as follows:

"I have witnessed the declaration of independence of the states of Chili and Peru. I hold in my possession the standard which Pizarro brought to enslave the empire of the Incas. I have ceased to be a public man. Thus I am more than rewarded for ten years spent in revolution and warfare. My promises to the countries in which I warred are fulfilled—to make them independent and leave to their will the elections of the governments.

"The presence of a fortunate soldier, however disinterested he may be, is dangerous to newly constituted states. I am also disgusted with hearing that I wish to make myself a sovereign. Nevertheless, I shall always be ready to make the last sacrifice for the liberty of the country, but in the class of the private individual, and no other.

"With respect to my public conduct, my compatriots (as is generally the case) will be divided in their opinions. Their children will pronounce the true verdict.

"Peruvians! I leave your national representation established. If you repose implicit confidence in it, you will triumph. If not, anarchy will swallow you up.

"May success preside over your destinies, and may they be crowned with felicity and peace!"

APPENDIX

ARBITRATION IN SOUTH AMERICA

1. The United States and New Granada in 1857.
2. The United States and Chili in 1858. Claim of compensation for silver bars and coin taken by a Chilian admiral from an American citizen. Referred to the King of the Belgians, whose award sustained the American claims.
3. The United States and Paraguay in 1859. Referred to a commission, whose award was duly given.
4. The United States and New Granada. Pecuniary claims. Referred to a commission.
5. Great Britain and Brazil in 1863. Imprisonment of British naval officers. Referred to the King of the Belgians, Leopold I., who decided that the action of Brazil was justified by circumstances.
6. The United States and Peru in 1863. Alleged illegal capture of ships. Referred in one instance to the King of the Belgians, and in another to a commission.
7. Great Britain and Peru in 1864. The Senate of Hamburg arbitrated on claim for compensation on account of the alleged false imprisonment and banishment from Peru of a British subject, and decided that the claim was based upon a partial and exaggerated statement, and was entirely inadmissible.
8. The United States of Colombia and Ecuador in 1864. Referred to a citizen of each state (Ecuador and Colombia), who, with an umpire or arbitrator, should undertake "the mutual adjustment of claims," which was done successfully.
9. The United States and Venezuela in 1866. Claims by citizens of the United States against the government of Venezuela. Referred to a commission. Award in favor of the former.
10. The United States and Peru in 1868.
11. The United States and Brazil in 1870.
12. Japan and Peru in 1872. Seizure of the bark *Maria Sury*, engaged

in the coolie trade, and the liberation of those on board. Referred to the Emperor of Russia, whose decision was in favor of Japan.

13. Great Britain and Brazil in 1873. Dundonald claims. Referred to the United States and Italian ministers at Rio. Gross amount of award against Brazilian government nearly £40,000.

14. Chili and Colombia in 1880. Dispute relative to the transportation of arms for Peru across the Isthmus of Panama. Referred to the President of the United States.

15. Chili and Argentine Republic (about the Straits of Magellan and their land boundaries) in 1881. Referred to the United States ministers to those countries. Boundaries settled, Straits of Magellan neutralized.

16. Great Britain and Chili in 1884 (about damages incurred by their subjects in the war between Chili and Peru). Referred to a commission consisting of three members, one to be nominated by the Emperor of Brazil.

17. France and Chili. Similar claims. Referred to a similar commission.

18. Italy and Chili. Similar claims. Referred to a similar commission.

19. In 1889, between Brazil, La Plata and the Argentine Republic. A question of boundary. Referred to President Harrison of the United States, whose decision was accepted.

For the benefit of those who wish to pursue the study of this subject more in detail, I append the following list of books and authors.

"Agriculture in South America," Almond Barns. Published by the Department of Agriculture, Washington.
"Bureau of South American Republics," State Department, Washington.
"Antiquities," Wright.
"Life of William Wheelwright," Alberdi.
"South American Trade," Balcazar.
"Equatorial America," Ballou.
"South American Travel," Baxley.
"A Thousand Miles' Walk," Bishop.
"Spanish-American Republics," Child.
"Visit to South America," Clark.
"Tropical America," Ford.
"Life and Nature under the Tropics," Myers.
"Andes and Amazon," Orton.
"South America" (illustrated), Macoy.
"Equatorial Forests," Stuart.
"Cuba and Porto Rico," Trumbull.
"Wanderings in South America," Waterton.
"Colonial History of South America," Markham.
"Spanish and Portuguese South America during the Colonial Period," Watson.
"San Martin," Mitre.
"America Poetica."
"Mexican and South American Poems."
"The Neglected Continent," Guiness.
"Notes of a Naturalist," Ball.
"Life in the Argentine," Sarmiento. Translated by Mrs. Horace Mann.

Bartolomé de las Casas.
Garcilasso de la Vega.
" Peru," Markham.
" L'Empire des Incas," Wiener.
" Rites and Laws of the Incas," Markham.
" War between Chili and Peru," Markham.
" Conquest of Peru," Prescott.
" Myths of the New World," Brinton.
" Peruvian Antiquities."
Helps.
" Fables and Rites of the Incas," Molina.
Sarmiento.
" History of America," Robertson.
" Travels in Peru," Temple.
" South American Republics," Curtis.
" Antiquarian Researches in New Granada, Ecuador, Peru and Chili," Bollaert.
" Ornaments from the Huacas (Tombs)," Bryce M. Wright.
" South America," Humboldt.
" Basil Hall's Journal."
" From China to Peru," Howard Vincent.
" South America," Niles.
" Between the Amazon and the Andes," Mulhall.
" From Lima to Peru and down the Amazon," Smith.
" Up the Amazon," Mathews.
" The Arbitration of the United States," Professor Moore.
Documents relating to President John Q. Adams's message in regard to the conventions in South America (in 1825).
Official reports of International American Congress (1889–90).
" History of Don F. Miranda's Attempt to Effect a Revolution in South America," James Briggs.

" Memoirs of Simon Bolivar," Ducoudray-Holstein.
Mosquera.
" Life of Bolivar," Felipe Larrazabal.
" Narrative and Critical History of America," edited by Winsor.
" North American Review," January, 1829.

PRESIDENTS OF COLOMBIA

1819. Bolivar.
1831–32. José Maria Obando.
1832–37. General Santander.
1837–41. José Ignacio Marquez.
1841–45. Pedro Alcantara Herran.
1845–49. General Mosquera.
1849–52. General Lopez.
1854–55. José Maria Obando.
1857–61. Marino Ospina.
1861–64. General Mosquera.
1864–66. Manuel Murillo-Toro.
1866–67. General Mosquera.
1868–70. Santos Gutierrez.
1872–74. Manuel Murillo-Toro.
1874–76. Santiago Perez.

PRESIDENTS OF ARGENTINA

1826–27. Bernardino Rivadavia. His administration was followed by the government of the tyrants, from 1829 to 1852.
1852–53. General Urquizà, provisional Dictator.
1853–60. General Urquizà, constitutional President.
1862–68. Bartolomé Mitre.
1868–74. Domingo Faustino Sarmiento.
1874–80. Nicolas Avellaneda.
1880–86. General Julio A. Roca.
1886–90. Miguel Juarez Celman.
1890–92. Carlos Pellegrini.
1892–98. Dr. Luis Saenz Peña.

APPENDIX

PRESIDENTS OF PERU

1827–29. José Lamar.
1829–33. Gamarra.
1835–36. Salaverry (the poet).
1836–39. Santa Cruz.
1839–43. Gamarra.
1845–51. General Ramon Castilla.
1851–55. General Echenique.
1855–59. General Ramon Castilla.
1862–63. San Roman.
1863–65. General Pezet.
1865–68. General Prado.
1868–72. José Balta.
1876–79. General Prado.
1879–81. Nicolas de Pierola.
1881–83. Francisco Garcia Calderon.
1883–85. General Iglesias.
1886–90. General Caceres.
1890. General Bermudez.

PRESIDENTS OF CHILI

1817–23. General O'Higgins, Dictator.
1823–27. General Freire, Dictator.
1827–29. General Pinto, under a constitution.
1830–31. José Tomás Ovalle.
1831–41. General Prieto. The present constitution was promulgated in 1833.
1841–51. General Bulnes.
1851–61. Manuel Montt.
1861–71. José Joaquin Perez.
1871–76. Federico Errázuriz.

PRESIDENTS OF VENEZUELA

1813. Bolivar, Dictator.
1831–35. General Paez.
1839–43. General Paez.
1864. Present federal constitution proclaimed.
1870. Guzman Blanco, Dictator.
1873–88. Guzman Blanco, constitutional President.

PRESIDENTS OF ECUADOR

1830–35. Juan José Flores.
1835–39. Vicente Rocafuerte.
1839–45. Juan José Flores.
1845–49. Vicente Ramon Roca.
1850. Diego Noboa.
1856–59. Francisco Robles.
1859–61. Gabriel Garcia Moreno, chief of the provisional government.
1861–65. Gabriel Garcia Moreno.
1868–69. Javier Espinosa.
1869–75. Gabriel Garcia Moreno.
1875–76. Borrero.
1876–83. Ignacio Veintemilla.
1883–88. José Maria Placido Caamaño.
1888–92. Antonio Flores.

PRESIDENTS OF BOLIVIA

1826–28. Antonio José de Sucre.
1828. Marshal Santa Cruz.
1829–33. General Agustin Gamarra.
1836–39. Marshal Santa Cruz.
1839–41. General José Miguel de Velasco.
1841–47. General José Ballivian.
1847–48. General José Miguel de Velasco.
1848–55. General Manuel Isidoro Belzu.
1855–58. Jorge Cordova.
1858–61. José Maria Linares.
1861–65. José Maria Achá.
1865–71. General Mariano Melgarejo.
1871–72. General Agustin Morales.
1873–74. Adolfo Ballivian.

APPENDIX

PRESIDENTS OF BRAZIL

1889–91. Republic proclaimed. General Fonseca placed at the head of the provisional government.
1891. General Fonseca elected President.
1891–94. General Peixoto.
1894. Prudente Moraes. Elected for four years.

POPULATION OF SOUTH AMERICAN CITIES

(*Census* 1890)

Buenos Ayres............. 720,000
Rio de Janeiro............ 700,000
Montevideo............... 175,000
Bahia.................... 200,000
Pernambuco.............. 130,000
Valparaiso............... 125,000
Bogotá................... 110,000
Lima..................... 101,000
Pará..................... 100,000
Rosario.................. 100,000
Quito.................... 80,000
La Paz................... 80,000
Caracas.................. 70,000
Barranquilla.............. 65,000
Cartagena................ 16,000
La Guayra................ 14,000
Bolivar................... 11,000
Concepcion............... 11,000
Araure................... 10,000

THE HIGH CITIES OF SOUTH AMERICA

FEET.
Oroya Railroad (tunnel)...... 15,645
Potosí (Bolivia)............ 13,330
Cuzco.................... 11,380
La Paz................... 10,883
Quito.................... 9,543

FEET.
Bogotá................... 8,732
Arequipa................. 7,852

THE HIGH PEAKS OF THE ANDES

FEET.
Aconcagua................ 23,910
Chimborazo............... 20,498
Sorata................... 21,286
Illimani.................. 20,952
Tupangato................ 21,149
Cayambe................. 19,534
Cotopaxi................. 19,600
Tolima................... 18,420
Antisana................. 13,300

THE GREAT RIVERS OF SOUTH AMERICA

MILES.
Amazon.................. 3,270
Orinoco.................. 1,600
Rio de la Plata............ 2,500
Magdalena............... 960
Marañon................. 450
Uruguay................. 1,020
Parana................... 2,200
Paraguay................. 1,800
San Francisco............. 1,400
Xingú................... 1,300
Tokantuis................ 1,300

MILEAGE OF RAILWAYS (1889)

Argentina................ 6,940
Brazil................... 5,700
Peru..................... 1,630
Uruguay................. 445
Venezuela................ 183

VALUES IN SOUTH AMERICAN COIN (1897)

U. S. GOLD (CENTS).
Argentine Republic, *peso*...... 96.5
Brazil, *milreis*............ 54.0
Chili, *peso*............... 36.5

APPENDIX

	U. S. GOLD (CENTS).
Venezuela, *bolivar*	19.3
Bolivia, *boliviano*	48.6
Peru, *sol*	48.6
Colombia, *peso*	48.6

GOLD PRODUCTION OF SOUTH AMERICA

	FINE OUNCES.	VALUE.
Argentina	4,838	100,000
Bolivia	3,628	75,000
Brazil	120,950	2,500,000
Chili	33,866	700,000
Colombia	188,682	3,900,000
Ecuador	3,870	80,000
Guiana (British)	125,000	2,583,965
Guiana (Dutch)	26,685	551,618
Guiana (French)	78,700	1,626,941
Peru	7,256	150,000
Uruguay	7,256	150,000
Venezuela	41,123	850,000

INCA MUSIC

A HARAVI, OR ELEGIAC SONG, IN SOL MINOR

www.ingramcontent.com/pod-product-compliance
Lightning Source LLC
Chambersburg PA
CBHW022025240426
43667CB00042B/1152